LIM[illegible]

Helen [illegible] the elde[illegible] years, until she [illegible] Liverpool – a city that fea[illegible]ly in her work. For the past fort[illegible] she has lived in Alberta, Canada.

Helen Forrester is the author of four bestselling volumes of autobiography and a number of equally successful novels, including most recently *Madame Barbara.* In 1988 she was awarded an honorary D.Litt. by the University of Liverpool in recognition of her achievements as an author. The University of Alberta conferred on her the same honour in 1993.

By Helen Forrester

Fiction

THURSDAY'S CHILD
THE LATCHKEY KID
LIVERPOOL DAISY
THREE WOMEN OF LIVERPOOL
THE MONEYLENDERS OF SHAHPUR
YES, MAMA
THE LEMON TREE
THE LIVERPOOL BASQUE
MOURNING DOVES
MADAME BARBARA

Non-fiction

TWOPENCE TO CROSS THE MERSEY
LIVERPOOL MISS
BY THE WATERS OF LIVERPOOL
LIME STREET AT TWO

HELEN FORRESTER

LIME STREET AT TWO

TED SMART

HarperCollins*Publishers*
77–85 Fulham Palace Road,
Hammersmith, London W6 8JB

www.harpercollins.co.uk

This edition produced for The Book People Ltd,
Hall Wood Avenue, Haydock, St Helens WA11 9UL

This paperback edition 1994

Previously published in paperback by Fontana 1986
Reprinted nine times

First published in Great Britain by
The Bodley Head Ltd 1985

ISBN 0 00 775006 4

Typeset in New Baskerville by
Palimpsest Book Production Limited,
Polmont, Stirlingshire

Printed and bound in Great Britain by
Clays Ltd, St Ives plc

To my husband

The generals, the institution can
select a strategy, lay it all out,
but what happens on the battlefield
is quite different.

Count Lev Nikolaevich Tolstoi
(1828–1910)

CHAPTER ONE

The huge clock still hangs in Lime Street station, Liverpool, and marks a convenient spot for travellers to be met. During World War II, almost every girl in Liverpool must have written to a serviceman coming home on leave, 'I'll meet you under the clock at Lime Street.' There were always women there, dressed in their shabby best, hair long, curled and glossy, pacing nervously under that indifferent timepiece. Every time a train chugged in, they would glance anxiously at the ticket collectors' wickets, while round them swirled other civilians, and hordes of men and women in uniform, khaki, Navy blue, or Air Force blue, staggering under enormous packs and kitbags. Some men wore foreign uniforms, with shoulder flashes of refugee armies, navies and air forces. No matter who they were, they all shared the same expression of deep fatigue.

This huge vortex of uprooted humanity was supervised by stolid-looking military police standing like rocks against a tide. Some of them were American Snowdrops, so nicknamed because of their white helmets. Occasionally a single English civilian policeman stood out amongst all the other uniforms, a reminder of peacetime and sanity, when a quiet, 'Now move along there, please,' was enough to reduce a pushing crowd to order.

The station may be rebuilt, the generations pass, but the ghosts are still there, ghosts of lovers, husbands, sons, withered like flowers on distant battlefields long forgotten, and of mothers, wives and sweethearts long since dead. Amongst those kindly shades stands Harry O'Dwyer, the fiancé of my youth, a ship's engineer, lost at sea in 1940.

I do not know how I got through that dreadful summer of 1940, after the news of Harry's death, or the long, hopeless year of 1941. It was a period when the Merchant Navy was decimated by German submarines and aircraft. Once a man was at sea, there was not a moment when he was not in acute danger. Over the bar, in Liverpool Bay, the U-boats waited, like cats at a mousehole, for the slow, ill-defended freighters entering and leaving the ports of Liverpool and Birkenhead. If they survived the submarines, they could strike acoustic mines, magnetic mines and other menaces plopping about in the heaving waters.

Even snugly moored in dock, ships were often the target in air raids; and the homes of their crews, packed in the dockside areas, were frequently destroyed.

I lived within a mile of the south docks, with my father and mother, four brothers and two sisters. I was the eldest child. We were a most unhappy family, our lives fraught with the bitter quarrels of our parents, and our considerable penury.

When I was a child we had lived in comfortable circumstances, but in 1930, my father had gone bankrupt, as a result of the Depression. In an effort to find employment, Father had brought us to Liverpool, his birthplace. Like most of the people living in the south of England, he had no notion of the horrifying effect of the Depression in the north. The unemployment rate was 33 per cent and there was almost no hope of work. We had sunk into an abyss of poverty, which I have described in earlier books.* By 1940, however, we had begun

* Helen Forrester, *Twopence to Cross the Mersey*, *Minerva's Stepchild* (published in paperback as *Liverpool Miss*) and *By the Waters of Liverpool* (London: The Bodley Head, 1974, 1979, 1981, and Fontana Paperbacks, 1981, 1982, 1983).

to climb out of the pit into which we had fallen, though we were still very poor.

My parents were still filled with the Public School snobbery of their youth, so I had told them nothing of my engagement to Harry O'Dwyer. They would have immediately condemned such a union as beneath me. Harry was from a respectable Irish working-class family and a Roman Catholic, originally intended by his family to be a priest. Since I was a Protestant, we had agreed to be married quietly in a Registry Office soon after I was twenty-one, when I would not need my parents' consent. Harry had bought a little house, which was not quite complete when he was killed. I was twenty-one years and two months old when his mother told me of his death, under the very odd circumstances that she did not know she was talking to her son's fiancée.

In 1940, I was a neophite social worker in Bootle, a small town sharing a common boundary with Liverpool. It was a Roman Catholic area tightly packed with overcrowded terrace houses, factories and timber yards, hedged in by the docks along the river. Though the poverty was very great, Harry was proud to say that he was a Bootle man; men had sailed from Bootle since the Anglians settled there in AD 613, and perhaps even before that.

One morning in August, our waiting room at the

office was packed with the widows of men lost at sea, who wished to seek our advice regarding claiming pensions. Among them sat Harry's mother, long since estranged from him because he had refused to enter the Church. She was now bent on benefiting from his death by claiming a pension. I thought I would faint when she explained her business, and I quickly referred her to my colleague, Miss Evans. Then, deserting the waiting crowd, I fled to the unused cellars of the old house in which the office lay, and there in the clammy grime of a disused coal cellar, I stood shivering helplessly, so filled with shock that I hardly knew where I was. When, after a few minutes, my mind cleared a little, I was nauseated at a woman who could order her son out of their home because of a religious difference, and yet could coolly try to get a pension at his death.

I heard Miss Evans calling me and automatically I ran back up the stone steps. She met me on the upper staircase and scolded me for leaving clients waiting. Like a zombie, I moved to obey her orders. I did not cry.

I did not want to know this cold, grasping woman, Harry's mother, nor did I say anything to my own parents; there was no point in facing their probable derision at such a humble marriage. I could almost hear their cultured voices ripping apart a man I had loved dearly, and I could not bear that they should do it.

Somehow, I kept my mouth shut, but the unexpressed grief was like a corrosive at work inside me. It caused such damage that I never truly recovered from it. In a body made frail by much illness and, at times, near starvation, it worked its will. In a character already very introspective from childhood, filled with fear of grownups, its effect was devastating.

As a little child, I learned early that my parents were simply not interested in me, and that I had to face all the fears of childhood alone. As a young adult, I continued that early attitude of solitary suffering, and it was reinforced by the loss of the one person I trusted implicitly.

Though I did not consider it at the time, I had lots of fellow sufferers and, as a social worker employed by a charity working in the dock areas, I had to help to look after them. Our waiting room was daily filled by rows of weeping mothers and wives; every ship that went down seemed to have a Bootle man aboard. My mind is filled with memories of the overwhelmed resources of our little office, when the *Athenia*, the *Courageous*, the battleship *Royal Oak*, and hundreds of others, big and small, were lost in 1940 and 1941.

Sometimes the position was reversed, and a seaman's family was lost in an air raid.

My senior, Miss Evans, and I often faced a stony-eyed or openly weeping merchant seaman or a serviceman, sent home on compassionate leave because his home had been bombed and his family killed. Commanding officers did not always tell them why they were to go home. A few would go straight to their house, see the wreckage and realise what had happened. But quite a number reported directly to our office, as instructed by their Commanding officer, and we would have to break the news to them. Because extended families frequently lived in adjoining streets, a man could find himself left with only a badly injured infant in hospital, and neither sister, aunt nor mother left alive to help him to care for the baby.

These heart-rending cases intensified my own sorrow to such a degree that I could not bear it any longer, and I decided I must try to obtain other work. Not only was I grief-stricken, I was also hungry. The salary that the charity was able to pay me was so small that I could not even afford lunch; I was poorer than most of the clients who thronged our waiting-room.

CHAPTER TWO

Even in 1940, there was much unemployment in Liverpool, and the competition for any job was still very keen. At first, when the war began, the number of unemployed was increased by firms going out of business as a result of the war. For example, my mother, so acid-tongued at home, used her superior-sounding Oxford accent to good effect as the representative of a greeting card firm. The company was suddenly faced with an acute paper shortage, and, in order to remain in business, they had to turn to printing products essential to the war effort; they did not need a sales force. Mother, by this time very experienced and quite nicely dressed, soon found a new job as an accountant in a bakery. Girls like me, however, were in direct competition with a large population bulge made up of babies born after the servicemen came home from World War I. We were now in our early twenties.

Though by this time I was a skilled shorthand typist, as well as having had experience in social work, I was turned down again and again when I applied for secretarial posts.

The supercilious head clerks and typing pool supervisors looked me over as if I were a horse up for sale, often asked the most impertinent questions and always demanded references as to my moral character. They also asked about my education, and I had to own up that I had had only four years in school.

'Why?' they would snap suspiciously. 'Were you ill?' and I would have to reply that my parents had kept me at home from the age of eleven, in order that I might keep house for my parents and my six younger brothers and sisters; it was essential to impress on them that I was extremely healthy, because no employer would consider a person who might miss days of work through ill-health.

They looked disdainfully at a sheaf of evening school certificates showing high marks, and then would often change the subject by making disparaging remarks about my poor appearance.

I could not help the way I looked. My complexion was a pimpled white from insufficient food. My homecut hair hung lankly from lack of soap. In spite of working days and evenings, I could not earn enough to dress myself properly, even in second-hand clothes. When I could manage it, I bought little tins of Snowfire makeup from Woolworth's, at threepence a tin, to improve my looks, but often enough the expense was too great for my limited funds. I was neatly shabby to the point of beautifully stitched patches on patches, darns on darns.

Seventeen shillings and sixpence a week, which was what I earned, was only two shillings and sixpence more than I would have received on unemployment pay. Before I received my wages, deductions were made by my employer for National Health and Unemployment Insurance and for hospital care. The remainder was demanded of me by Mother. In those days, many mothers believed that they owned not only their daughters, but also everything their children earned, and my mother was no exception.

Money for my own expenses was earned in the evenings, by teaching shorthand to pupils in their homes.

I always fell into a panic when I lost a pupil, because it often meant that I had no tram fares and must walk the five miles to work in Bootle, through quite dangerous slums. In winter, the walk had to be done in the dead dark of the wartime blackout.

Mother was not prepared to help me. She had at that time no intention of ever being a fulltime housewife herself. Before Father went bankrupt, she had always been able to afford help with the children, had never had to care for them herself. She used every pressure she could think of to make it impossible for me to work, so that I would stay at home and be a free housekeeper. Even during the time that my younger brothers and sisters, Brian, Tony, Avril and Edward, were evacuated, she nagged and made my life a misery on this subject, presumably in order to have me ready at home to care for the children when the war ended. This remorseless battle between us had gone on for years, but I had always refused to give in.

I was quite sympathetic about Mother's preference to go to work, but I never could see why I should have to shoulder the burden of her responsibilities and become, once more, an unpaid, unrespected slavey to an uncaring bunch of siblings and two indifferent parents.

Perhaps Mother's lifetime repression of me had become a habit and closed her mind to the possibilities of other domestic arrangements. I knew from infancy that my very existence was a trial to her – she had always made that point extremely clear to me – and I tended to apologise continually to her as if I had no right to live.

Some time back, when, because of her callous attitude towards me, I had nearly suffered a nervous breakdown, she had become suddenly afraid; mental instability was much feared as a dreadful blot on a family's reputation. She promised she would treat me exactly as she did my pretty, compliant sister, Fiona, the third child of the family, now aged eighteen. Until I could command a better wage, she promised, she would take from me only about seven shillings a week, which would cover amply the food I ate.

She soon forgot her promise and fell into a series of tremendous rages, until I again gave up all my wages.

Fiona, three years younger than me, earned the same amount as I did, but the money was, in practice, left with her for her expenses and clothing, as was often done in middle-class families. She always looked well dressed.

Alan, the brother next to me in age, was in the Air Force. Out of the miserable fourteen shillings a week which he was paid, he allotted seven shillings to my mother. I felt that this, also, was pressing too hard on someone who had very little. I was unwise enough to say so, and Mother blew up like a time bomb.

'It's the only way in which I can claim a government pension, if he is killed,' she stormed.

As far as I was concerned, this remark put her into the same cold-hearted category as Harry's mother.

Before he was killed, Harry, my fiancé, had been on several voyages to New York, and at different times had brought me three very nice dresses from the Manhattan garment district. Anxious not to give an indication that I was engaged, I had told Mother that I had bought them in a second-hand store. Together with a pair of satin slippers, bought for my Confirmation and subsequently dyed black, the frocks enabled me to look appropriately dressed when I went to a local Dancing Club. Mother and Fiona often borrowed them. Since both of them were bigger than me, the seams were now showing signs of splitting.

Despite Mother's ruthlessness, from the spring of 1940 I had endured my lot more philosophically. I would be twenty-one in June and would marry Harry in the summer, when he hoped to have earned enough to furnish his house with the essentials, so that we could move into it.

Now I was alone again and so distressed that I

believe that sometimes I was out of my mind. I would cry as I walked home through the darkness, and often cried through the night, while Fiona slept contentedly on the other side of the bed, and poor little Avril aged twelve, squirmed uncomfortably between us.

One very hungry day, I inquired at the Employment Exchange about joining the Wrens, the naval service. I saw myself trim and smart in the navy blue uniform and tricorn hat of an officer.

The clerk told me sharply that, with my qualifications, I might get into the ATS, the women's service attached to the army; they needed kitchen help and drivers. I could not drive, and my present work demanded more skill than cooking for the Army, so I turned down this suggestion.

Feeling crushed and lonely, that evening I spent an extravagant shilling and went to the dance club, where I had first met Harry; I craved warm, friendly people round me.

Norm, the owner, had a new record of *In the Mood* on his wind-up gramophone, and over the cheerful noise of it, he greeted me genially.

At first those dancers who had known Harry and me were a little shy about asking me on to the floor. When they discovered that I was not going to weep for him on the padded shoulders of their best suits, I was never short of a partner. They were nearly all skilled workmen, for the moment exempt from military service; they were earning bigger wages than they had ever enjoyed before and had money to spend.

As a joke, I mimicked the pompous clerk in the Employment Exchange, who had so mortified me when I asked about joining the Wrens. A group of us were waiting for Norm to change the record, and the men gravely assured me that for a girl to join the Services was a fate worse than death.

With eyes averted, one man said, 'It's not suited to a nice girl like you. You'd have a rotten time.'

Another said with a grin, 'Nice girls don't leave home; they stay close to their mams.' He nodded towards his friends, and added, 'When these lads get into uniform it brings out their tomcat instincts; regular tigers, they are.' He exchanged playful punches with the others, and the conversation became ribald, so I left them. Truly, I thought, there is no one so conservative, small c, as a skilled craftsman. I trusted them enough, however, to feel that I should keep on trying for work as a civilian.

One of Harry's acquaintances escorted me home, and left me politely on my doorstep.

During that night, as I lay sleepless, I think I

began to realise that I could not live my life alone, and that I hoped to meet someone a long time in the future, who would fill the frightful gap in my life. I was used to a large family round me. Homes were, indeed, more crowded in those days. Sometimes there was a grandparent or other relation living with a married couple with children, and a lodger or two; single men frequently rented a room and were boarded by their landlady, who sometimes became the target of malicious tongues. Elderly women, widowed or single, occasionally doubled up and also endured the disparaging remarks of their neighbours, in these cases, with regard to their sexual preferences. The concept of birth control was barely beginning to penetrate the densely populated area in which I lived; and in Bootle, a Roman Catholic district, it was almost unknown and, in consequence, families were huge.

If I could keep myself, I thought rather pitifully, one of my brothers, when they married, might allow me to live with him, if I were still single. At least then I would have some male protection. In the meantime, it was necessary for me to earn sufficient to satisfy my mother, and have enough left over to buy a decent lunch each day, pay tram fares, clothe myself and, if possible, put away something for my old age. I rarely dreamed of anything more, except to be able to go to a dance or to the theatre occasionally. The idea of holidays or of buying books, pictures or music never entered my head – they were untold luxuries.

During the following few weeks, kind, familiar faces began to vanish with alarming rapidity from the Dance Club. Though many members were exempt from military service, Ernest Bevin, the Minister of Labour and leader of the powerful Transport and General Workers' Union, was re-directing skilled manpower to war production, often in other parts of the country. The men's places on the dance floor were taken by soldiers from the nearby barracks, and they brought in women picked up from the streets. These new members of the Club were harder for the owners, Norm and Doris, to control; they were transients with no local reputation to maintain.

Very shortly after, a tight-lipped and disapproving Norm and Doris announced the closure of the Club. They would both go to work in a munition factory and would re-open their business after the war. Their dancing shoes were put away and they passed out of my life, two kind people who believed in a certain standard of conduct and refused to deviate from it.

It was only when I saw the hastily scrawled note pinned on the dusty black door, *Closed for the duration*, that I realised how much I had depended upon the Club for company. Because it was so late before I got home from work, it had been my sole source of social life, except for occasional visits to the Playhouse theatre with a friend called Sylvia Poole.

After reading the note, I stood looking up at the door with its blistered paint and soot-covered portico, and I felt again, for a moment, the same scarifying loneliness of my first days in Liverpool as a child of eleven.

A savage air raid was in progress, but, despite the whistling bombs, I had, on my way home from work, crossed the double width of the parallel boulevards of Princes Road and Princes Avenue, to look once more at the old house where I had first met Harry. It had brought me such intense, though short-lived happiness. A greenish flare, dropped by a German bomber, lit up every detail of its simple, graceful architecture and gave it an almost dreamlike air.

'Goodbye, youth. Goodbye, happiness,' I muttered bitterly, as amid hissing flak, I crossed back over the road and the avenue, and went home to face the inner loneliness, the sense of being lost, which is the lot of the bereaved.

I wanted to die.

CHAPTER THREE

Alan had been in the Air Force since July, 1939, and I missed him very much. I did not see much of Fiona, who came next after Alan in the family. She worked as a clerk in a magazine distributor's office and had a number of men friends who took her out in the evenings to dinners, dances or the cinema. My parents rarely spoke, except to quarrel. The four younger children, Brian, now aged seventeen, Tony, aged fourteen, Avril, twelve, and Edward, aged nine, had in August, 1939, been evacuated to the country for safety, but early in 1940 Mother brought them home again, because the Government had demanded a modest financial contribution to their upkeep while they were away.

Brian finished school that year, and went to work for a shipping agent in the city. He also joined the City Police ARP Messenger Service, a group of boys with bicycles who, when the telephone lines were blown down during air raids, acted as messengers between hospitals, police, air raid wardens and rescue squads, and rest centres for the homeless. Father used a bicycle to get to work, and Brian borrowed the machine at night.

On their return to Liverpool, the youngsters faced almost immediately four sharp, frightening air raids. No damage was done in our district.

I had suggested to Mother that, with the fall of France, it would be easier for the Germans to bomb the north of England, and perhaps we should leave at least the younger children in the country, where they were being fairly well looked after by my father's sisters and, in the case of Avril, by a friend of my aunts. Mother would not hear of it; it was cheaper to bring them home.

Now she said to me, 'See, the Germans are only interested in bombing the north end of the docks. We are quite safe, down here at the south end.'

I held my tongue.

Fortunately for our children, the Government had reopened the city schools. At the beginning of the war they had been closed, because their teachers had to accompany the evacuees to the country. Some children, however, were never evacuated;

they ran wild in the streets, and vandalism and theft became widespread. When the trickle of children returning from evacuation became a torrent, many teachers were recalled, and the small predators went back to learning to read and write.

It says a great deal for the dedication of the teachers at that time, that despite the upheavals in their own lives and the dislocation of being evacuated, they managed to teach Tony and Edward well enough for them to win scholarships to grammar school. This made it possible, later on, for both boys to gain university degrees.

Nobody seemed to give much attention to little, blonde Avril, the second youngest member of our family. She was only a girl, equally frightened of being re-evacuated and of the air raids. In a chaotic world, she plodded on through elementary school as best she could.

The return of the children made Mother reopen, yet again, the question of my giving up my work and staying home to look after them.

As I washed the dishes and she dried them, she said without preamble, 'Now the children are back, Helen, I expect you to stay at home. You can give your notice in on Friday.'

The idea of keeping a daughter permanently at home, often denying her marriage, died hard.

But I felt I had endured enough in my early teens when I had been forced to keep house and, as the housekeeper who did not have to go to work, found myself reduced to a point bordering on starvation – the workers were fed and clothed first, the children next, and the woman at home was often left with nothing.

I did not, at first, answer Mother. This was before Harry's death and I was buoyed up by the thought that in a very few months, I would have only a loving husband to care for.

'I don't think it is necessary, Mother,' I replied carefully. 'Couldn't we manage the house between us? I'm getting good training as a social worker – it should lead to something better.'

Mother put the last pile of plates on to the kitchen shelf, while I emptied the washing-up bowl. She said scornfully, 'You'll get nowhere without a degree, so what's the use?' She glanced impatiently round the tiny, stone-tiled kitchen, with its greasy, deal table, and sandstone sink with a solitary cold water tap. 'Now, where are my curling tongs.'

'On the mantelpiece in the living room,' I replied mechanically, and I followed her into it, as I shook out the wet tea towel, ready to hang it to dry on the oven door of the old-fashioned range. The range took up nearly the whole of one wall of the room, and I noticed that its iron frontage badly needed blackleading.

Mother found her tongs and thrust them into the fire, and I silently draped the tea towel over the oven door. While the tongs were heating, she combed her hair quickly, in front of a piece of mirror balanced on the mantelpiece.

'You know very well we can't mange, Helen,' she began again. 'It was difficult enough to manage when the children were evacuated.'

'They're not babies any more, Mother. They could all help. Brian and Tony are big enough to queue in the shops, or even help with the cleaning. Or why can't Fiona take a turn at keeping house?'

'Fiona is too frail – and she doesn't know how. And boys can't do domestic work. How stupid can you be?'

'Well, why can't they?'

Mother paused with hot tongs poised to make a curl at the side of her face. She said angrily, 'Helen, you are being impudent. When I say you are to do a thing, you do it, my girl.'

'No, Mother,' I responded with unusual temerity. 'I am not staying home again.'

I thought Mother was going to strike me with the hot tongs, and I stepped back hastily.

'Don't talk to me like that. I won't have such nonsense. I'll talk to your employer. I'll have you dismissed.' Her face flushed with anger, and she seized a piece of her hair and rolled it on the tongs, as if she were about to pull it out.

I was scared. I had no idea what the ladies at work might do, if approached by an angry mother. They might very well agree to let me go to get rid of a shouting harridan on their doorstep. Mother saw her chance in my frightened face, and she pointed the tongs at me, and said, 'You have to learn, my lady, the facts of life. You can't choose what you want to do. You have to do what I say.'

How I wished Harry was there. I would have turned and run to him, begged him to find me a place to shelter until we could marry; it was, after all, only a little while until we would be married. But Harry was at sea. I thought of Father, the weaker parent, and burst out, 'I think we should talk about this with Father.'

But Mother was not listening. She was ranting about feckless daughters and how she would be worked to death, as she continued feverishly to put curls in her hair. Occasionally, she would pause in her endeavours to shake the tongs at me, as I stood like a paralysed rabbit in front of her.

I was saved by Edward's coming in. He had fallen

down and grazed his knees. They were bleeding and I took him into the kitchen to wash them, while Mother went upstairs to find a piece of old sheeting we kept for bandages.

By the time we had mopped up the blood and the tears, it was time for Mother to go to the cinema, and with a sharp, 'I'll talk to you later,' she put on her hat and coat and shot out of the house. I was left to put Avril and Edward to bed and to wonder whether I should, perhaps, just capitulate, and leave when I married.

We might have been able to afford a little help in the house, between all of us, but my parents were great fritterers of money. They both smoked heavily, and my father drank. There was always money for Mother to go to the cinema, which she did twice a week at least; always money to buy, for show, a piece of furniture for the sitting-room, paid for on the hire purchase system, a most expensive way to buy anything; money for clothes for Mother and Fiona. But there was never enough for good, plain food, for coal, blankets, soap, for underwear for the younger children. We were always short of necessities, and I knew from experience that, made to stay at home, I could be the most deprived person of all.

A beshawled neighbour of whom I had once asked

the time, because our single clock had stopped, had said to me disparagingly, ''Asn't your Dad got a watch? All lace curtains and nothin' in the larder, that's your Mam and Dad.' And she had sighed, as she looked me up and down.

A scared waif of a girl, I had not known how to answer her, so I had hung my head and shuffled away with Baby Edward in his squeaking pram.

Whenever Mother was short of ready money, she would collect any spare clothing lying about or some of our sparse bedding, and pawn it. Because I took great care of my few clothes, it was the shelf in the girls' bedroom which was first raided.

I was frequently reduced to the clothes I had on, and then had to save up, penny by penny, to retrieve the rest from Uncle Joe, the pawnbroker.

It was a game I could not win. Years later, however, I bought very cheaply a chest of drawers which had been badly seared by fire. A kindly man friend, aware of the problem, made a key to fit the old-fashioned locks on the drawers. Mother had one of her bigger tantrums on the subject of these locks, and she immediately demanded a key. I refused her, and carried the single key threaded on a piece of string round my neck, with Harry's ring.

When I heard from Harry's mother that he had

been killed, I was devastated not only by grief, but, in the background of my pain, also by the knowledge that I had lost my sole defence against my mother. As my friends in the Dance Club had sharply reminded me, nice girls did not leave home – they might have added, except, of course, to be married.

Sometimes, in those early weeks after Harry's death and after the row I had had with Mother about being the family housekeeper, I would stand behind the high shelves of files in the office of the charity for which I worked, and hold my head, while I shivered helplessly. Father had tried to act as peacemaker between Mother and me, by saying we should first try if we could manage without someone at home. Mother had reluctantly agreed, but she continued to nag at me about it. I wondered if between sorrow and Mother and hunger, I would go mad. Then I would renew my efforts to find better paid work. At least, I thought, that might settle the problem of being always hungry.

CHAPTER FOUR

Mother had many small ways of trying to make it impossible for me to go to work. One was to pilfer any money I had, so that I had no tram fares for the five-mile journey to Bootle where lay the office of the charity who employed me.

I kept a close eye on my handbag, but sometimes not close enough. I also tried secreting tram fares in the bedroom which I shared with Fiona and Avril, but a room furnished only with a double bed, a single shelf and no floor covering, does not offer many hiding places. Several times, I put a week's fares up the chimney, getting very sooty in the process, but she either found the money herself or, perhaps, Fiona mentioned it to her as an idiosyncrasy of mine.

Fiona was always *asked* if she would lend money

and always wailed miserably that she had none. Her ability to burst into floods of tears, her gorgeous light blue eyes welling up piteously, always defeated Mother, whereas my verbal fury merely bred acidity in return.

A few weeks after Harry's death, of which, of course Mother knew nothing, she had done one of her lightning swoops on my belongings and had pawned them. The blouse and underwear which I had been wearing that day had to be washed and dried overnight, ready to put on the next morning. In a world where washers and dryers had not yet been heard of, this meant putting on damp clothing every morning. Frequently there was no washing powder or soap, so my white blouse had, in Liverpool's polluted air, become grey.

It was some time before I managed to save up two shillings (ten pence in today's money) in order to redeem a change of garments from my old friend, the pawnbroker.

The only method of saving which I could think of was to walk most of the way to and from work. My two shorthand pupils paid me one shilling and sixpence a lesson, but I had recently lost one of them when I tried to increase my charge to two shillings. To get another one, I would have to advertise in the *Liverpool Echo or Evening Express,* and I had yet to find the money for that.

At the same time, as the Battle of Britain progressed, air raids became frequent.

The raids usually began about six o'clock in the evening and lasted until eleven or twelve. It was everybody's ambition to be safely at home, or wherever they were going to be in the evening, before the air raid warning howled its miserable notes across the waiting city. This was usually an impossibility for me, because, as the raids gained in intensity and the bombed-out sought our aid, the load of work in the office increased proportionately.

We worked later and later. My colleague, on whom devolved the ultimate responsibility for the office, looked ever more careworn; her skin was pasty from lack of fresh air and her eyes black-rimmed. She was a wonderfully caring person who gave of herself unsparingly to our distraught clients.

The five miles to work seemed to take a lifetime to walk. I went down the hill and through the city, and out again, along Byrom Street, Scotland Road and the eternity of Stanley Road, through some of Liverpool's worst, festering slums. Like many English people who commonly travelled long and inconvenient distances by public transport to their employment, I arrived already very tired. Because roads were blocked by fallen debris or railways were out of commission, many others beside myself were forced to walk. A walk which I would have cheerfully undertaken, however, if it had been necessitated by an air raid, depressed me beyond measure because it was totally unnecessary.

Only people who have had to walk without a torch or cycle without a lamp through the total darkness of a blackout can appreciate the hazards of it. Innumerable cats and dogs trotted silently through it, to be tripped over by cursing pedestrians; pillar boxes and fire hydrants, telephone poles and light standards, parked bicycles and the occasional parked car, not to speak of one's fellow pedestrians, all presented pitfalls for the unwary. Many times I went home with a bloody nose or with torn stockings and bleeding knees from having tripped up. Another problem was the ease with which one could lose one's way; it was simple to become disoriented while crossing a road or a square and end up on the wrong pavement, hopelessly lost.

A new hazard appeared later in the war, and was the cause of Father's having a painful fall, when the batteries of his flashlight failed. Lack of sufficient water pressure to douse the fires raised by incendiaries had necessitated the laying of extra water pipes directly from the river. The pipes ran along the street gutters or the edge of the pavements, and even in the daytime, people occasionally fell over these unaccustomed barriers. Father, one night, tripped over a newly laid pipe and bruised himself badly. He lay on the pavement in the dark, too shaken to get up, until he heard footsteps approaching.

He cried for help, and was immediately answered by a male voice. He was located, helped up and asked about his injuries. Father said that he was all right, that the fright of the fall had given him heart pains which had now ebbed.

'I'm lost, however,' he said.

The stranger asked his address, and Father told him it.

'Oh, that's easy. I'll have you home in a couple of shakes,' promised the man. 'Put your arm in mine.'

'Have *you* a torch?' inquired Father, very puzzled at his rescuer's self-assurance in the total darkness.

The stranger laughed. 'I don't need a light,' he said. 'I'm blind. Didn't you hear my stick on the pavement?'

'No, I didn't,' Father answered. 'Do you think

we could find my spectacles? They fell off, as I went down. They must be just here somewhere.'

The stick was used to sweep the pavement round them, and the spectacles, fortunately unbroken, were returned to their owner. A very grateful Father was safely deposited on his own doorstep by a man who, in ordinary circumstances, would have been regarded as seriously handicapped.

Bearing in mind the distances I often had to walk, it was as well that I had inherited my mother's stamina, if not her temperament; even so, the strain was very great.

In the safe knowledge that no one could see me, I would stumble along in the dark, weeping openly, and wishing I was dead. Yet, when a stick of bombs began to fall nearby, and the whistle of each succeeding missile became closer, I would instinctively duck for shelter in the nearest shop doorway and crouch down, hands clasped over head, until the last resounding bang. I discovered that to survive is a fundamental instinct of all living things, and in such situations instinct takes over.

Sometimes the planes would dive fast, one after another, and other pedestrians would dash pell-mell into my refuge, to huddle tightly round me, like sheep in a storm, until the danger had retreated. Then, with shy apologies and light jokes directed to unseen faces, we would issue forth again into the street.

While we sheltered, the blackness was occasionally lit by the unearthly green glow of flares floating slowly in the sky, while the Germans tried to locate their specific targets. For a moment we would see fellow shelterers in the greatest detail, and all of us would feel naked and helplessly exposed to our enemies in the sky. The flares and bursts of tracer bullets were in one way useful, however, because they gave us a sufficiently good view of our route that, when we all set out again, we were less likely to have a fall.

The flares also showed up ARP messenger boys racing recklessly along on their bicycles; regardless of danger, they sped from air raid wardens' posts, to hospitals, to fire stations and rescue squads, wherever a message needed to be delivered. Most of the boys were under seventeen years of age, too young for military service; yet nightly they took chances which even the military would have considered risky.

Motor traffic crawled along with heavily shaded lights; ambulances and fire engines rang their bells continuously. Lorry drivers, tram and bus drivers normally kept going until a raid was overhead, when they would park and take refuge in the nearest shelter. There were few private cars on the streets, because of petrol rationing; those out at night were, for the most part, carrying walking casualties, rescue squads, tradesmen like telephone men and electricians, air raid wardens and medical personnel. More than one vehicle ended up in an unsuspected bomb crater in the middle of a road, the driver and passengers killed or injured.

So when my mother riffled through my handbag with her tobacco-stained fingers, to take my fare money, she created cruel hardship for me, and it was not only for my lost love that I wept.

CHAPTER FIVE

When attacking convoys, particularly at night, the Germans began to use packs of U-boats working in unison, rather than single submarines. Although the escort ships of the convoys now had a listening device, called Asdic, with which they could detect the presence of submarines, the noise of the convoy itself often confused the listeners and made it difficult to identify a submarine with certainty. It was also ineffective if the U-boat was on the surface.

To avoid the Asdic device, the U-boat commanders would come up steeply into the middle of a convoy, and, in a few moments, create havoc. Then, still on the surface, they would race away into the darkness, outrunning the escorting corvettes.

Once my first grief over Harry's death had become

more controllable, I again began to feel very deeply for the frantic mothers and wives of merchant seamen and Royal Navy men, alike, who died during September, October and November of 1940. The women threatened to overwhelm our little office, with its limited resources.

During one dreadful Saturday morning, when weeping women stood in the waiting room because all the chairs were full, and queued along the passageway and stairs, I was so distressed that something seemed to break inside me, and I cried out in fury to a startled voluntary worker, 'It's madness to send men to certain death like this!'

The words rang through the crowded, untidy room, and all the voluntary workers stopped their bustle and turned to stare at me. My weary colleague, Miss Evans, seated at her desk at the hub of the turmoil, put her hand over the mouthpiece of the telephone, and said sharply, 'Miss Forrester!'

In the ensuing dead silence, I mumbled, 'I'm sorry.'

I snatched up a pile of files and began feverishly to put them back on their open shelves, my fury unassuageable. The tears coursed down my cheeks. 'Why couldn't seamen have enough sense to stay ashore?' I raged inwardly. Most of them had skills which would have given them protected jobs in war factories. On the other hand, Harry had said that, if he had come ashore, he would have been called up, sooner or later, for the Army or the Navy; he might just as well remain a merchant seaman, and earn better wages.

Based on my utter frustration, a dull anger at Harry surged in me. He was old enough not to be amongst the first to be conscripted. We could have been married by now and had some happiness together; I could have been carrying his much desired baby. The fool! The stupid idiot, to go and get himself killed! I was terribly, unreasonably furious at him.

In those wild moments, I gave no thought to the fact that unless freighters went to sea, to carry on the country's trade, we would soon starve. I also forgot that, though Harry often complained about the conditions under which seamen lived aboard ship, basically he enjoyed going to sea; like everyone else, he hoped the war would soon be over. Few civilians knew enough of the true situation to realise that it was bound to drag on for years. Wars are very easily started; the problem is in bringing them to a close.

Now Harry was gone, and I had not the faintest idea what to do, as I struggled to help women equally distressed. My mind refused to concentrate;

my body longed for rest, preferably eternal rest. Normally I was always hungry; now I sometimes found it difficult to eat.

Even Mother noticed my unusual dullness and told me to stop looking so sulky. 'Laugh and the world laughs with you,' she would say, so truly, 'Cry, and you cry alone.'

'It's easier for her,' I would think sullenly. 'She's doing quite nicely now.' I forgot that she had been through an earlier war, a war which had been in many ways much worse.

'Why aren't you going dancing?' Fiona asked.

I looked at her blankly for a moment, and then replied, 'I'm too tired – the office is so busy.'

I don't think that Father noticed anything much. He tended to live a life of his own amongst his friends from the office; Mother never accompanied him either to the public houses or to the concerts and plays to which he went. Sometimes he would inquire of Tony or Brian what they were doing in their spare time. Not infrequently, he had a tremendous row with Mother, usually on the subject of money.

He may possibly have noticed that, at that time, I was not quarrelling much with Mother, and consequently the house was quieter. I was too exhausted to face her verbal barbs, and no matter what she did, I accepted it and did my best to cope with the consequences.

On the Saturday on which I had exclaimed so explosively in the office about the lunacy of the war, I worked all day, and arrived home just as Mother was putting on her retrimmed, turban-type hat before going to the cinema. She was peeking at herself in the broken piece of mirror on the mantelpiece. It was still the only mirror in the house and was consequently very precious. During the war, mirrors were hard to obtain.

She nodded to me, buckled up the belt of her leather overcoat and picked up her handbag. 'Back at eleven,' she threw over her shoulder, as she went through the back door.

As I took off my own coat, I listened to the click-click of her high-heeled shoes on the stone flags of the back alley. I remembered how, as a child, I would lie in bed after Edith, our nanny, had tucked me up, every limb tensed, eyes screwed tight in case those clicking heels came upstairs. Nothing made her crosser than to find that Alan and I had failed to go to sleep promptly at six o'clock. An extremely nervous child, I was afraid of the dark, afraid of the flickering shadows made by the candle which Edith always left on the dresser, but, most of all, I was afraid of my stormy mother.

While I put together a meal for myself, Father leaned back in his chair and closed his eyes. It was a habit he had acquired after a heart attack which he had suffered at the age of thirty-three. Now, he was dozing while he waited for the arrival of his friend, Tom, a school teacher, still in his late twenties. Before Tom had gone to attend a Teachers' Training College, he had worked in Father's office, and, despite the difference in age, they had interests in common, including Father's long-standing study of French history; they also argued about politics by the hour.

I knew that they would go to town, to drink in *The Vines* in Lime Street and in other public houses. *Ye Hole in Ye Wall* was another of their favourite haunts. Once Tom took Father to *Ye Cracke* in Rice Street, and subsequently, if Father was alone, he always went there. It had a tiny parlour with a transom labelled *The War Office* over its entrance. Men used to sit there and refight the Boer War, and no doubt Father refought the First World War in the same place. He really enjoyed exploring the many quaint taverns in Liverpool. He would come in about eleven o'clock, gravely drunk, and proceed, with care, upstairs to bed, to sleep it off in time for his Sunday morning pint at nearby *Peter's*, another of his favourite public houses.

Father woke up from his nap, and sat cracking his fingers for some minutes. He looked up at me. I was seated at the table, a sheet of cheap writing paper in front of me.

'Are you not going to a dance?' he asked.

'No. I thought I'd write to Alan. He must be having a terrible time at Biggin Hill; it's been bombed like anything.'

Father nodded agreement. Though he could write well and amusingly, he rarely wrote to any of his children while they were away, and I think that in many other houses this task was left to the womenfolk.

'He's ground staff; he should be able to take cover,' Father said heavily.

I wondered at Father's indifference to the danger his sons were in while they were in the Services. Perhaps, after the horrors of trench warfare in the First World War, bombing, aerial combat and the dangers at sea seemed petty in comparison.

Mother had heatedly forbidden me to write to or visit our little evacuees while they were away. 'You'll do nothing but upset them,' she had accused me.

Despite my protests, she was so vehement that I never did write.

Alan was my old and trusted friend, as well as my brother, and she knew better than to come between us. I wrote to him as often as I could. He did not always reply, for reasons which were painfully obvious from the headlines in the newspapers. The Battle of Britain was in scarifying flood. His base, Biggin Hill, was an airfield of crucial strategical importance and a frequent target of the Luftwaffe. He had continued to be trained as ground crew, had been promoted to Leading Aircraftsman, and did not normally fly. Our inadequate number of Spitfires and Hurricanes had, however, at all costs, to be kept in the air, and boys like him worked like devils to do it; at night he often slept under the aircraft on which he had been working, because time was so precious.

In the gorgeous summer of 1939, he went away a gangling youth. When we opened the door to him on his first leave in January, 1940, it was as if a young giant stood on our doorstep. He seemed to have grown a foot in height, his shoulders had broadened, and his face was that of a man. Though thin, he was healthier than I had ever seen him.

As we sat around our frugal fire, he told us that he had done six months of square-bashing, drilling very much as if he had been in the Army; then he had gone for further training in the maintenance of aircraft.

On his more recent leave, he had divulged,

'Some of the crates we have to deal with look more like colanders than aircraft when they land. And we have to get them back up again within hours.'

'And the crews?' I asked.

'We're losing an awful lot,' he replied, his face strained and sad.

I had guessed at the losses; we were getting Air Force families in the office, as well as those of seamen. Tears welled at the back of my eyes.

During his leaves, we gave all his clothing, which was usually soaked with oil, a thorough wash, and Mother fed him with everything she could cajole out of arrogant shopkeepers. He brought his own ration card, but it was inadequate, and, as well, we gave him our own rations of cheese, bacon and meat.

He seemed happy to be at home, and yet, by the end of the week, it was always apparent that he would be glad to return to his RAF station. Though war is horrifying, it brings excitement and drama into dull lives. As yet, he was only a Leading Aircraftsman, hardly trained, but his uniform gave him a certain prestige; and he always performed at his best when facing a high level of stress.

So, seated at the scratched, living-room table, I tried to forget my own pain and to put myself in his position. I wrote as cheerfully as I could about the neighbourhood, as yet little damaged by bombs. I told him about Nickie, our tan and white mongrel, who knew the sound of the air raid warning and the all clear, and came and went, without any direction from us, to his own private air raid shelter, which he had established in a little cupboard by the side of the fireplace.

My second brother, Brian, had brought the animal home, some years before. A publican had thrown it out of the door of his public house, and the tiny whimpering puppy had landed at Brian's feet. Dreadfully upset at its obvious hunger, Brian brought it home to a house where hunger was endemic; yet we were unanimous in adopting it, and it shared our meagre meals and learned to eat anything. Faithful and intensely loving, it lay on my feet as I wrote.

I did not mention in my letters the nightly air raids we were enduring; they seemed small in comparison with the battles that the Air Force were fighting.

On the 30th and the 31st August, Biggin Hill received two dreadful poundings which nearly put it out of action. Planes were damaged on the ground, as well as in the air, and there were numerous casualties.

Alan, not yet twenty and with less than a year's full-time experience, had, like all the other youngsters there, to cope with repairs that would in normal times have called for skilled engineers and mechanics. Above their heads, pilots who were no older, fought to break up the waves of German bombers and Messerschmitt fighters, as Goering tried to wreck the Royal Air Force, and thus open up Britain to the invasion armies then gathering in French ports.

The fall of France had been devastating for Britain. The German Air Force was now operating from French airfields just across the English Channel. Based in French ports, the U-boats could hunt the eastern Atlantic to their hearts' content. As I wrote, I realised, with a pang, that it was probably one of those very U-boats from France which had caught Harry's ship. I knew that Alan, too, was now in deadly peril; but letters must be optimistic.

Optimistic? Most of Britain was in a state of quiet despair. The British Army had been thrown out of Norway. Our men had been pushed out of France, though, to console us, the saga of the rescue from Dunkirk of the remnants of our army was on everyone's lips – once or twice, I heard of men who had arrived on their mothers' doorsteps, filthy, bloody, ragged and exhausted, rifle still in hand, having come straight home after landing; a few of them never went back – protected by their families, they simply deserted.

Now London was being bombed unmercifully, and there was a steady trickle of Londoners fleeing the capital. Some came to Liverpool, only to be caught in the lesser, though still frightening, raids on our city.

Almost everyone suffered nightmares at the thought of a German invasion, and superhuman efforts were made by the Home Guard and civilians to be ready for it. So that the Germans would not be able to find their way, signposts were uprooted and names of railway stations painted over. Nobody seemed to realise that a professional soldier would, in thirty seconds, make any hapless civilian he came upon say exactly where he was. All that happened was that, throughout the war, people got lost like pennies running down a sewer drain. Fortunately the Air Force did not need sign posts to know where it was; otherwise, they might have got lost, too, and the war would have had a different ending. The Army was not so fortunate, and many times, during my long walks in the Wirral, I directed lost, khaki-clad lorry drivers. Once I came upon a stranded tank, its flustered crew kneeling over a map at the roadside. They not only wanted to know where they were but where they could get a cup of tea!

There was a rap on the front door, and Father got up to let in his friend, Tom.

He came into the living room and stood uneasily fingering his trilby hat, while Father put on his overcoat.

'Good evening, Helen.'

I smiled up at him rather shyly. I did not like him, because I felt he was responsible for Father's drinking so much. This was not fair, because Father had always drunk quite heavily, perhaps to soothe his shattered nerves when he returned, from the First World War, a shell-shocked neurasthenic.

Tom was a big, heavily built man, a little under thirty years of age, extremely dark, his well-shaven chin still almost black from a threatening fresh growth.

He said to Father, 'I got my call-up papers this morning.' He ran the brim of his hat nervously through his fingers.

Father stopped buttoning up his coat. 'Well, I'm blessed! Army?'

Tom did not look as if he regarded it as a blessing. 'Yes,' he replied. 'Have to report next week.'

'Ah, well, I suppose it was bound to come. At least you're single. No family to worry about.'

'Mother's very upset.'

'I'm sure she must be.' Father sighed, as he picked up his hat. 'I shall miss you very much.'

Tom half-smiled. 'Thanks. Are you ready?'

They both said goodbye to me, and left me to my letter. I could hear Avril laughing in the back yard, as she played a game of ball against the house wall, with another little girl. She did not laugh often enough, I thought.

Nickie put his nose on my knee and I patted him absently. Apart from the disintegration of my personal life, the further world around me was changing fast. The war kept nibbling at unexpected aspects of life. Men like Tom were being whisked away, and women like his widowed mother suddenly had to face a society which did not care much what happened to them, a society from which fathers, husbands and sons had given them a good deal of protection.

I tried not to think about my own unhappy situation, but the fact that I did not have the money for a stamp for Alan's letter reminded me forcibly of my dire financial straits.

What should I do? What *could* I do when I had so little formal education?

I had recently been for two interviews for secretarial jobs. I was turned down immediately it was obvious that I had hardly been to day school at all. My experience in a charitable organisation did not, I discovered, rank very high. Charities were, in the minds of head clerks interviewing me, run by bumbling amateurs, do-gooders, cranks, a lot of old women. Humbled by the sharp tongues, I had thanked the gentlemen for their time, and had gone home.

CHAPTER SIX

On 7th September, 1940, London suffered a dreadful bombing; it went on day and night, until the news was that the city was on fire from end to end. As verbal descriptions of it were passed from mouth to mouth and reached the north, we became more and more apprehensive that our turn would be next.

In a hastily scribbled letter, Alan told me that about five hundred bombers were involved, and that the raiders were very well protected by fighter planes.

Londoners hardly had time to recover before the Germans, on 9th September, mounted another huge operation, in which they stoked up the fires still burning from the earlier raid. On the 11th they hit Buckingham Palace, which seemed incredible to many Liverpudlians. Who would dare to hit the palace of a king? The King seemed almost thankful that he himself had been bombed out; he said that he could now look homeless East Enders in the face!

Liverpool was under nearly continuous nightly attack. Alan said he never went to bed for weeks during that period, but neither did we. We nodded on the basement steps, trying to get what rest we could, while the diving planes screeched overhead and the guns in Princes Park roared unceasingly. I learned a lot of German irregular verbs during those long, sleepless nights, in an effort to continue studies that I had pursued through seven years of evening school attendance. Such schools had been closed at the beginning of the war.

Working in the dock area, I could see that it was daily becoming more difficult to keep the port of Liverpool open, and Bootle, lying immediately to the north, was to have, for its size, the doubtful honour of being the most heavily bombed area in the British Isles. The ingenuity of the population in keeping going amid the ruins was a wonder to behold.

The civilian casualty lists began to lengthen. Amongst other places, the lists were posted outside our main office in the city, and I remember so clearly the tired, anxious faces of the people scanning them. But the faces of a few readers had an expression of morbid fascination, eyes glazed, lips parted, as they read – the same expressions that you can, nowadays, see in the faces of onlookers at an accident or a street murder or rape; they just stare and do nothing about it, getting pleasure out of other people's agonies.

For many of us, life was solely long days at work, work which in the Bootle area consisted largely of trying to continue normal operations amid the wreckage of a factory or office or warehouse or dock. Then a quick rush for home, into the air raid shelter – if one was available.

As I write, I can feel the burning tiredness of my eyes at that time, and the acute discomfort of the ridged stone basement steps. I can smell the odour from the cellar of damp coal and of cats. I can see the flaking whitewash on the stairway's walls and a century of cobwebs hanging from its ceiling. It never seemed to occur to any of us to make some cushions to sit on – we had none in the house – or brush down the dirty walls, perhaps rewhitewash them, to cheer the place up. We were singularly unenterprising and simply endured the long, chilly nights.

If we were lucky, we would get an hour in bed,

before we had to get up at six o'clock to go to work. I often felt worse after that hour in bed than if I had stayed up; but it did help to reduce the swelling in one's feet, which came from never putting them up.

Picking one's way to work in a long procession of pedestrians winding through shattered or blocked streets is a memory which must have remained with many people. It always astonished me how clean and neat we managed to make ourselves, despite interruptions in the water supply and the appalling dust raised by the bombing.

Because I had frequently to walk onwards to Bootle, in the north, I was often amongst the earliest people to set out from the south end of the city. I found myself part of a long line of much older women, their heads wrapped in turbans or kerchiefs, a pair of old shoes under their arm or sticking out of a shopping bag. They plodded along stolidly on swollen feet, their varicose veins lumpy under their woollen stockings. Occasionally, they would shout, 'Mornin',' to each other or stop for a word or two, but for the most part they walked in silence, putting first one cautious foot over scattered chunks of brickwork or electric cables and then lifting the other one over. Sometimes they paused to stare back at some unusual object, like a bath, lying in the road, or to watch the firemen and rescue workers at a particularly large scene of destruction.

They were the cleaning ladies of Liverpool, often leaving homes that had been damaged in the previous night's raid, to go into the city to make ready the offices and shops before their staff arrived. Increasingly frequently, they found nothing left to clean, only a dangerous mountain of rubble or a burning skeleton of a building. Many businesses, however, had reason to bless them, when the building was still standing, but all the windows and doors had been blown out and stock or papers were scattered everywhere. Imperturbable, they would pick up, shake and sort, until they had the floors fairly clear. Then, if the electricity was still working, they would plug in their vacuum cleaners and assail the all-enveloping dust. If there was no electricity, out came brooms and mops, buckets and floor cloths. To the nervous, excited clerks and shop assistants, when they arrived later, these women were quiet symbols of stability.

As the winter crept in, loss of windows became hard to bear, both at home and at work. The sweeping rain soaked many a home and office, despite people's efforts to keep it out by nailing old rugs or linoleum over the gaping frames.

Our office in Bootle was no exception. I arrived one morning to find snow thick on the ugly brown linoleum of our second floor office, and a great drift up against my desk.

With icy fingers, I carefully shook the flakes off the precious files on the top of my desk and that of Miss Evans. I lifted the telephone receiver and wiped it. Immediately a sharp voice asked, 'Number, please?' I thanked heaven that it was working, as I quickly put the receiver down again.

Using a piece of cardboard, I shovelled the freezing piles out through the glassless windows. But there was still a lot on the floor when the rest of the staff arrived. 'Be careful not to slip,' I warned our voluntary helpers, as they tiptoed through the puddles.

As the day progressed, the remainder of the snow melted under tramping feet, leaving the office dank and miserable for days afterwards.

I learned to be very afraid of looters.

On the ground floor of the old house which was our office, we had a room filled with clean, second-hand clothing, for the reclothing of the bombed out. Not only were people sometimes clad only in their nightclothes, when their house came down about their ears, their day clothes could be ruined by such a catastrophe; every stitch in the house could be torn, impregnated by glass or ruined by spouting water-pipes and thick dust. Everything had to be replaced – and Bootle was poor, terribly poor.

One frosty morning, as I hastened up the street, I saw that the office had again lost its windows during the night. My exhausted colleague had succumbed to influenza, and I wondered who I should talk to in the Town Hall in order to get a fast replacement of the glass.

As I unlocked the front door I heard the sound of voices. At first I thought it was the women who ran another charity on the ground floor, but then I realised with alarm that it was men's voices I was listening to.

The door of the clothing room was ajar, and I ran forward and flung it wide.

A sheet had been spread over the centre of the floor and two men and a woman were tossing clothing on to it.

'What on earth are you doing?' I asked indignantly.

One man paused and looked up at me. He was burly, in shirt sleeves, with huge muscular arms covered with black hairs. A docker, I guessed.

'You get out of here,' he growled. 'And mind your own business.'

'This is my business.' My voice rose in anger. 'You don't belong here. Get out yourself before I call the police.'

The three dropped the clothing they were holding, and looked uncertainly at each other. They did not move.

'OK. I'll call them.' I moved towards the door.

'Oh, no, you don't.' Both men advanced on me, their feet tangling in the pile of clothing lying on the sheet.

I quickly pulled the door shut in their path. The lock was broken, but it might hold them up for a second or two.

Light and fleet, I sped up the stairs, thrust the key into the lock of our office, slipped inside and locked it from the inside. I seized the telephone and thankfully asked the operator, 'Police, quick.'

After a solid night of bombing, the police number was engaged. The men were pounding on the door and shouting threats. 'Call the ARP. There are probably more people there,' I told her.

Though she had been afraid of interrupting a police telephone conversation, the operator unhesitatingly broke into the conversation on the ARP phone, and asked for help.

The men outside must have heard the relief in my voice, as I said, 'Thanks very much.' By the time two volunteer wardens pounded up the stairs, the looters had fled.

I was still trembling when the first volunteer member of our staff arrived. I asked her to re-sort and hang up the clothing again, and a little later on, presumably as a result of the wardens' report, our windows were boarded up by workmen, who arrived unbidden by me.

We had some funds which could be lent to men who had lost their tools in a raid or to replace smashed spectacles, and alleviate similar woes, which were not covered by any governmental source. Ready cash was kept in an old-fashioned cash box, locked in a cupboard overnight. On a bleak November day, while my superior was still sick, I put the cash box out, ready, on the desk, and went to the waiting-room to check the number of people there.

A boy passed the waiting-room door. I presumed he had brought a message from his family; it was a common occurrence, and I went back to deal with him.

The boy had flitted silently out, taking the cash box with him.

I was appalled, and immediately sent for the police.

Two plain clothes men, they sat and warmed

themselves by our dim electric fire, and sighed and rubbed their hands.

'Normally we could pick 'im up as quick as light,' one of them said. 'Anybody with that much money to spend sticks out like a sore toe. But now . . .' he shrugged, 'with all the high wages . . . well.'

The thief was never traced. It was a sore loss to our small organisation.

During my harsh days of mourning, I learned a lot of sad truths. It was a revelation to me that the poor would steal from the poor. Working-class solidarity had been preached to me consistently by Communists working in the main office; the poor stood shoulder to shoulder against the wicked, exploiting upper classes. But, in truth, they prey on each other, with a ruthlessness which was, and still is, hard to swallow. Who has not seen decent city-built housing, built specifically to help those who could not afford much rent, stripped bare as a skeleton, of tiles, fittings, lead for the roof, by people who must have been close neighbours, to know even that the house was not yet occupied?

There is a saying in Liverpool, 'If it isn't nailed down, sit on it.' I now understood what it meant, and I became very careful.

Particularly during the war, great targets for thieves were the gas and electric meters in the cellars of damaged houses in the poorer areas. These meters had to be fed either by pennies or shillings, and their cash boxes were temptingly full of money. In peacetime, they were often rifled at night. A slender youth would lift the manhole in front of the street door, normally used for the delivery of coal directly into the cellar, and slide through the opening. He soon prised open the drawer in which the money was collected, and was then hauled quietly out by an accomplice.

Though our house was not damaged at the time it happened, we twice had our meters broken into, and found, to our sorrow, that we had to pay the gas and electricity companies all over again.

One exasperated old man near us had had to pay a huge gas bill because thieves had robbed his meter. Afterwards, he carefully tied a ship's bell to the underpart of the manhole cover.

One early morning, as I was washing myself in the kitchen, I heard the sonorous ding-dong of the bell, and about half a minute later, shrieks and curses in the street. The old man had caught a youth and was giving him a sound beating with a broom stick, a far more effective punishment than a lecture from a magistrate.

CHAPTER SEVEN

It was October, and nearly five months since I had bid Harry a hasty goodbye, when he embarked on his last voyage. I still felt very forlorn and terribly alone, despite a large family. I had spent this Saturday afternoon walking over to see the pawnbroker, to retrieve a cotton-wrapped bundle containing two of my dresses, a skirt and cardigan, which Mother had pawned. My return journey took me past the house in which we had rented two freezing attic rooms, when we first came to Liverpool.

Seated on the stone steps which led down from the pavement to her basement home was Mrs Hicks. Bundled up in a series of woollen cardigans, she was enjoying the late October sunshine.

She was an old friend, and when she saw me, she

got up from the steps and dusted her black skirt with her hands.

''Allo, luv,' she greeted me in surprise. ''Ow are yer? Come in. Haven't seen you in ages.' She pulled open the cast-iron gate which protected the steps.

I smiled at her and carefully eased myself past the gate and on to the narrow steps, to follow her down and through the heavy door under the sweep of steps that led up to the main entrance of the house.

The basement rooms in which she lived had originally been the kitchens of the house. Thick, vertical iron bars still guarded the windows, and the interior still smelled of damp and much scrubbing with pine disinfectant.

The sun did not penetrate her home, and in the gloom, she beamed at me, every wrinkle and crease of her face suggesting battles won or lost, patience learned. She had been very kind to all of us in the bitter days when, up in the attic, we had nearly starved.

Brian had been her particular friend, and she asked after him, as she shut the outer door. I told her he was well and had work.

'Sit down, now. We'll have a cuppa tea. See, the kettle's on the boil,' and she pointed to an iron kettle on the hob, belching steam like a railway train. 'And how've *you* bin, me duck?'

While I sat down by the fire and put my bundle on the floor, she moved swiftly round the room on tiny booted feet, while she collected the tea things and put them on a table beside me.

'I'm all right,' I lied. 'And how are you? It's lovely to see you again.'

'Och, me? Never nuthin' the matter with me. And me hubbie's a lot better, now he's workin'.'

Mr Hicks, I learned, had become a timekeeper at a new factory in Speke, and Mrs Hicks said that, after so many years of unemployment, it felt strangely nice to have regular wages coming in, although it meant a long bicycle ride for him each day.

I congratulated her. Provided they were not bombed out, people like Mr and Mrs Hicks benefited greatly by the war.

Mrs Hicks finally came to rest in the easy chair opposite me, and, as we sat knee to knee, she stirred her mug of tea vigorously, and remarked, 'You don't look at all well, luv. Has your throat bin botherin' you again?'

'No, Mrs Hicks.' My throat was husky, but not with the tonsillitis which plagued me from time to time. I put my mug down on the little table, put my head down on my knee and burst into tears.

In a second I was pressed to Mrs Hicks' pillowy chest. 'Now, now, dear.' She stroked my hair, which I was again growing because I had no money for hairdressers. Then she turned my face up to her. 'What's to do? Has your Mam been at you agen?'

No love had been lost between Mother and Mrs Hicks; she must have heard Mother raging at me many a time.

'No, Mrs Hicks. It's not that.'

Gradually she wormed out of me my loss of Harry, and I said tearfully, 'I don't know what to do, Mrs Hicks. I just don't.'

'You're not expecting, are you, luv?'

Mrs Hicks was a most practical woman, and I had to smile at her through my tears.

'No, I'm not. We – we agreed we would wait. But I wish I was. I'd have something to live for, then.'

'Nay. It's better as it is – you'll see that later on. And him bein' an older fella, he sowed his wild oats years ago, I'll be bound. He knew what he was about – he must've really loved you.'

'He was awfully good. He didn't want me to be left single, with a child, like so many.' Fresh tears burst from me.

She let me cry, and it did me good. The tea went

cold, but when I gently loosed myself from her arms and leaned back in my chair, full of apologies for being such a badly behaved guest, she wiped my face with a corner of her apron, and then made me sit quietly while she made a fresh, black brew.

'I don't blame you for not telling your Mam; hard case, she is, if you'll forgive me for sayin' so. Will you tell her now?'

'I don't think so, Mrs Hicks. It's past now.' I sipped my new cup of tea gratefully. 'You know, she'd dissect the whole thing and be so disparaging – mostly about his being a seaman. You know her.'

'Humph. What's wrong with goin' to sea?'

The question was rhetorical; I did not have to explain my mother's snobbery to Mrs Hicks; she had suffered from it herself often enough.

'Have you bin to see his mother?'

I had already told her how I had met Mrs O'Dwyer when the lady came to my office to consult the Society for which I worked about claiming a pension. Now I added, 'She seemed so hard and bitter, Mrs Hicks. Harry said she never forgave him for leaving the priesthood; and yet, there she was, trying to benefit from his death. Frankly, it made me feel sick.'

The tears welled again.

'Aye, dear, dear. What you need is a body and a good wake. Gives you a chance to cry yer head off.' She sighed. 'There's lots like you, luv, and all they can do is light a candle.'

I agreed wanly, and often, in later years, when I saw forests of candles twinkling before bejewelled Madonnas, I thought of all of us who did not have the privilege of burying our dead.

I said, depressedly, that I must go home, and she rose and put her arm round me as I walked across the room. 'Now, you come and see me again – anytime you like. And I won't say a word, if I see your Mam. I won't say nuthin' to nobody, if it comes to that.'

'Thank you, Mrs Hicks.' I put my arms round her and kissed her.

I went to see her two or three times. Then I lost touch with her when, on the sudden death of her landlady, the house was sold, and she had to move. Nobody seemed to know or care where she had gone. The new owner of the house simply shrugged his shoulders and said, 'Half the world's on the move.' When I stopped the postman on his round, to inquire if he had a forwarding address, he remembered the old lady, but he nodded his head negatively. 'They didn't have no letters to speak of. She couldn't read, you know. Nice old girl, she was; let me shelter in her hall, once, when it were raining.'

CHAPTER EIGHT

Being able to talk frankly to Mrs Hicks during several visits helped me immeasurably. She encouraged me to cry and talk as much as I wanted, and she never used the platitudes that come so readily to the lips of those trying to comfort the bereaved. Illiterate she might be, but she understood people very well, and I began to accept that I really had to pick up my life again and go on living.

Everyone in Liverpool needed as much strength as they could muster. That autumn, we endured over fifty consecutive nights of air raids. Brian, Tony, Avril and little Edward looked washed out and old, because of fear and lack of sleep. They never complained, however, and the three younger ones went to school daily, no matter how late they had had to sit up. Fiona was rarely at home during these raids; she continued her social life as if the bombings never occurred. She would return home after the raid was over, with stories of playing cards in hotel shelters or eating in a restaurant while the lights dipped from time to time, as the building rocked.

We worried when Brian was on duty during a raid. The more intense the attack, the more likely that telephone wires would be brought down, and the more messages he would have to carry through the pandemonium of the streets. A cyclist has not even the protection of a vehicle roof over his head; and, for once, Mother and I were united in our worries. He would turn up, however, soon after the all clear had sounded, covered with dust, eyes bloodshot, triumphant and cheerful, after having helped the police and wardens dig out victims.

After one particularly heavy raid, he breezed in rather later than usual, saying casually to our horrified mother, 'Sorry I'm late. We had to find the heads.'

Without the production of the head of a victim, a person could not immediately be pronounced dead – arms, legs, even torsos, did not count, and this caused boundless difficulties to many families. So, quite phlegmatically, seventeen-year-old Brian had been hunting heads at the site of a bad incident.

I wondered if the highly strung, imaginative little boy had really grown into an iron-nerved man, or whether he had just learned, of a necessity, to live with his fears. In any case, his experience as a police messenger must have helped to prepare him for the greater horrors he saw later in the Royal Navy. He never lost his compassion, though; the small boy who took pity on a whining puppy and brought it home grew into an immensely understanding man.

Sometimes I was myself caught in a raid, while still at the office or when walking home; once or twice, when the siren sounded, I was at a dance with my friend, Sylvia Poole.

I had known Sylvia for a number of years. She had a lively mind and we enjoyed discussing topics of the day. I was interested in the forces that shaped history, and in individuals, like Churchill and Hitler, who seemed to be born at a pivotal moment in time. Did they shape our history or had our history shaped them? Ideas about the economic forces surging beneath the surface of the news turned my attention to appropriate books and newspapers, as did the plight of European Jews.

I knew more than most people about the dreadful situation of European Jews, because since 1933

I had seen a steady stream of refugees go through our office, and each of them had his own shocking story. When I put the individual stories together and saw the general trend of them, I was both horrified and terrified.

After the war, when I talked to demobilised friends who had served in the army of occupation in Germany, men and women who had seen Belsen and other death camps, I knew that even my worst imaginings had under-estimated what had happened. I had been taught that the Germans were the best educated, most advanced people in Europe; yet they had condoned genocide.

Sylvia and I never discussed our personal affairs. Looking back, I do not really know why not. Girls are supposed to giggle and confide in each other. I never did. Sylvia was precious to me because of the way we hammered out ideas.

Sometimes, during that hard winter of 1940–41, I accepted a date with the acquaintance of Harry's who had escorted me home on the day that the Dance Club closed. I was glad of company, and had no thought of anything more than that; indeed, I found it hard to think beyond the day I was living. He was a pleasant, shy young man in a reserved occupation, but when he wished to deepen the friendship and began to speak of a possible engagement, I sent him on his way. Though I liked him, I could not love him.

There was an inner core of me which was extremely fastidious. Though I was a passionate young woman, I lived in a time when many girls would not settle for less than marriage; and for me marriage had to have real love as one of the ingredients.

As a good dancer, I had the opportunity of meeting throughout the war a great number of young men. Far from the roots of home, men who normally would not have been seen dead in a ballroom, sought company on the dance floor. Friendships and romances flourished, but for me the chemistry was never right. And I further longed to meet the kind of cultivated man who visited our home in the long-ago days before Father went bankrupt. Though Harry had fought his way up from nothing, he had had the company of scholarly men during his youth; he knew how to study and he read widely. His mother might be a most unreasonable woman, but I think it must have been she who taught him good manners, and this, added to a naturally kindly character, made him a very pleasant person to be with.

On 28th October, the *Empress of Britain* was sunk, and on 5th November, the armed merchant cruiser

HMS Jervis went down while escorting an Atlantic convoy. Despite brave efforts by the *Jervis* to defend the convoy, five other boats joined her at the bottom. In December, U-boats off the coast of Portugal played havoc with several convoys. The sorrow caused was reflected in our office, the names of ships whispered by weeping women becoming a monotonous litany.

We became expert at guiding womenfolk, many of whom could hardly read or write, through the voluminous red tape in which they became enmeshed when they applied for pensions. Some women took a double blow; they lost a husband or son to the German navy and, during the air raids, they lost their home, and, sometimes children, as well. It became a relief to deal with more ordinary problems, like a cripple's special needs or a bastardy case.

Increasingly, I sought diversion during the long hours spent seated on the cellar steps, when there was nothing to do except consider how sleepy and how miserable one was. So I continued to study my German grammar book, until the humour of it struck me; then I laughed and put it away – I never wanted to speak to a German again. Crouched on the steps with a lap full of cotton reels and darning wool, I sewed and mended. Whenever I had a few pence, I went with Sylvia to a new dance club or to the theatre, regardless of the heaviness of the raid.

I danced mechanically with anyone who asked me, glad when the man was a good dancer, so that I could give myself over to the rhythm of the music and find some relaxation. While exchanging the usual pleasantries, I would, over my partner's shoulder watch the door, look at the other men on the floor, always hoping, half believing that Harry would be there. Outside, I searched the faces in the bus queues and in any group of seamen walking in the town; wherever there were men, my eyes hunted automatically. I began to understand Mrs Hicks' remarks about the need for wakes and funerals, to be convinced of death.

The owner of the new dance club which Sylvia and I attended converted his lessons into a permanent wake. He had lost his wife in the blitz and had had her body cremated; her ashes were put into a fine vase, and the vase was set on a special shelf in the ballroom. The idea was so macabre that we ceased to go there and, in fact, neither of us ever went to a dancing class again.

Father asked me to write periodically to his friend, Tom, now training with the infantry. To please him, I did write for some considerable time, giving news of Liverpool and, since he was a teacher, sending press cuttings about the plight of teachers, which I thought might interest him. Perhaps Father hoped for a match between us, but I found him as dull as a January day. His replies were pedantic and grammatically perfect; I used to scribble *Ten out of Ten* on the bottom of them.

Father was very disconsolate at losing his drinking companion. He used to go alone to the concert halls and public houses they had previously frequented, but, since he was a sociable man, he probably found people to talk to.

He was on friendly terms with his colleagues at the office, but they had other interests. In their spare time, many of them were air raid wardens, and some joined the Home Guard when it was set up. Most took the Government's instruction to *Dig for Victory* very seriously and, according to Father, raised mammoth crops of vegetables on what had once been their lawns. We had only a brick-lined yard, so gardening was not possible, but, in any case, Father's bad heart precluded his doing much heavy work.

There is no doubt that during those years he was often very lonely. Mother and he were never the good companions that older people can become. At best, they carped at each other continually.

Father was a clerk in the Liverpool Corporation.

He was transferred by them to work in the administration of Rest Centres for the bombed out and of warehouses used to store the possessions of the dead or of the temporarily homeless.

When members of the Polish Army straggled into Liverpool, he was sent for a few days to help to take the history of the ragged, disillusioned men. Some who could not speak English could speak Russian, and the language he had learned under such painful circumstances in the Russian campaign in the First World War was suddenly put to use. He enjoyed the work, but he would come home to sit in his ancient easy chair, eyes closed, hands trembling with fatigue. Like all of us, he lacked sleep; and I think, also, that the company of soldiers in such adversity reminded him of his own anguish in the Great War.

The constant barrage of the guns during the raids also wore him down. I could see his face grow steadily more grim, as the nights progressed. He would sit very quietly on the cellar steps, while overhead the racket was continuous. Occasionally, however, he would bury his face in his hands, and once he muttered that it was exactly like being on a battlefield with a jammed machine gun, unable to return the fire.

There was little that I could do for him, except

let him talk to me whenever he felt like it. He enjoyed telling his war stories over and over again. They were excellent vignettes of the lives of primitive Russian peasants, who had rescued him from certain death when he lay half frozen amid his dead comrades in the bloodied snow. He told me of sharp encounters with the enemy, in pathless forests, where his greatest fear always was that he would get lost. Many of his wounded friends died, when a shed made into an improvised hospital was set alight by the enemy during a raid. He still shuddered at the memory. 'It was a hopeless inferno in seconds,' he said. He spoke with praise of a Japanese unit which, at one point, served with him, of the utter savagery of the Russian revolution, of the people of Archangel dying of starvation and the smallpox. He was himself immune to smallpox, because his mother had caught it while she was pregnant with him; so he helped to nurse and to bury the victims of the disease. He had innumerable scarifying tales of the personal agony of war and revolution, so often forgotten amid cold statistics. He taught me that revolution rarely solves anything.

When the noise of the bombs was very bad, he would give a shaky laugh and say, 'And we thought we had finished with war!'

'It will be over in a few months,' I would say to him. He would smile faintly – he knew better – from experience.

Once he said with great bitterness, 'It will never be over – it will go on and on.'

How right he was. The war died down amid exhausted European populations, only to blaze up in Korea, Vietnam, India, Afghanistan, Iran, Iraq, Egypt and Israel, while embers smoulder and threaten Africa and strange outposts, like the Falklands.

In October, Sylvia celebrated her twenty-first birthday with a party, one of the first grown-up parties I attended.

Her plump, patient, little mother must have collected bits of rationed food over many months. Someone had contributed a bottle of blackcurrant wine of surprising strength; unaccustomed to alcohol, we all became quite merry.

On my twenty-first birthday, the previous June, Mother's employer, a baker, hearing that I was approaching my majority, baked for me an exquisite little birthday cake. It was a rich fruit cake, which he had decorated himself with delicate flower wreaths of white royal icing. It was illegal to make such an extravagant cake, and he must have taken the ingredients from some illicit hoard stored away at the beginning of the war. He presented the cake to Mother as a gift.

The family had joined together to buy me a leather shopping bag, popularly known as a zipper bag. In these bags, carried by almost all business girls, were transported makeup, lunch, a change of shoes and stockings for wet days, a novel to read on the bus or train, and innumerable oddments like safety pins and aspirins. I was delighted by the gift; they must have hunted through most of Liverpool's many shops to find such an article.

I arrived home from work, that evening, about eight o'clock. The family had given up hope of my arrival, assuming that I was working late and was having a snack in the office. They ate the sandwiches and scones which Mother had kindly provided to celebrate the day. The cake, however, was kept untouched.

I remember being moved almost to tears at the effort that had been made to find me a gift and a cake. I immediately cut the cake and passed it round the family. It was strange to eat cake for my birthday – but no dinner!

CHAPTER NINE

Small financial problems which, looking back, seem laughable, presented me with dreadful headaches.

In the early part of the autumn I forgot to switch off the cloakroom light before leaving the office.

The room had no blackout curtaining, and the light blazed forth across the old, walled garden at the back of the building. Our outraged warden reported it, and the Society was fined seven shillings by the local magistrate. This amount was deducted from my wages at the rate of one shilling a week, and for nearly two months my already penurious state was reduced to near disaster; I remember being torn between a decision to walk to work and thus wear out my precious stockings, which would have to be replaced, or nurse my current pair of stockings along, by hooking up the ladders with a fine crochet hook and darning and redarning, so that I could ride on the tram to work. It was a very long seven weeks.

It always astonished me that Mother never got fined for similar offences. The warden frequently remonstrated with her about the lack of curtaining over our back bedroom windows and the consequent glow of candlelight through them, a glow which in his opinion would guide the Luftwaffe straight to us. Perhaps because he was a neighbour he was loath to report her. Towards the end of the war, she did buy some second-hand curtains and put them up, but I suspect that she rather enjoyed baiting the unfortunate warden.

It was on a foggy day in late November that, after a heavy raid, I was very tired and decided to travel the whole distance to work by tram. On the first tram I took, to the city centre, the clippie told me that the whole system had been disorganised by the air raid, and that I might get a tram to Bootle more easily from the Pier Head.

At the Pier Head, the Transport Supervisor was about to dispatch a tram to my destination. It was evidently the first tram which would travel along Derby Road that morning, and I heard him tell the driver, 'The police say the timber yards is burnin' fierce. I tried to telephone, but the wires must be down 'cos I couldn't get through, and nobody seems to know what's really happening. So you mayn't get to the end of the line.' He paused uncertainly, and then ordered, 'Go as far as you can. There's no end of people as will be going on and off shift at the other end.'

The driver, his face almost purple from constant exposure to the elements, wound a huge scarf round his neck and climbed wearily on to his unprotected platform. He tinged his bell irritably with the toe of his boot, and his clippie threw away her cigarette end and skipped quickly on to the back platform. I followed her more sedately. The rush hour had not yet begun, so I was the only passenger.

The clippie was a gaunt woman in a navy blue uniform, too short at the sleeves. She collected my fare and handed me a ticket. Then she closed the door of the passenger compartment and sat down opposite to me, to have a cosy gossip on the hardships and dangers of being a tram conductor.

'I'm that scared sometimes at night, with no proper lights, like, and the pubs let out. It's all right if they're merry drunk, if you know what I mean; the worst that'll happen is that they'll be sick all over the floor. But if they're bevvied and ready for a fight, or if they start to slobber all over you, well! And me man away in the Army, an' all.'

I sympathised with her. I wondered if I could do her job. Cope with drunks, and the impertinence she would endure as a woman doing a man's job? I doubted it.

While, out of the corner of her eye, she watched the scenes of destruction that we passed, she smoked incessantly. 'Lot of fires,' she remarked, and then added with a sigh, 'I'd rather be in an air raid, at times, than face some of the men as gets on this tram.' With the heel of her flat, laced-up shoe, she ground a cigarette end into the floor.

'Couldn't you get a better job?'

'Well, it's handy, 'cos I do split shifts, and in between I can get home to see to the kids. And the pay's good – for a woman.'

When the tram slowed, at a point where men were still hastily clearing pieces of debris from the tram lines, she got up abruptly.

'I'll ask Hisself how he's doin',' she said, and strode forward between the bench seats, which faced each other the length of the vehicle. She shoved back the door which connected with the driver's platform, and smoke rolled into the passenger compartment; the poor driver must have been nearly blinded by it. I hastily pulled out a cotton handkerchief and dabbed my smarting eyes. In seconds, I could barely see anything myself.

The tram stopped.

Shadowy firemen and wardens bobbed round the vehicle and shouted up to the driver. As the result of their encouragement, the driver edged the tram forward, tinging his strident bell persistently.

As we sailed slowly past, a warden called up to him, 'The overhead wires is still up all the way. It's a bloody miracle.'

The tram stopped again. From behind the hanky pressed to my nose, I peeped at the stout back of the driver. A warden had swung himself up on to the platform beside him. The warden's face was black with soot, his eyes and mouth a startling red.

'I can't see a thing in front of me,' the driver protested.

'I'll get down and walk in front of you,' the warden offered. 'I'll watch for anything on the line.' He hopped down on to the road again, and shouted up to the driver. 'Now, mind you listen hard for me – and don't, for God's sake, run me down. You can see better than you think – it's more steam than smoke now.' Then his voice came more faintly from the cloud of vapour. 'Couple o' hundred yards and you'll see all right. And they'll have this bit o' trouble damped down by the time you come back.'

Once again the tram eased forward. It seemed a very long two hundred yards.

When visibility improved, the warden left us with a brisk wave of his gloved hand, and the driver accelerated. Timber flamed and crackled, as we passed the yards, and sometimes waves of heat swept through the open door at the front.

I should have been frightened, and yet I was not.

I was let down at the stop nearest to the office, and, as I walked up the side road to the dilapidated building, I was thankful to find that the immediate area appeared undamaged. It was extremely quiet, and I met no voluntary workers hurrying up the road at the same time. These middle-aged ladies were normally extremely conscientious about being prompt, and I put down their absence to the transport system being disorganised by the raid. No clients were leaning against the front door, waiting for me to let them in. Sometimes, however, if the raid had been severe, they would come streaming in from the rest centres later in the morning.

I unlocked.

The postman did his morning round very early, so I emptied the letter box, and slowly climbed the stairs, sifting through the letters as I went.

I unlocked the rooms the organisation occupied

and put on the lights. The silence oppressed me. The raid must have been so bad the previous night, that people were not yet able to move around, I decided, or were still having breakfast in the rest centres.

The mail consisted largely of Government circulars, which would have to be studied, so that we could advise our clients of the latest foibles of civil servants, on the subject of servicemen's debts, rationing, pensions of every kind, and so on. Many civil servants were tucked away in huge mansions or commandeered hotels in different parts of the country, and were in a fair state of confusion themselves; this was reflected in the muddled bureaucratic gobbledygook of their epistles.

After the letters had been scanned and sorted, I wandered round the office and went into the waiting room, to open the only window which had any glass in it. Though the air that rushed in was smoky, it smelled better than the fetid atmosphere of the room, and I leaned out to see if the buildings at the back had been damaged.

Below me, amid the weeds of the brick-walled garden, squatted a solitary soldier. He was bent over, as if taking cover.

I smiled. From the back, he looked like a Home Guard practising guerrilla tactics, and I expected that in a moment I would see one or two more of them sneak over a broken part of the wall, rifles at the ready; retired men or men on night shifts would sometimes get together in the daytime to do this. Like mothers-in-law they were a favourite cartoonists' joke, but they tried very hard to prepare themselves to face the Germans' professional invasion troops.

The soldier stood up slowly and signalled with a wave of his arm to someone outside my line of vision. In response, two other soldiers appeared, carrying spades instead of rifles.

The first soldier moved aside. And then I saw the object of their interest.

A dull metal pillar box was resting half on its side, much of it buried in the earth. After circling slowly round it, the men with spades began very gingerly to dig it out.

A bomb disposal squad! And a very large unexploded landmine which, presumably, the first soldier had now defused.

But if it were damaged, it could still explode.

The instinct of self-preservation sent me across the room and down the stairs quicker than the bomb could have blown me. Coatless, hatless, out of the front door I flew into the cold, smoky road.

An unattended army lorry was drawn up by

the side gate, presumably waiting to transport the bomb to an open area to be exploded.

In the middle of the road, I paused uncertainly.

An angry shriek came from further up the road. A warden beckoned me wildly. I ran towards him, where he stood behind a rope tied across the street.

He lifted the rope for me to duck underneath it, as if he believed that the rope itself would protect us from the possible blast.

Furiously, he thrust his thin, bespectacled face close to mine. 'And how did you get down there? When we cordon off a place, it's cordoned, and you're not supposed to go there. You might be killed.' He was genuinely concerned.

Gasping for breath, I muttered, 'I came into work from the Derby Road side. I didn't see any barrier. Perhaps the soldiers undid the rope to get their lorry in, and forgot to tie it across the road again. No wonder I didn't have any clients or staff in the office. I *think* it's defused now.'

'Well, you stay right here, young woman, till they've taken it away. It can go off, defused or not defused, if some of its innards is ruptured.'

It is strange how strong the instinct to live is. I stood shivering by the warden for nearly an hour, until we saw the lorry roll slowly down the other end of the road, with its horrid burden in the back.

While I waited, I thought about Coventry, which, on 14th November, had been decimated in one enormous raid. I wondered if we would be the next victims.

Raids did continue, though none as heavy as that which destroyed Coventry. Amid the turmoil that they engendered, the problem of Christmas asserted itself.

We were determined to give the younger children the best possible Christmas. To Mother, it meant squeezing out of a reluctant butcher one of his few turkeys; to me, it meant contriving from nothing a gift for each child; and to all of us, it meant we could get a good sleep sometime during the daytime hours. The Germans, however, had other ideas. On the night of Friday, 20th December, we endured a very heavy air raid, with an even more severe one on the 21st. On the Sunday night, we shared a third intense raid with Manchester.

After the first raid, I went out and stood in the middle of our empty street, while the all clear howled eerily round me. Though there was no sign of damage in the street itself, the sky was suffused by the reflection of fires, and I wondered what would be awaiting me in the office that Saturday morning. Shivering with cold and apprehension, I went back into the house, to snatch a couple of hours of sleep before setting out on my long journey to work; I was thankful that my kind superior at the office had, at last, returned after her long battle with influenza. The raid had lasted ten hours, ten solid hours of bombardment. What a mess there would be for us to clear up. What a tremendous number of ruined lives to try to put together again.

Despite having to take several detours, the city bus and tram service was working very well. We passed scurries of activity where fires still burned, victims were being dug out, and dangerous, teetering walls pulled down. The Adelphi Hotel, the pride of Liverpool, had suffered badly from blast, and my fellow passengers on the tram viewed it with surprised exclamations, as if it should have been exempt from damage.

'It was a land mine,' the clippie told us. 'Fell at the side of the building – in Copperas Hill.'

Copperas Hill was a narrow street of early 19th century houses, some boarded up as uninhabitable, a few used as offices, the rest still lived in by very poor people, who would that morning be a lot poorer – if they were still alive.

Feeling physically and mentally drained, I left

the office very late that Saturday evening. The Luftwaffe had already been extremely busy for some hours.

I dithered on the office steps. The roar of flames, the whistle of bombs, seemed concentrated in Bootle and in the north end of Liverpool itself. I would have to pass through the area in order to get home.

Miss Evans had decided to work later, to catch up with her records, and then to sleep in the office. She insisted, however, that I should go home. 'There isn't much you can do to help me now – you'll be safer at home,' she said.

She was very brave. Looking up at the sky, all too full of shrieking, diving planes, it seemed likely that the office would not survive. Very reluctantly, I left her in the cold, empty building.

I walked up to Stanley Road, to see if, by chance, there was still a tram running to town.

The whole normally busy road was almost deserted, though in the distance I could hear the bells of a fire engine and, as I crossed the street, a van nearly ran me down. I listened for the answering guns in their emplacements in Bootle, but could not hear them. The searchlights were busy, though, flicking like metronomes across the sky.

In the light of flares, fires, tracer bullets and searchlights, it was easy to see. I felt cross; I was not going to be kept from home by any German planes. I began to walk.

When the even explosions of a stick of bombs seemed to be coming very close, I dodged into doorways, pressing myself tightly against whatever door presented itself. Twice I found a public shelter, crowded with people, some singing, some praying, rosaries in hand, and was urged by wardens to remain there. But I was obsessed with the need to get home, and immediately there was a slight pause in the racket, I slipped out and pressed onwards. At several points, the raid passed right overhead at a time when there seemed no place to hide. I went down on my knees in the road and then flattened myself against the kerb, face tucked into the tiny corner of protection that it offered; and listened to hasty footsteps running on the pavement, as others tried to find a refuge, while I eased myself slowly along the gutter. Further down the road, I heard someone cry out in pain and the sound of anxious voices, as a person was struck, presumably by flak. A series of bombs appeared to hit the next street, and I was suddenly glad that I had been faced with a blank wall on my side of the street, and was consequently, sprawled in the gutter; if there had been a house or shop doorway in which to shelter, I could well have been speared by glass slivers bursting from the windows.

On the theory that a moving object was harder to hit than a stationary one, I ran like a frightened alley cat, in the hope of avoiding an incendiary bomb or heavy piece of debris falling on me. Incendiary bombs, though quite small, were deadly if they fell on someone, and flak from our anti-aircraft guns or flying pieces of rubble and glass from bombed buildings, were more of a menace than the chance of being caught directly by an exploding bomb. Another great danger was from falling power lines, still live and spitting like angry dragons.

At the junction of Cazneau Street with Scotland Road, which is the continuation of Stanley Road towards the city, I hesitated. The violence of the raid had momentarily decreased, and the blackout appeared to have taken over again. If I went up Cazneau Street, I could bypass the city centre which was probably under attack. Cazneau Street was, however, a fearsome slum with which I was not familiar, and I feared that once I crossed London Road, a main artery which bisected that particular line of streets, I would get lost. Mind made up, I trotted along Scotland Road. I was shivering with nervous determination to outwit the Luftwaffe and get home safely.

As I neared the city centre, there was more traffic about and more pedestrians; raucous male voices called after me as they glimpsed the outline of a young female. I increased my speed and panted onwards towards the Old Haymarket, a vast open space into which the Mersey tunnel debouched from under the river.

'I'll cross William Brown Street, where the Picton Library is, and skirt around the wall of St John's Garden. It'll give me a bit of protection,' I told myself. By doing this I avoided the wide open spaces of this handsome part of Liverpool and would be less likely to be hit. I would also bypass most of Lime Street, still the main walk for prostitutes in the city, where I had no doubt it would be business as usual, blitz or no blitz; it was not the ladies I feared, but their pimps and hangers-on.

The city was in turmoil, with service vehicles zipping recklessly through the battered streets. There seemed to be a very big fire at the beginning of Dale Street, and behind the buildings past which I ran up to the far end of Lime Street, there was obviously another heavy conflagration, which I afterwards was told was St John's market burning. Roasted in it were most of the turkeys which Liverpudlians had dreamed of eating on Christmas Day, and to hear the talk in the shopping queues after the holiday, one would imagine that the loss of the turkeys was more deeply mourned than the loss of three hundred and fifty-six men, women and children who died during the three days of the blitz.

As I ran, incendiaries fell like rain, and magnificent St George's Hall was alight; I was told later that there were hundreds of people sheltering in the cells underneath it, unaware that the building above them was in flames. Though I was aware only of a blizzard of bombs, flak and hazardous litter on the pavements, a short distance away a bomb fell in front of the Court Theatre, and a fire engine, racing to a call, fell into the crater, killing the entire crew of seven; so much for speed in such a situation. I was lucky that I did not fall over something or into something myself.

I felt naked as I left Renshaw Street behind me, and climbed the hill towards Catherine Street. To my right, the Anglican Cathedral was outlined against a rosy sky. It seemed less noisy here, and was totally deserted. The quiet rage, which had sustained me through the city, began to drain, and I was aware of intolerable fatigue.

There were several hospitals at the top of the hill, where cars and ambulances were coming and going steadily. I wondered if I should give up, and take refuge in one of them. But I was very close to home, and hospitals could be hit, too. In fact, during that night the Royal Infirmary and the Mill Road Infirmary were severely damaged.

I dragged onwards slowly, bothered by the smoke and dust in the atmosphere as well as by the sound of bombs whistling down on the city centre.

At the sound of the front door being opened and closed, Father, his face filled with anxiety, came up from the cellar steps. 'God! Whatever happened to you?' he exclaimed.

I licked my parched lips. 'I walked,' I said simply.

He caught my arm and led me to a chair, where I sat until I regained my breath. I remember the flashes of light from explosions, coming through cracks in the wooden shutters over the window, as I sat there.

Mother came up, the inevitable cigarette in the corner of her mouth, and despite the scream of bombs and diving planes overhead, she cut bread and margarine and boiled a precious egg for me, while, at the kitchen sink, I washed under our single cold water tap. Mother was extraordinarily brave under fire; I do not remember her once showing any sign of fear, and she accepted my ghastly appearance without comment, while she prepared a meal for me. I was grateful to her.

As I crouched on the cellar steps and ate from a tray balanced precariously on my knee, I told the sleepy family what I had seen.

Mother heaved a big sigh. 'I hope Brian and Fiona are all right – Brian is doing his messenger service, and Fiona went to a Christmas dance at the Grafton, with some of her friends.'

For the benefit of the three younger children present, I said cheerfully, 'I'm sure they will have taken cover and be all right.' Mentally, I was angry with myself for having described in front of them so vividly what I had seen on my walk home. I must have frightened them. They did settle down again, however, on the mattress which Mother had put down for them on the coaldust-laden floor of the cellar.

When small snuffles indicated that they had fallen asleep, I told my parents of the incident which had most upset the office. 'It isn't in our district – it's in Sandhills – but we had people inquiring about it at our office – some of them relations of those trapped. It's in Bentinck Street, where the railway line crosses it. There is – there was – a row of four or five railway arches there, really well built – solid; a first class air raid shelter, where lots of people slept every night. And last night, you know, Mum, it got a direct hit and the arches came hurtling down on the shelterers. Most of them are dead, but it is believed that some are alive – and they can't get them out – the stone blocks of those arches are so big that they have nothing they can move in which will lift them.'

'What are they going to do?' asked Father.

'Last thing I heard, they are going to bring something in to split the blocks, to make them moveable. But by the time they've done that, it will be too late. Even if some are alive, they'll be horribly injured; they'll wish they were dead. Every time I think about it I feel sick.'

'Poor souls,' Mother whispered.

'One of our wardens told me that there isn't a hope in hell for them – somebody built that bridge all too well.' I crunched up my eyes. We all had a kind of faith in the heavy rescue squads, that we would always be dug out. Now that trust was shaken. I wondered how long it would take the living to die.

I sighed. 'I can't imagine what Bootle will be like after tonight. I'll go back first thing tomorrow.'

'On Sunday?' exclaimed Mother.

'Well, of course. What else can I do?'

About six in the morning, Brian returned, as filthy as I had been. His grin was as great as ever, when he said, 'Helped to dig out at Mill Road Infirmary.'

He was followed almost immediately by a white and shaken Fiona, who had managed to get a taxi from the Grafton, after agreeing to share it with three other people.

'It was awful, Mum. We'd hardly got there – I'd just walked into the ballroom and was looking for the others, when there was a most horrendous explosion. A whole chunk of the roof blew off, and bits came raining down round the alcove in which the band sits. Poor Mrs Hamer – you know, the lady who conducts – dived under the grand piano! It's funny now.' She gave a sheepish giggle. 'But it was really scary, and I turned to run outside; I was afraid of being buried. One of the men hanging around the door stopped me. He said I'd get hit by flak, and to stay put.'

'That was wise,' said Father, as he helped her off with her coat.

'Well, I'm glad I stayed. Mrs Hamer picked herself up, and the band went on playing as if nothing has happened. They tidied up the floor a bit, and we all danced until the all clear went, around five o'clock. We had a good time, though sometimes I was a bit frightened when I could hear the bombs dropping nearby.'

Mother was bustling round, making early morning tea. 'You shouldn't be out on nights like this,' she scolded.

'Oh, Mummy, I might as well be there as here; they could easily have attacked the south side instead.'

'I get worried about your getting home, as well.'

'That was easy. There was this young army officer wanting to get back to the barracks here. He got a cab from somewhere and shared it with three of us; he was really nice.'

Still gossiping, everybody went to bed and I had my breakfast and went to work.

CHAPTER TEN

That chilly Sunday morning, for the first time, I had to show my special identity card, which indicated that I was a social worker.

I was stopped by a police constable on duty near the Rialto Cinema, where Princes Road, Upper Parliament Street and Catherine Street all meet. I had hoped to pick up a tram or bus there.

'Nobody allowed in the town this morning,' he told me, as he handed the little green card back to me. 'Where was you wanting to go?'

'Bootle.'

'Ye Gods! Ye'll have a job.' He watched me put the card safely back into my shabby handbag, and then looked past me. ''Alf a mo', they might give you a lift.' He signalled someone approaching from behind me.

A police car, with two constables in it, drew up beside us.

'This young lady's with the Welfare. She's got to get to Bootle – to work. Could you take her?'

'Goin' down to Dale Street,' answered the heavy, redfaced officer at the wheel. He turned to me. 'Could drop you at the corner of Scotland Road, or rather Byrom Street, for starters,' he offered.

A police car would certainly be allowed through any road blocks, so I gratefully accepted. Though there were few civilians about, air raid and fire personnel were clustered round dusty heaps of rubble, some still smouldering, and our driver had to edge his way through several streets which were littered with debris from homes and little shops ripped open from top to bottom, to show an assortment of wall-papers looking garish in the dancing light of lanterns and torches carried by the air raid wardens and rescue workers. It was the coldest and darkest time of the year, the worst time to lose one's home. I hoped it would not snow.

At the corner of Byrom Street, along which I had flitted through the blitz only a few hours before, the driver honked his horn at a WVS canteen van. The van drew into the kerb.

'What's up?' the lady driver shouted.

The constable in the passenger seat leaned out

of the car's window and bellowed an inquiry as to their destination.

'Bootle.'

'I guessed right,' the constable said to me, with some satisfaction, and it was arranged that the WVS driver would give me a lift.

Sandwiched between two volunteers, both housewives who had been up most of the night and were now taking food to stricken Bootle, I heard their stories of the raids.

When I saw the office still standing, I muttered, 'Thanks be.'

Miss Evans and the first voluntary worker to come in were already besieged by bewildered people, many of whom had been bereaved the previous night and had lost their homes. A greater number of dusty, dishevelled inhabitants had homes only partly damaged. They had, however, had their little store of food ruined, tins squashed or pierced, bread, milk and margarine filled with dust or sand, and their handbags or precious ration books lost in the mess. They had no money to buy fresh food and did not know where to get a new ration book on a Sunday.

One elderly lady, brought in by a neighbour, had lost her spectacles and could barely see. A man's tools had been blown away. Neither had money to replace their loss. Harassed mothers, the usual representative of families, told us that their whole families were so covered with soot falling from the chimney that they were hardly recognisable; there was no water to wash in and they had no change of clothing. And almost every person complained of cold, because, at the very least, their windows had been blown out.

As the day progressed, our small funds were rapidly depleted and our store of clothing shrank.

Apart from giving help ourselves or directing people to other sources of aid, we represented the Red Cross Society. The Red Cross had set up a system by which a letter of twenty-five words could be sent to a prisoner of war, who otherwise rarely got any news at all from Britain. It was always a surprise to me that, after an air raid, many of our clients gave first thought to reassuring their husband, son or lover in a German prisoner-of-war camp that they were safe. It was as if they expected that news of a raid on a man's home town would be immediately transmitted to him by some unknown means.

I marvel at how much love and caring was conveyed in those twenty-five-word messages, by semi-illiterate women often carrying an unbearable burden themselves.

The most pressing need that Sunday morning was water; water to wash people in, water to wash clothes, water to make tea, water to wash out houses filled with dust and debris. I was told that the municipality opened the public swimming pool, provided soap and towels, and invited the soot-covered bombed-out to come to have a bath. We still had a water supply in the office, so our small stock of coal was used to make a fire in the old basement kitchen range to heat it, and we were able to bath a number of children in the big, old-fashioned iron bath, which still stood in our cloak-room. Then we dressed them from the store in our clothing room.

People were strangely quiet and very practical. We had odds and ends of families much in need of comfort; two young girls, who had slipped down the street at the beginning of the raid, to visit friends, had stayed while the bombing continued. They had returned to a hole in the ground where their home should have been, and no family survivors; an unknown baby picked up in the street and howling lustily for food was brought in by a young boy, who did not know what to do with it; an electrician still in pyjamas, anxious to get to work the following morning, despite his flattened home, had neither clothing nor tools left; two elderly women needed doses of special medicines, their supply having been lost in the ruins of their homes. And so it went, all day long.

At four o'clock, my colleague, who had worked most of the night, and I, who had had little sleep, were both exhausted. We went together to the waiting room and said sadly that we could do no more. 'Could any of you come back in the morning?' we asked in despair.

Everybody sat firm; they were equally desperate. One woman said kindly, 'You go and have a cup of tea, luv, and rest a bit. We'll wait.' Everybody nodded gently in agreement.

We sat quietly by our one-bar electric fire, while a volunteer in a rather better state of repair than we were made tea. We shared the bread and margarine I had brought from home and a chocolate bar provided by the volunteer; we drank our tea in quick, scalding gulps. Then we went on again.

We closed the office at seven o'clock. By that time bombing had recommenced, and nobody fresh had come into the waiting room since the air raid warning had blasted out over the ruined little dockside town. We dealt with everyone remaining, and then set out for home.

My colleague had the use of a little car owned by the Charity, so I presume she went home in that;

the Society's petrol ration was so small, however, that there was no possibility of her driving me home to the south side of Liverpool. A tram trundled slowly along Stanley Road and I thankfully swung myself on to it. In the harried city centre, however, there seemed to be neither tram nor bus going in the direction of the Rialto cinema, so, drunk with fatigue, I walked the rest of the way home.

Though all around me an orange sky and persistent explosions proclaimed more disasters, the need to get home was paramount, and I concentrated on putting one weary foot in front of the other.

The whole family came up from the cellar steps, to greet me. Each vied with the other to tell of the devastation they had seen during their Sunday walks. They were electrified by the drama of it all.

'It's too bad,' Father exclaimed, 'St Nick's has gone.'

The loss of the Sailors' Church, Our Lady and St Nicholas, hurt. It was part of our waterfront, part of our heritage.

'And Wallasey!' Fiona chimed in. 'Not Liverpool at all – across the river. It's got nothing to do with the war – it's just houses. And it was bombed like anything! What would the Germans want to do that for?'

I shrugged helplessly.

'The biggest bang was Evans, Sons, Lescher and Webb going up,' announced Tony, in reference to a chemical company for whom my old friend, Sylvia Poole, worked. 'They said it was like an enormous firework display!'

'Poor Sylvia,' I said. 'That will put her out of work.'

I drew up a chair to the living-room table and hastily ate a very dried out Sunday dinner, which had been keeping hot for me in the oven of the big iron range, since midday.

'Where's Brian?' I asked, suddenly realising that he was missing.

'The fool's gone upstairs to bed,' Mother snapped crossly. 'He refused to take cover on the steps with us – the stupid boy said he was too tired. I'm worried to death about him, up there. Supposing the bedroom window is blown in? He'll be cut to pieces.'

I did not reply. While Mother poured herself another cup of tea and took it back to the cellar steps, I took my dinner plate and cup to the kitchen sink and washed them under the cold tap; a rime of gravy refused to come off the plate, so I left it to soak.

Suddenly, my senses began to reel and I clutched

at the draining board for support. Then I staggered to the open cellar door.

The family looked up. In the warm candlelight their faces reminded me of a mediaeval painting; the children's innocent looks, their parents' care-worn visages, could have been the detail filling the corner of some great canvas from Siena.

'I'm sorry, Mother,' I said flatly, 'I have to lie down; otherwise I'll collapse. I'm going to bed.'

At the foot of the cellar steps was a single mattress on which Tony, Edward and Avril would soon curl up together. Behind it lay a small pile of softly glittering coal, and to the left I could see the dim outline of a big clay and brick wash-boiler, and in front of it an open space. It was not considered safe to put another mattress in this space, because of the weight of furniture in the room above it. So the older members of the family always sat on the steps during raids.

Followed by Mother's fretful clucking, I staggered through the living-room and up the stairs. Through the uncurtained window of my bedroom the sky looked like Guy Fawkes Day. I kicked off my shoes and fell on to the bed. I did not hear the all clear sound, but the next morning, Monday, I was up at six and went back to work. In Bootle, there was no sound of carols in the streets, no busy last-minute shopping for Christmas amid bright lights. Instead, there was dire need amid the almost total darkness of the blackout.

The Germans left us alone during the Christmas holiday itself. I imagined, with a wry chuckle, the entire Luftwaffe, all overweight and ash blond, standing round Christmas trees and singing *Holy Night, Silent Night*. I did not wish them joy. I was at work throughout that time. If the family had a Christmas dinner, I did not share it. I left my humble gifts on the living-room table for them to find on Christmas morning. I suppose they must have given me gifts, but I have no memory of them. I was so exhausted that I forgot my own grief.

CHAPTER ELEVEN

A girl named Belle, whom I was to meet later in the war, was in Mill Road Infirmary when it was bombed during the Christmas blitz. She told me how scarifying it was to lie helpless after having her appendix out, not daring to move in case she burst her stitches and bled to death, while bits of plaster from the ceiling fell on to her bed and she expected the roof to cave in on her any moment.

'When the nurse came and put my pillow over my face, I thought I'd suffocate,' she said. 'But she was only trying to save me from being cut by flying glass. As if a pillow was much good – I've seen glass slivers go right through a mattress!'

The memory of the bravery of the nurses remained with her for many years afterwards;

they were true heroines, and it was the same at the Royal Infirmary.

I wondered why they – that almighty They – did not paint red crosses on the roofs of hospitals; and then I realised that it would be difficult in the case of our hospitals; most of them had been built in Victorian times, with fancy turrets, twisting chimneys and steeply sloping roofs, not a very practical surface on which to paint a cross.

When I suggested this to Father, he laughed cynically.

'They wouldn't show any mercy, anyway,' he assured me. 'There isn't much mercy in hand-to-hand fighting. And killing from a distance, as they are doing? I don't suppose they feel the slightest qualm.'

I thought of the babies born during the blitz – life going on, despite the fear of death. There were some hair-raising stories of babies being born in air raid shelters, and at least one made his way into the world under the counter of his parents' tiny corner shop. When her birth pangs began, his mother crawled into the shelter of its heavy oak slab. The midwife, when she arrived after cycling through the raid, crawled in after her, and delivered the baby by the light of a candle. We actually had a terrified girl begin to give birth to her baby on our office floor. Mothers in shock sometimes produced a dead child, which was an added grief, and in Bootle a lot of miscarriages were blamed on the frightening experiences of expectant mothers whose homes were damaged or demolished.

Doctors were another group who, with wonderful courage remained at their posts. Raids began in the middle of operations; lights failed, when crackling electric cables were knocked down; floors caved in under them or fell on them, incendiaries falling slantwise came crashing through roofs and windows at the most inopportune moments; injured civilians buried under menacing piles of fallen masonry had, somehow, to be reached and their agonies assuaged. More than one gave his life for that of his patient.

On the Boxing Day of that sad blitzed Christmas, our old alarm clock clanged at six in the morning, and I shot out of bed. I had to go to work.

While the rest of the family slept on, I ran downstairs. In order to see what the weather was like, before I put the light on, I folded back the heavy wooden shutters of the living-room window.

It was bitterly cold and the unheated room still smelled of soot from a bad shake which our house had received, when a bomb had fallen a few streets away and had brought down all the soot from the chimney. I lifted the window in the hope of letting out some of the sooty odour, but the still air outside was so full of fine dust particles from the raids that it did not smell any better.

I leaned over the sill and looked up at the sky. It was still very dark, and the dust haze made it worse; it seemed to me, however, that there was some cloud cover as well as dust.

'Dear God,' I thought, 'if you are up there, send us some snow. Send it now, while we've got the people under cover at least – before we get more homeless on our doorstep.'

Snow would clean the air. Snow would blur the image of the city, partially camouflaging it. If the snow were heavy enough, flying would become difficult and the Luftwaffe might be deterred from a further raid.

Shivering with cold, in my nightgown, I leaned out and prayed passionately, 'Snow, O Lord, snow! Enough to give us time to clear up a bit before the next raid, please.'

And it *did* snow, fine, soft flakes sizzling into the still glowing furnaces which had been buildings, covering churches and public houses, shops and warehouses and homes. It covered our wounds and made everything virginally beautiful with its glittering whiteness.

Few people were about, as the trams I caught took me out to the office. I sat and sewed as I travelled. I always carried with me either knitting or embroidery, and in this way made little gifts for the family, for Christmas and birthdays. With a few scraps of old garments or bed linen, I could make soft toys, handkerchiefs, clutch handbags, night dress cases and matching hair tidies – hair tidies were small embroidered or lace-decorated pokes, hung by a ribbon from dressing table mirror stands. All the loose hairs from brushes and combs were put into them, and they were emptied when the room was cleaned. No bedroom was complete without a pretty hair tidy. From second-hand wool, unravelled from worn-out sweaters, I knitted mittens, gloves, scarves and berets.

Often, when I travelled after air raids, I went into the unknown. Telephones were so few that it was rarely possible to ring to inquire from a friend or a business or an institution how they had fared during the night, to ask, for example, if a train or bus was still running. Very often, what few telephones there were were unreachable, because the lines were down. In my working-class world, nobody had a telephone, except the doctor or the chemist. There were, as yet, no public telephone boxes in our district, and the instant transfer of personal news and reassurances was far in the future.

When public transport was disrupted, it was not very easy to communicate with the shorthand pupils I taught in the evenings. The students never replied to letters, although the post office was still extraordinarily efficient. Increasingly, when I arrived on my students' doorsteps, after a difficult journey, I would be told that our Em, or our Marjie, was working overtime and would not be home for her lesson. There was also a growing feeling, well expressed by one of my pupils, originally a shop assistant and now in a munitions factory. She tossed her brilliant golden mane, and said, with a shrug, 'I'm earnin' that much on munitions, more'n any typist. What's the point in lairnin'?'

I suggested gently that, after the war, she might be glad of shorthand and typing skills.

She laughed. 'I'll be married afore then. I won't have to work.'

Knowing that without money from teaching shorthand I would not be able to continue working in Bootle, I renewed my efforts to find more lucrative employment.

A cold, depressed New Year came and went. Slowly Bootle picked itself up, and the office returned to near normality. There were further sporadic bombings, but nothing so terrifying as the Christmas blitz.

One blustery February morning, after a short, sharp raid, I found on our doorstep a flurry of faded, yellow pages from a large book. The script was alien to me, so, out of curiosity, I made a neat pile of them and took them inside to show Father.

Father spread the pages on the table and turned them over carefully. He was as intrigued as I had been.

'I think it's Hebrew.' He rubbed a page gently between his fingers. 'The paper is very good, and, see, the pages have been hand cut with a paper knife; you don't see that very often nowadays. The book must have been quite old.' He pondered over my find for a moment or two, and then said, 'I wonder if the book belonged to Mr Cohen. He was killed last night, you know. Direct hit on his shop, poor old man. His daughter survived, though. She's in the Royal Infirmary – the warden told me, when I went out to have a look round after the all clear went.'

'Do you think she'd like to have them?' I asked. 'They could be all that she has left, in connection with her father.'

So, in the hope of bringing some small comfort

to a badly injured elderly Jewish lady, Father and I combed the adjoining streets and alleyways and asked our neighbours to look in their back yards for any further pages. We collected quite a number. We wiped the dust off them, dried them where necessary, and made a neat parcel of them.

Since it was the weekend, and father did not have to go to work, he undertook to cycle over to the Royal Infirmary to see Miss Cohen.

Miss Cohen was still under the anaesthetic after surgery for her injuries and was, therefore, not able to receive a visitor. Father explained to the Ward Sister the purpose of his journey, and she undertook to give the parcel to Miss Cohen, with a hastily scribbled note from Father. 'If the book is not hers, the pages can be thrown away,' Father told the nurse.

Weeks went by and we forgot about the incident. Then Father received a letter written in a stiff, upright hand. Miss Cohen had been touched beyond measure by Father's kindness; the pages did, indeed, belong to the book her father had been reading during the raid. As we had suspected, the pages were the only thing left from her old home, and she would treasure them always. She was in a convalescent home in Wales and was now walking with the aid of sticks.

Father and I looked at each other. Though we did not say anything, it was obvious that we were both struck by her quiet acceptance of what had happened to her. I wondered what it was like to have to begin again when one was about fifty-five years old.

Another person who had unexpectedly to begin again was Fiona. She received a week's notice to leave, from the magazine agency which employed her. The agency was closing down for the duration, because its subscribers were now so scattered, and it was also difficult to obtain the magazines normally ordered for them from the United States.

'What am I going to do?' she wailed. 'They were so nice to me.'

'You'll have to report to the Employment Exchange,' Mother told her briskly. 'Perhaps they'll put you in the Forces.'

Fiona was aghast. Though she had stayed at school until she was fourteen, she, like me, had not much education, and she was scared at the thought of where she might be sent by the omnipotent Employment Exchange.

CHAPTER TWELVE

Fiona was directed by the Employment Exchange to work in a factory in Speke, a suburb on the south side of Liverpool. The factory manufactured components for aircraft. The journey to work was not difficult but, since her shift began at eight o'clock, she had for the first time in her life to get up early.

She was most excited at the prospect of earning the much higher wages offered to her, and enjoyed the period of training she was given.

'The girls are very rough,' she told me. 'Their language is unbelievable.'

'Did the Employment Exchange give you any other choices?' I inquired.

'No. Except that I could have gone into the ATS, if I could have passed the army medical. And I didn't want that, really. At least I can come home at night, if I'm in a factory.'

She really was not very strong; we had always protected her from heavy work, and I hoped the job she was given would not require great muscular strength.

Another change was pending in the family. The severity of the Christmas raids had, at last, been enough to convince Mother that the younger children should have remained in the country. Tony was now over fourteen though, and she felt he should remain in Liverpool. During his earlier evacuation he had, like Brian, won a scholarship to the Liverpool Institute. The Institute had originally been evacuated to Wales, so he had gone there to join it. Because so many boys returned home, the Institute had been re-opened in Liverpool, so when Mother arranged for his return home, he was able to continue school.

Now, once more, Mother wrote to the Aunts, my father's sisters, who lived across the river, to ask if they would again accept little Edward and Avril into their home.

Because the Aunts originally faced having Liverpool slum children billeted on them, they had asked that some of their nephews and nieces be sent to them, to be their evacuees. We had thankfully accepted their offer. Tony and Edward had been well cared for by them, and Avril had been most kindly looked after by a friend of theirs.

We all waited impatiently for a reply to Mother's request. Despite the disruptions of the war, we could reasonably expect an answer within forty-eight hours.

No reply came. Then Father discovered from files in his office that the authorities had decided that the Aunts' village, Hoylake, was now considered too close to badly bombed Birkenhead and Wallasey to be safe for evacuees; the Aunts were, therefore, exempt from billeting.

A subsequent letter to their friend who had looked after Avril elicited a polite reply saying that they had another child staying with them.

A scattered raid which damaged property near to us, finally prompted Mother to consult the children's school teachers. Within a couple of days, Edward and Avril were whisked away to Wem, a small village in Shropshire.

There they really suffered. Billeted on poor families with few facilities, people who also did not want them, they were even colder and more hungry than they had been at home. The local school had to accommodate the village children as well as the evacuees, so pupils were taught in two shifts, which meant a very early start to the day for our young ones. They had a long walk to the school and back, and then a dreary afternoon when they were not wanted in their hosts' houses and yet had nowhere to go. Far more than the heavy raids they had endured in Liverpool, the bitter experiences of their second evacuation were engrained in their minds for the rest of their lives. I could cheerfully have shot Mother for removing them from the comfort and safety of their original billets.

Tony had never talked much about his earlier experiences in Wales, except to say that he was first billeted with a very old lady, who lived alone in a huge, neglected house. Though she was kind, she had no idea how to manage a strange little boy. He must at first have been very frightened, but he never complained of being unhappy. Perhaps his life there was marginally better than it was at home, and his unquenchable sense of humour carried him through. When the subject of re-evacuation was brought up, he said simply, 'I won't go.'

Once the two younger children were re-evacuated, our household was reduced to Father and Mother, Brian, Tony, Fiona and me. Except for Tony, all of us had work. Mother's irritation at my refusal to become a full-time housekeeper was reduced to a steady grumble. I still did my share of housework and standing in queues. My days were very long, however, particularly those on which I had to walk to work. In an effort to cope with the needs of our war-weary clients, the staff continued to work long into the evening and through the lunch hour.

During this period, as I tried to overcome my sense of hopeless loss, to stop myself glancing along the rows of anxious faces in the waiting room, in the hope of seeing one cheerful, broken-nosed, beloved countenance, I began to understand better the turmoil within an apparently coherent, calm client; I looked for the real person behind the mask. Later on, it gave me strength not to flinch, when faced with a pilot whose face had been burned off or with frightfully misshapen, civilian cripples. I sought the valiant, hurt personality within the shattered frame, the truest bravery sitting silently, uncommunicatively, in a wheelchair.

In my mind, also, the difference between black, white, yellow and brown people lessened. I lived in a district with a fairly large black, West African population and the Chinese community was not far away. Bootle itself had a number of seamen from the Far East, some Indians and Negroes; most of them had white wives and gorgeous-looking children. As the bitterness of the blitz drew us all closer together, I learned that we all shared the same needs, the same fears, the same bigotry; we were simply the human race.

At the time, having met hundreds of fleeing Jews, I found it difficult to include Germans and, later on, the Japanese in the human race! In the face of the licensed cruelty and murder of a war, it is hard to stand back and view the faults of one's own beleaguered nation, and then judge.

Though ignorant and very innocent, caught in the trap of a lonely, narrow life, in a few months I seemed to grow from adolescence to maturity, just as the boys who went into the Forces suddenly became men.

I often wondered what a normal life was like. Was there such a thing? What was it like to live all one's life in one house, go to one school for twelve years, be trained for a profession or go to university? I could not recall what it was like to eat three meals a day as a matter of course. What was it like to have friends you had known all your life, people you never had to explain anything to, because they knew of, and had shared many of your experiences? Go out to dinner? To parties? I had been to only one adult party in my life – Sylvia's twenty-first birthday celebration. What was it like to stay in the house of a friend? How should one behave in such circumstances?

The novels I read dealt with the crises of life, not the humdrum everyday. Being moved about as a child, like a tiddly-wink counter being neatly pinged into ever-new cups, was not a great deal of help to me in answering these questions. A child visitor was not treated in the same way as an adult. One was often put to sleep in the corner of someone else's bedroom, someone who, often enough, found a child a nuisance. Frequently, in my grandmother's house, I was very lonely and fell back upon a morose charwoman for company. Above all, I was expected to be quiet, which immediately stifled many of the questions a child might have asked in normal circumstances.

Moving to and fro, from Grandma's house to my parents' house, parents who often moved themselves, meant that I was, during my few years at school, usually 'the new girl', and I grew ever shyer and more diffident as I moved from school to school.

My parents and their friends, caught up in the mad gaiety of the early Twenties, after the First World War, had lived a life separate from that of their children. We were penned up in a nursery with a nanny. Except for glimpses of other children's parents when we went, occasionally, to play with families like our own, grownups and their behaviour were something of a mystery to us. Grandma, two aunts and an older cousin, who lived together, were probably more familiar to me than any other grownups, but I was always acutely aware of being an outsider amongst them, and, looking back, I am surprised how little I really knew them.

In the long, noisy nights of the blitzes, when it seemed that we might all be dead before morning, I pondered for hours on these gaps in my knowledge.

I knew my crisis-ridden clients quite well. I had seen their dreadful poverty, though it was not as acute as mine had been. I admired their bravery and resourcefulness. But their world was totally different from the world from which I had sprung. They had deep-rooted family ties. Most of them had always lived in the same street and had a strong sense of neighbourliness. They worked in the same places that their fathers and grandfathers had done. They belonged to trade unions and benevolent societies and to churches and chapels. They had networks.

Normally, was it like that in the middle classes?

Was Grandma's household, where I had spent so many healing months as a little child, a normal household? No man lived in that house, and a male visitor was rare indeed. Did not the four staid women who lived there have wild desires like me? How did they subdue them? What had lain behind their gently smiling faces?

Being a surrogate parent from the age of eleven had cut me off from ready discussion with my siblings, of their experiences and ideas. To me they were our children, whose needs must be met; I never thought of them as people in whom I could confide or ask difficult questions of. The three younger children, Tony, Avril and Edward, had no memory of our earlier life, and Brian had very little; theirs was a totally different upbringing. Only an occasional word dropped by Fiona and Alan indicated their remembrances, and their lack of shared early experience with the rough, though quite friendly, youngsters living round us.

I never dared to ask Mother what she would regard as normal. She could demolish me with a word. When Father felt like communicating, he talked like a Canadian on the telephone, a flood of words which could last for an hour without stopping to take breath. He was interesting and witty but a difficult person of whom to ask straight questions.

Legally and in truth, I had become an adult, an adult without the experiences of my class or status. I was anxious to blend into my odd world as I found it, not to be thought of as unusual by my acquaintances at the office or by the neighbours, most particularly not to be thought of as uneducated. Though quite loquacious, I tended to avoid any expression of my own deeply held beliefs and ideas, and would often agree politely with anything people said to me, no matter what I felt; it was as if I papered over the cracks and voids of personality and experience with what I regarded as suitably patterned wallpaper. To many observers the result must have been quite eccentric.

Though my parents seemed unaware of the fact, Fiona, too, was grown up. She was becoming increasingly resentful because, like many parents, Father and Mother tried to dictate to her who should be her friends. They had one idea in mind, that she should make a good marriage. At nineteen, she was bent on pleasing herself, and it seemed to me that she chose quite well. She was not nearly so stupid as she pretended to be, and she had inherited Mother's ability to play a part if she wanted to – to avoid the persecution I endured from Mother, and to avoid taking a turn as family housekeeper, she had most successfully played for years the part of Mother's darling, empty-headed, little girl. I did not blame her in the least; I wished that I had been that smart. Now, however, she wanted to be her own woman.

Many years later, it was interesting to see her on stage in amateur dramatic performances. She was unusually adept at interpreting a character, and I felt sad that she had not had the opportunity to exploit this gift in the professional theatre. With this ability and her great beauty, she might have become a popular actress.

Now, feeling more independent as a result of her good wages, this usually placid, inoffensive young woman rebelled.

One raidless evening, while the rain beat down outside, she announced to my parents, seated finishing a last cup of tea after the evening meal, that she was considering becoming engaged to a young watchmaker, whose politics were known to be far left.

Father slapped down his newspaper, knocking over his cup, and blew up like a ruptured gas main. Mother, for once in total agreement with her mate, was equally noisy. 'Fiona, how ridiculous! He's not a nice young man at all, and you must know it!'

I could not remember ever seeing Fiona so angry as she became that night. Dry-eyed, but flushed, she said furiously that she would live her own life and make her own mistakes. Irritation, suppressed for years, came bursting out, and I realised how alike we were, except that she had had the self-control which I lacked. She suddenly ceased to be, to me, a rather distant saint, who, according to Mother, was always perfect, and became infinitely more loveable in her distress.

Finally, she snatched up her mackintosh and handbag, and stormed out of the house.

My parents were left facing each other, nonplussed and panting with rage. I had been in the back kitchen, washing the dishes. Not wishing to be caught up in the row, I had watched through the open door while I continued the greasy, sooty job. We were always short of soap, and a small kettle of hot water is not enough to clean saucepans used on an open coal fire. Dish detergents, now taken for granted, were still being tested in the laboratories; in any case, we probably could not have afforded them.

Now, I wiped my hands on our single, murky tea towel, and came into the living-room. For once, my parents looked dumbfounded, unsure of themselves. As I sat down, facing them at the table, I felt almost sorry for them. It was as if some quiet grassy slope had suddenly blown up under their feet, leaving a gaping hole.

'Don't be too upset, Mummy. Fiona will cool

down in a little while, and you'll be able to talk to her again.'

Neither parent answered me; Fiona had said too many bitter things to them. Home truths that they would have accepted from me as being just my vicious, bad-tempered character, came hard from a daughter noted for her gentleness.

I tried again. I was very anxious that Fiona should not marry in haste, out of defiance. 'She may not marry him, you know. Engagement isn't marriage – and they are often broken, nowadays.' I paused. The silence was oppressive. 'Try not to be too upset. Just wait and see what really happens.'

Mother suddenly collected herself. 'You mind your own business. Keep out of this. We will decide who she marries.'

Father, also, had recovered a little of his usual equilibrium, though he drummed his fingers on the table, as he always did when upset. He gave me a warning look, and then said to Mother, 'She is under age, don't forget. She can't marry without my permission.'

I nodded agreement, and sighed wearily. Then I edged my way round the back of Father's chair, to get at the fruit basket, which held the socks to be darned. I wondered wryly if I would ever be freed from mending woollen socks each night;

even a husband would need his socks darned, and I thought, with a sudden pang, that a seaman would have needed warm, hand-knitted ones – but that would have been a labour of love.

Rescue from these monotonous tasks was on its way; a wonderful thread called nylon was already being used for the manufacture of parachute silk; it would, in time, rescue women from hours and hours of work.

I studiously avoided meeting Mother's eye, by concentrating on threading the needle, as she got up impatiently from her chair, and flipped back and forth in the tiny space of the room, muttering, 'We have to stop this.' I thought how wise I had been to say nothing about Harry to them.

While they verbally tore the ill-starred watchmaker apart and discussed possible strategies, my needle flew swiftly in and out of sock heels. I said not a word.

I felt Fiona creep into our double bed late that night, but I feared Father or Mother might hear me, if I said anything much, so I just asked, 'You all right?'

She whispered, 'Yes,' and I turned over to sleep again.

She must have risen very early. I did not hear her. When Father and I went downstairs to start the fire and the breakfast, there was a note addressed to me lying on the table.

'I am leaving home,' she had written. 'I am so fed up. Don't worry about me. I will phone you at the office.'

CHAPTER THIRTEEN

'It's all your fault,' Mother shrieked at me.

She stood in her nightgown in the middle of the living-room, while my harassed father dodged round her, as he gathered newspaper, a bundle of wood chips and a bucket of coal, in order to build the fire in the Victorian grate, a task he undertook each morning, provided we had coal.

Normally, long before the rest of the family got up, the living-room was warm and cosy, and hot kettles of water stood on the stove, ready for them to wash in. So that the room continued to keep warm for the children returning at lunchtime, Mother would bank up the fire with damp slack before she left for work.

Both father and I appreciated being able to hold our cold hands over the flames before we went out, he because his circulation was very poor and I because I was cursed with rheumaticky pains in both hand and leg joints. Though I got up at six o'clock, I had such a long journey to work that I could not wait to heat water before getting washed, and I always washed in cold. This also chilled me.

Now, as Father struck a match and put it to the kindling newspaper, I went into the kitchen to wash myself. Angry that I had not replied to her, Mother flew after me.

'You've encouraged her to leave. Why else would she leave a note for *you.* Really, you're nothing but a trouble-maker!' She flourished Fiona's note at me.

I ran cold water into the washing-up bowl, and stripped off my nightgown. As goose pimples rose all over me, I wished that the gas stove would work properly, so that I, too, could have hot water; but I dared not waste time waiting for a kettle to boil.

Father had put a cup of water in a tiny pan on the only gas burner that worked reasonably, so that Mother could have early morning tea. Now, spitting like a fighting cat, Mother dumped the water into a small teapot and stirred vigorously. I gritted my teeth, partly to stop them chattering with the cold and partly to hold back the sharp tirade I would have liked to let loose at Mother.

I scrubbed my face and neck, and icy trickles went down my flinching back. Then I said carefully, 'Mother. I haven't had anything to do with it; I've hardly seen the boy. But we do know that they've been friends for a long time – and that he'll inherit his father's watchmaking business, so it could be worse.'

Mother poured herself a jam jar of tea; we had no cups. We had commenced the war with very few, and kitchen casualties had taken their toll. It was well-nigh impossible to replace them, so great was the china shortage in the shops.

Before turning out the gas, Mother stuck a cigarette in her mouth and deftly lit it by poking it into the flame; she occasionally lost part of her eyelashes and eyebrows from this habit.

'Humph,' she snorted. 'She *must* have had encouragement.' The tiny scullery was filled with smoke, as she exhaled.

'She's grown up, Mother. Nobody can tell her what she can do and what she cannot. Certainly, I have never given her any advice,' I replied, as I dried my goose-pimpled flesh on our grubby towel – the only advantage of being the first person to wash in the morning was that the towel was dry; everybody else had to use it damp.

'The minute she phones you, get her address.

Then telephone your father at the office, and he can go to bring her home.'

I sighed. Without answering, I slipped on my knickers and petticoat, and went into the living-room. I laid the towel on the fender in front of the fire, in the hope of drying it a little for Father.

Father had heard what Mother had said, and now he told me, 'You must tell us. I am really worried about the girl. Nice girls do not leave home.'

There it was again – the idea that women could not manage alone. And yet the whole population seemed to be on the move, either by Government decree or, equally involuntarily, because of the bombing of the cities.

Father gave the coals a careful lift with the poker and the fire blazed up cheerfully. He laid the poker in the hearth, and then took his razor from the back of the mantelpiece behind the alarm clock. I had left my newly pressed blouse and skirt on the back of a chair near the fire on the previous evening, so that they would air overnight. Now I put them on. They still felt clammy. My stockings hung beside Mother's, laid over a piece of string stretched between nails across the mantelpiece; they were rayon, and I washed and mended them each evening. They, also, were still a little damp, but I hauled them quickly up my long legs, and rolled the tops over a pair of elastic garters; it was customary to wear an elastic foundation garment with suspenders, but mine had worn out and I saw no hope of replacing it, so I was reduced to garters and continual, surreptitious hitching up of my stockings throughout the day.

Father had gone into the kitchen to shave and wash. Now he called, 'Did you hear what I said, Helen?'

'Yes, Daddy. But, Daddy, she must be very unhappy – otherwise, she wouldn't have left.'

Father did not reply.

Privately, I was filled with admiration for Fiona's temerity. But then, I told myself wistfully, she can easily afford a bed-sitting room with cooking facilities. I had considered following her into the factory, but I knew that the minute the war ended we would then both be out of work. She would easily find a husband, but I would not – I would always have to earn my living, and I must have skills and experience to enable me to do this. Moreover, she was not very happy in her new employment.

'The girls are horribly crude,' she had told me, 'and the men! They keep trying to catch you in dark corners, so that they can fondle you.'

'Good Heavens, Fi!'

'Well, I haven't much choice; I don't suppose it's any better in the ATS.'

'Be careful.'

'Oh, I am. I just mind my own business and try not to leave the assembly line, except with other girls. And the money is good.'

As I laid the breakfast and Mother took her turn to wash in the kitchen, she continued to grumble at what she called Fiona's ingratitude and lack of consideration.

Brian, yawning and red-eyed, wandered into the room, and inquired, as he heard Mother's complaint from the kitchen, 'What's up?'

Shaking cornflakes rapidly into six assorted bowls, I told him.

'What's the fuss? She'd have to leave home anyway if she were directed into one of the Services.'

'God forbid,' exploded Father, as I pushed a bowl of cornflakes towards him. 'At least she can live at home where she is. She was stupid to have accepted work like that – they could have found her an office job.'

Brian sat down to eat his breakfast. 'Looks as if they're going to call up all the girls, any time now,' he remarked.

I quickly made a cheese sandwich for Brian's lunch, wrapped it in the greaseproof lining from the cornflakes packet, and handed it to him. Then I scraped margarine over a couple of slices of bread to take to work myself. While I hunted through the sideboard drawer for something to wrap my lunch in, I asked Brian, 'Do you really think we'll all be called up?'

'Well, everybody's talking about it at the office,' he said.

My heart sank. With so little education, I would get the Army's most dirty, menial jobs to do. It was not a cheerful prospect.

A quick rat-tat on the front door announced the arrival of the postman; a faint rustle came from a letter being stuffed through the broken letterbox.

Mother had gone into the hall to get her hat, which she always put on immediately after arranging her hair, so that it did not get ruffled. She picked up the letter and brought it into the room.

'It's for you,' she said to me, suspicion in every line of her. As if there was something wicked about it, she added, 'It's a typed letter.'

She tossed it across the table to me.

CHAPTER FOURTEEN

The letter was from the Petroleum Board, a consortium of oil companies formed for the duration of the war. The letter asked me to go for an interview at their Dingle Bank installation, less than a mile from my home.

For the first time since Harry's death, I felt a tingle of real excitement. Nothing could bring Harry back or ease the pain of loss, but employment close to my home would alleviate the great strain and constant worry over getting to work each day.

On the morning of the interview, I telephoned the Bootle Office and told Miss Evans I did not feel very well, but would be there in the afternoon. She was accustomed to the disruption caused by the actue menstrual pain I endured, and accepted my excuses. I felt a little ashamed at deceiving her;

she had always been most kind to me, and it was not her fault that I was overworked and hopelessly underpaid.

I had washed all my clothes the previous evening. Now I scrubbed myself, and set my hair neatly; it was now shoulder length and I curled it with Mother's curling iron and pinned it back from my face. The result was an untidy mess, so I tied a shoelace round my head and tucked it into a neat roll, a fashion made common by the lack of hairpins and clips on the market.

The Installation lay next to the Herculaneum Dock, and, as I walked down Dingle Lane, a high wall on one side and neat, small houses on the other side, the wind blew freshly off the river; it smelled sweet after the acrid, fire-laden air of Bootle.

Shyly, I approached the policeman guarding the entrance and explained my business.

He smiled amiably down at me and inquired, to my astonishment, 'Got any cigarettes, lighter or matches on you?'

'No. I rarely smoke.'

'OK. Go to that office over there.' He pointed to a brick building more like a small house than an office. 'And good luck,' he called after me, as I picked my way across a rutted lane.

In a glass-walled office, I was interviewed by a

snappy little man in rimless glasses. Despite being indoors, he wore a bowler hat. His business suit was of a blue which Father would have instantly condemned as vulgar. I disliked him on sight.

He did not offer me a seat, but after standing in front of him for a couple of minutes, in a flash of anger I seated myself on the visitor's chair by his desk. As he fired questions at me regarding my experience, he looked me up and down, from ankles, neatly crossed, to the turban on my head.

Occasionally, the telephone on his desk rang and he barked instructions down it, while I looked around me.

Through the glass, I could see a number of people working at high desks. One of them was using a machine I had never seen before. He would tap the keys of it and then pull a handle. I learned afterwards that it was an adding machine, and very precious – like everything else, they were difficult to replace.

After one telephonic interruption, the man swivelled round to look at me again, and said, 'You'd be working in Wages.'

I answered primly that I had hoped to work in a Personnel Department, where my experience in social work might be useful.

'Well, Wages is Personnel, isn't it?'

I did not answer, and he continued, 'You'll be classed as a stenographer – two pounds, seven and sixpence a week, to start.' He turned back to the telephone and picked up the receiver. 'You'd better be tested,' he told me.

My heart sank a little. I did not want to be only a stenographer. Yet the wages seemed excellent – and I would have no travelling expenses. I did not know that the salary offered was not particularly high; throughout the war, Fiona was to earn much more than I did.

'Miss Hughes'll come and test you,' the man said, as he slammed down the receiver.

While we were waiting for Miss Hughes and the telephone was put to good use, I decided that if the post was offered to me, I would take it; the relief of having enough salary to enable me to buy lunch would be very great. I rationalised my decision by believing that I would gain experience which would lead me to a personal secretaryship one day.

Miss Hughes came quietly in and stood by the desk, until my interviewer deigned to notice her. She was a middle-aged woman with dull brown hair done in the same style as I had done mine. Her homely face was politely expressionless. Instinctively, I felt she shared my dislike of the man in the bowler hat.

'Take this girl and test her; she's for Wages.'

Miss Hughes' face broke into a friendly smile, as she took me into an empty office, dictated an ordinary business letter and left me to type it on a dusty Remington as heavy as a tank.

When she returned, she seemed satisfied with the result, despite two rubbings out.

'I am sorry about the corrections,' I said. 'I usually do better than that.'

There was a trace of cynicism in her laugh, as she said, 'I don't think Mr Fox decided to take you on because of the quality of your typing!' She looked down at the letter, and added in a kindly tone, 'But your typing is quite good.'

She left me sitting by the typewriter, while she went to confer with Mr Fox, and I wondered what her rather odd remark meant. I had been at work on the Installation for some weeks, before I discovered that I had been chosen to join Mr Fox's Young Ladies, everyone of them picked because they had nice legs! The steady stream of young women coming to take the places of men called up would have made a good chorus line, as far as legs were concerned, and most of them had the prettiness of youth.

I walked home feeling like a prisoner enjoying his first few moments of freedom. For the first time for months I was almost happy. No more nightmare worries about how to get to work. No more teaching shorthand at nights and on Saturday afternoons. No more going without or with only little lunch. I could even go to the theatre a little more often, something which had been a rare treat indeed up to then.

At the end of March, I said goodbye to my kind colleague in the Bootle Office, and, without a qualm, put behind me seven years of gross overwork and exploitation, the unhappiest years of my working life.

CHAPTER FIFTEEN

Despite my hopeful anticipation, I was as scared on my first day at the Installation as if I were about to be guillotined. I think that, when my friend, Belle, joined the staff a little later on, she, too, must have been quite nervous. She had had a wearying series of illnesses, and was in Mill Road Infirmary when it was hit during the Christmas blitz. Needless to say, she had lovely legs, and a very pretty face. She was vivacious and had a wicked sense of humour.

The policeman at the gate recognised me. He stood, arms behind his back, swaying gently backwards and forwards on the heels of his heavy, black boots, and asked, 'So you got in?'

I smiled up at him. 'Yes, I did.'

'Well, that's very nice. Got any matches or smoking materials?'

'No.' I paused, and then, perplexed, I asked him. 'Why do you want to know?'

'Well, it's in case of fire. No smoking allowed. Everybody has to leave their matches and pipes and cigarettes with me.'

'Oh, I see. Thank you.'

Though it was early, Miss Hughes was already at her typewriter in the small, brick building where I had been interviewed. When I inquired where I should go, she instructed me to follow the lane from the entrance until I came to the end of it. 'It's the building on the left,' she said.

So, on that fine spring morning, I followed a narrow, deserted, macadamised road which ran through the entire Installation. At intervals, I passed other small buildings, like the one in which Miss Hughes worked. Each one had the name of a famous oil company on it; presumably, they were, in peacetime, the local offices of their companies. Between them and behind them towered great round storage tanks, with a narrow ladder running up the side of each. Each tank was moated, so that if they leaked, the petrol or oil would be confined. Between the tanks ran pipelines over rough grass. Near one tank, two old lilac bushes were putting out buds, and other flowering bushes suggested that the area had once been a large garden. A high stone wall, patched with moss and lichens, marked the Installation's boundary. It, too, looked as if it had belonged to a garden.

At one point, I peeped into a huge garage, where it appeared that tanker lorries were being repaired. A man in greasy overalls looked down from the top of one of these behemoths and whistled after me as I passed.

I blushed and averted my gaze; I had never elicited a whistle from anyone before.

The sun shone brightly on the strange, circular storage tanks, making them look likc abandoned pieces of ancient, desert architecture. On the road before me, sparrows twittered and pecked, to rise and flutter away as I approached them. Seagulls sat on the edge of the tank tops and shrieked warning as I passed. Over all, hung the heavy, sickening odour of petrol, a very different smell from the close stench of Bootle slums. Above the boundary wall, I could see the chimneys of houses crowded near the adjoining Herculaneum dock. I was a little shocked that such a volatile commodity as petrol was permitted to be stored so close to people's homes; a well-placed bomb on a single storage tank could, I felt uneasily, set off such a violent series of explosions that the entire installation could be ignited in seconds.

Such a holocaust would take with it the whole neighbourhood.

It was the knowledge of this possibility which, during a particularly vicious raid, made a quiet, family man on the staff climb the deadly tanks near our office and heave off their floating roofs a series of incendiary bombs, for which incredible bravery he most deservedly received the George Cross.

I finally reached the last building on the road. Behind it loomed the boundary wall. It had a padlocked gate in it, which presumably led into Grafton Street and gave access to the Herculaneum dock. I looked up at the little office, and paused. About thirty years later, in a novel, I would make that building into a tiny cottage, facing the river, and I would break down the boundary wall, so that the inhabitant of the cottage had access to Grafton Street. The tenant's name and the name of the book would be *Liverpool Daisy.**

In front of the building was a large yard with a series of petrol pumps in it. Two big tanker lorries were being filled, and a man stood on top of one tank, dipping it, to check the level of its contents. Several men in overalls stood near the

* First published by Robert Hale Ltd, as *Liverpool Daisy* by June Bhatia. First issued in Fontana Paperbacks, 1984.

tankers, gossiping and shuffling papers in their hands. Such a strictly rationed commodity involved much paperwork, as the petrol passed down the lines of distribution. Not even the most involved checking system, however, prevented occasional theft, and there was a lively black market in petrol.

A youth of about seventeen, also in overalls, was placidly sweeping the yard, and whistling like a blackbird; he was the first *young* man I had noticed on the Installation. He was to be called up shortly and would become, before he was demobilised, a Wing Commander in the Royal Air Force, a feat which caused many earnest arguments amongst his fellow workers about the waste of talent during the Thirties, and how he might have spent his life as a labourer, had there been no war.

Shaking with nerves, I mounted the steep front steps and knocked at the door. Then, taking a big breath, to stall my sudden sense of panic, I turned the knob and walked in.

Though the lives of all my future colleagues had been upset by the war, I sometimes think that opening that door allowed me to leave a world of nightmare and enter a normal world. Yet, I was truly terrified, particularly when I caught a glimpse, through an inner doorway, of two men working. It brought home to me that I had, in giving up social work, left a segment of society run almost entirely by women, a whole way of life based on caring for others. Now I was entering a man's world, in which women played only a subordinate role, a world run solely for profit.

How was one supposed to behave? It was one thing to dance or converse with men, be pleasant for a few minutes; quite another to work alongside them. Fiona was having a difficult time, I knew, amongst men who regarded her as a sexual object to be preyed upon, not as a fellow worker. I wanted to turn and run. Better the devils of hunger and privation which I knew, than the devils I did not know.

'But it's too late to turn back,' I reminded myself, as I stood awkwardly before two girls a little older than myself.

At the sight of me, one girl swung out of her seat behind a desk. She was tall, rosy-cheeked and merry-eyed, uncannily like my childhood nanny, Edith.

As she came towards me, she said, 'You must be the new shorthand typist. You're just in time for tea. What's your name?'

I told her, and she showed me where to hang my hat and coat. One of the men, who proved to be the Departmental Manager, came from the inner office. He told me where to sit, and suggested that I try the typewriter for a few minutes. Then he would dictate some letters to me.

Two other small offices yielded the peacetime manager of the oil company which normally occupied the building, and his quiet, unobtrusive secretary. Their work involved the design of a pipeline to run under the English Channel, and I did not see much of them, except when the secretary was ill. I then deputised for her. Because we laughed and talked so much, the two of them must have been acutely aware of the invasion of their peaceful building by the Wages and Personnel Department of the wartime consortium of the oil companies. They were, however, very patient with us.

Over a cup of tea, I relaxed a little, but I had been so cut off from my own age group, so alienated by privation, that it was months before my voice lowered its nervous, defensive pitch, to its normal, deeper key. It was months before I understood the Department's racy, youthful badinage; in fact, I doubt if I ever did truly understand its more subtle inferences. I suspect that my bewilderment was a source of much good-natured amusement to all of them.

I found, to my dismay, that amongst my duties

was the calculation of a payroll. At night school I had, in bookkeeping classes, been taught only how to keep a simple set of account books; and, on the side, one teacher had tutored me in basic arithmetic. I had had little practice at either. In all my years in that office, I doubt that I ever got the weekly payroll absolutely correctly put together. The men whose wages I mixed up were extraordinarily kind and patient with me, and the Department Manager was never more than wittily caustic about it. I was, however, deeply ashamed of my inability to do basic arithmetic. Once again, the lack of schooling had caught up with me.

To a generation brought up in a period of pocket calculators, the urgent need to be able to do mental arithmetic quickly and accurately must seem strange. Yet, without mechanical help one needed such an ability at every turn, and I am sure there are still elderly people who can add up a column quicker than their grandsons can do it with a calculator. Certainly the girls in my office were very accurate.

I dreaded being dismissed as inefficient. Probably, with all the red tape which would have had to be waded through to dismiss anyone under wartime regulations, it was easier to put up with me. It came as a great surprise at the end of the war, when employers and employees were freed from Government restrictions, to be offered employment by one of the oil companies.

Throughout that summer, and for many summers after, I wore to work the three dresses Harry had given me – up to then I had always regarded them as being for best occasions only. From New York, they were beautifully cut and far superior to anything the other girls wore. Two of them were black, trimmed in subdued colours, and to me they were mourning dresses. Ironically, I had no decent underclothes to wear with them.

Out of my improved wages, I gave Mother thirty shillings a week, more than I would have had to pay a landlady in our district for dinner, bed and breakfast. At last, her pressure on me to stay at home to keep house eased; I was rapidly becoming a financial asset. We managed the home between us, and I thankfully stopped teaching shorthand at night.

The first six weeks of my new employment seemed very leisured. Despite the battle with the payroll each week, the weight of work was negligible, compared with the tremendous load carried in Bootle. The extreme fatigue began to seep out of my tired limbs and exhausted mind.

During that six weeks, I did three wonderfully exciting things.

In all my life I had never been to a dentist, and during our years in Liverpool I had, like the rest of the family, endured some excruciating bouts of toothache. Because of a poor diet and lack of a toothbrush, Mother had lost most of her teeth – they simply loosened and fell out. Some of mine were loose and several had large cavities. When they had ached, the holes had been stuffed with a tiny piece of cloth dipped in bitter oil of cloves. Feeling very daring, I made an appointment with a local dentist. It was taken for granted that a visit to a dentist was always painful, so I had to screw up my courage, as I waited in the front room of his house, for my turn.

He must have been used to neglected mouths, because he simply listed a formidable collection of fillings to be done, and two extractions, one because a tooth was beyond repair and a second because it was too loose to be filled. 'They also need a good scraping,' he told me, as he filled a needle to lessen the pain of the two extractions.

It was enough work to keep a modern dentist busy for half a dozen appointments, but this was in the days before dentistry was covered by Health Insurance, and the dentist had to keep his fees within the bounds of what the patient could pay. He therefore did the extractions immediately. They were painful and I bled sufficiently to cause him anxiety, probably because I was so ill-nourished. The following Saturday, he drilled and filled and scraped and polished until my mouth was sore and my head spinning.

'Come in next week, and I'll give the fillings a final polish,' he ordered, as he scrubbed his hands in a tiny corner wash basin.

When the final grinding was done, so that the fillings matched the teeth above or below them, I was so happy at being free of pain at last that some of my exuberance was communicated to the dentist, and he grinned under his grey moustache, before he opened the door of his surgery, to let me out. 'Feel better?' he asked.

'I feel wonderful.'

'Good.' His smile faded, as he surveyed his crowded front room. He must have been very tired. So many dentists had been called up that the weight of work on older men must have been very heavy, but not so heavy for him that he failed to remember ingrained, old-fashioned courtesies, like opening the door for me. I was touched that he should bother to do so.

Marks and Spencer's store was to me an Aladdin's Cave. There, I bought a pair of glistening black shoes with higher heels than I had ever worn before, all of one and a half inches high, and two pairs of rayon stockings – I had never before been able to buy *two* pairs at one time – and I felt very rich. The purchases proved to be a good investment, because shortly afterwards all clothing was rationed.

Except for a pair of satin dancing shoes, bought for my Confirmation in the Cathedral, these were the first new shoes I had had for ten years. I had always managed with secondhand ones.

Lastly, I opened a Savings Account at the post office nearest the Installation. I would put money into it each week. Post Office Savings Accounts had the advantage that one could save in them as little as sixpence a week. The customer was provided with a book into which he stuck six-penny stamps, as he was able to purchase them. The money was to be accumulated for new spectacles. I was still wearing, at twenty-one, the glasses prescribed for me when I was eleven. The frames were too small and had been mended and re-mended through the years, and the lenses distorted my vision. I tended to manage without them. Now, faced with the tightly packed figures on the payroll, I suffered frequent headaches.

I carried the Savings Bank book in my handbag, and guarded the bag from Mother as if it held the Crown jewels. Though she could not draw money from the account without forging my signature, I felt that she might easily do this, or, if she knew I had any money, she was capable of making my life such a misery that I would finally give it to her.

Many goods we take for granted were either no longer available, or were kept under the shop counters for specially favoured customers. Amongst these were makeup and hairpins and hair clips. The American seamen on the tankers docking at our Installation soon discovered this. Nylons, lipsticks and all the other small pleasures of life were soon circulating round the Installation and were eagerly bought by the girls. No Customs Officer at the exit gate of the Installation had time to bother about a single lipstick or pair of stockings carried out in a girl's zipper bag; their staff was so depleted by the call-up that they were already harassed enough. I bought a lipstick and some hair clips, and felt very wicked indeed.

Occasionally, as cigarettes, also, vanished under counters, I bought Mother a packet of Camels. She always thanked me politely for them, and would then complain steadily, as she smoked them, that, compared to Player's Navy Cut, they were horrible.

We were, of course, not allowed to smoke on the Installation because of the fear of fire, so we looked forward to a morning cup of tea instead. A tea break in the morning, however, was expressly forbidden by the management. It was considered an unnecessary indulgence. Nevertheless, we always made an illicit morning cup.

Because the office staff was scattered across the Installation in the numerous small offices owned by the individual oil companies, it was difficult to supervise us, but the trying little man in the bowler hat would zip around the entire complex between ten and eleven o'clock, in an effort to surprise us sipping tea.

He roared into our little office one morning, like an autumn gale. While banging the space bar of the typewriter noisily with my right thumb, I hastily slipped my contraband cup of tea into the stationery drawer of my desk. The resultant slop ruined a pile of typing paper and dripped with a noise that seemed unnaturally loud, on to the brown linoleum beneath my feet. I typed nonsense industriously to cover the persistent tip-tap.

I do not know where the Departmental Manager hid his cup or what the other girls did, but the picture of unnatural industry which we all presented was a miracle of instantaneous reflexes.

He said nothing, just snorted, and strode through the rooms, rattled down the basement steps to ensure that none of the yard staff was being so intemperate as to take tea and biscuits down there, came up again, glared at us and bolted out of the front door. We could hear him outside loosing his frustration on the unsuspecting yard men. We rescued our teacups and put the kettle on again.

Something had to be done, we all decided. We enlisted the help of the telephonist on the central switchboard in the main office, where the bowler hat had his glassed-in desk, at which I had been originally interviewed.

This lady was regularly informed by the wardens of the district, before the siren went, that an air raid was imminent. It was her duty to telephone each office to alert them to the impending danger. One of us would answer her ring, and she would announce, 'Yellow Alert,' or 'Red Alert', according to the closeness of the German planes. Occasionally, she would say, 'Purple, purple,' which meant that the raid was likely to be upon our area. On receiving such warnings, we were supposed to take shelter in the basement, with the yard crew. Warnings in the daytime had, however, become very infrequent, so we took over this system.

When the bowler hat moved out of his office, all the offices on the Installation got a whispered, 'Yellow!' Other offices would report sighting him to the operator, and the girl would hastily ring the phones of offices it seemed likely he would visit. She would say, 'Hurry, it's red!' And tea would vanish and biscuit crumbs would be swept into the waste-paper basket. The dreaded Purple warning was reserved for the Manager of the entire Installation. When, with suitable ponderous gravity, he emerged from his office – a rare occurrence – the whole Installation was on Purple alert, as if the entire Luftwaffe was overhead.

It is very important that management be sometimes blind, and to separate an English woman from her teacup, even when it contained the anaemic looking brew of wartime, takes more business acumen than it is worth spending. The bowler hat knew when he was defeated and gave up.

Though they were spent in a maelstrom of war, those six weeks were for me a time of recovery, and of learning to laugh and to enjoy the light-hearted company of my own age group. They were, in a sense, my first unworried, happy times, as I adopted my fellow employees as a second family. It seemed that the worst had already happened to me and was gone. I was moving forward into a new world.

And then came the May blitz.

CHAPTER SIXTEEN

As a result of the Lend-Lease Agreement with the United States, Liverpool was one of the primary ports through which flowed help in the war effort. The May blitz, which commenced on 1st May, 1941, was a week of night bombing aimed at destroying completely the city and its satellite towns. It was also the headquarters of Western Command, and the eradication of such an important Command Post would, alone, have made the attack worthwhile to the Germans.

Since previous raids had usually begun about six o'clock in the evening, I was thankful to be working close to my home. The office normally closed promptly, a luxury I had rarely enjoyed before, and I trotted through the fresh spring greenery of Princes Park as quickly as I could in order to be home before a raid began. A secondary reason for my haste was that there were soldiers in the park. They manned the anti-aircraft gun emplacements and, because there were few civilians about during the week, I was a little nervous of them.

Throughout the previous four months, there had been scattered raids causing a fair amount of damage. But we had slept undisturbed for a week or two before the May blitz, and had been lulled into a false sense of security.

We were all in our night clothes, and Brian and Tony had been in bed for some time, when, on the first night, the siren went. The clatter of incendiaries, the sound of bomb explosions and the roar of guns all seemed to come together immediately after the wail of the warning, and we tumbled down the stairs to shelter on the cellar steps. Now we shivered in the dank cold, heads on knees to protect our faces – of all injuries, young people seemed to dread most being blinded or having their faces disfigured. The family were shivering but none of them panicked, and we talked and made jokes to sustain each other, though our voices sounded oddly muffled through pyjamas and nightdresses.

After a stricken moment or two, I remembered the sound of incendiaries and that I was on fire duty that night, so I left the top step on which I was sitting and, with a muttered explanation to Mother, went through the shaking house, snatched up my overcoat from its peg in the front hall and slipped it over my faded, pink nightgown. Then I cautiously opened the front door. No one was in the street and there was no sign of flares on the opposite roofs. Keeping my head down between my shoulders, I ran across the road, bare feet pattering clearly in tiny breaks in the noise. I looked up at the roofs on our side of the road.

Nothing.

Very thankfully, I ran back into the house, through it and out of the back door, to look at the rear of the houses in the next street. They seemed all right, so I opened the yard door and went into the smelly alley which ran between our yard and the adjacent ones of the next street. I looked up at our roof and the other roofs in the block. All were dark, though the sky above looked like a Coronation firework display.

Sickened by the odour of urine round me and acutely aware of my bare feet in the filthy alley, I turned to go indoors again, and bumped into someone else.

I was more frightened by the sudden contact than I was by the raid itself, and I nearly fainted.

A pair of arms were pushed under mine and I was unceremoniously heaved to my feet again.

'Aye, luv, what's to do?' asked our faithful air raid warden.

'Oh,' I said in relief. 'I was checking the roofs. It's my turn tonight.'

'Miss Forrester?'

'Yes.'

'You was falling. Are you faint?'

'You frightened me so much,' I laughed shakily.

'Sorry. You get indoors. I'll shout, if there's need.'

'Thanks.' I felt my way back to the door. Before entering, I scrubbed my feet thoroughly on the bit of coconut matting which served as a door mat. Not even the zooming planes above and the sharp rap of ack-ack fire outweighed the sense of sick revulsion at what I had probably walked through in the alley.

The tremendous throbbing of aeroplane engines above our heads and the quick response of the guns immediately after the warning, told us that this was probably going to be a very heavy raid, and so it proved. Both sides of the Mersey were pounded.

As the house shuddered over us from a nearby explosion, and a slate slid down the roof and shattered in the street, Mother said, 'I hope Fiona is all right.'

'I hope so, too,' I agreed through the folds of my nightgown covering my knees.

As promised in her parting note, Fiona had telephoned me at the office, and had given me her address, a bed-sitting room in a southern suburb, not far from the factory in which she worked. She had made me swear that I would not tell our parents where she was, and I had unwillingly agreed, knowing very well what a fierce family battle there would be if Mother suspected that I knew her address. All I told Mother was that Fiona had said, over the telephone, that she was living in a most respectable house.

Now, feeling sorry for Mother, I said hesitantly, 'She's living well away from the city centre.'

'I am glad.' Mother's voice sounded flat and tired. She had always leaned on Fiona for company because she was hopelessly isolated from her own kind.

It obviously had not occurred to my parents that they could have traced their errant daughter through her employers. Perhaps a factory seemed so huge and alien to them, a place where anonymous employees were simply swallowed up every morning, their identities unknown, that it seemed an impossible task. While I sat listening to the fierce detonations outside, I decided that one night I would tell Mother I would be working late, and then go to see Fiona; I wanted to be sure that she was really taking good care of herself.

As the clock crawled towards midnight, we became very silent, each one of us nursing his own fear, afraid to say anything lest we lose our courage and become hysterical.

We all jumped with surprise when, soon after one o'clock, the all clear sounded. While the rest of the family stumped back up the stairs to bed, Father and I followed our usual practice after a night attack, and went out into the street to take a look round. Several of the neighbours were doing the same thing.

Towards the city centre the sky was red, sparks eddying amid heavy clouds of smoke, while white pillars of flame from broken gas mains lunged upwards.

The streets on either side of us and our own street were apparently undamaged, and we whispered to our neighbours our relief that it should be so, as if speaking in normal voices would wake the neighbourhood. If there were anyone left asleep after such pandemonium as we had just endured, it would have been the sudden silence that would have woken him!

Like everyone else, Father and I were very shaken

by the intensity of the raid, and before he went up to bed, Father sat down to smoke a cigarette. Knowing from childhood how even a thunderstorm could evoke again in his mind the roar of the battlefield, and reduce him to tears, I was loath to leave him, so I pulled a chair out from beside the table, and sat down to gossip a minute or two. He offered me a cigarette, and I laughed and took it. He had to demonstrate to me exactly how to smoke it, and I found it soothing. After that, I kept in my handbag a packet of cigarettes, mostly American ones culled from the purveyors on the Installation, and I smoked through the long, boring periods of waiting which a war brings. I smoked in innumerable queues, fish queues, sausage queues, greengrocer's queues, and bureaucratic queues for ration books or Government information, for stamps or a turn in a public telephone booth. Sometimes I smoked while waiting for dates under the clock in Lime Street station.

Walking to work through Princes Park the following morning, it was as peaceful as untouched countryside. The guns stood silent amid their camouflage, and, overhead, silver barrage balloons floated like cuddly toys put there for the amusement of children. Outside the park the tranquillity was not so apparent. An ambulance came out of a side street where there was a flurry of uniforms. The driver was going very slowly, indicating that she was ferrying someone in great pain, and I trembled at the amount of suffering being endured. It must have been a bad incident, I decided.

Incident had become a word which, to me, made little of death and destruction. There had grown up a sickening gobbledygook, as the Government, to avoid panic, sought to minimise what was happening. The upbeat stories in the newspapers were often nauseating in their hyperbole. The true bravery of the survivors and the dying, in the face of appalling suffering, was often overlaid by a description which made a raid sound like a football match we had unfortunately failed to win; better luck next time.

Sadly, I marched on to work. In the office, we silently looked round the desks, a quick glance by each arrival to see who was missing. When all the desks were full, we settled soberly down to work. Each day of that dreadful week we did the same. If someone was late, our hearts sank, and we would see the same worry in each other's eyes.

Towards the end of the week, our office boy who lived considerably further up the coast, in Southport, failed to arrive.

'He's as safe as houses up there,' we told each other. 'He must be ill.'

He came in after lunch, fair hair rough and uncombed, the rest of him smudged and untidy. He grinned broadly when he saw our anxious faces. 'It took a bit of time to dig us out,' he announced casually.

A bomber with a fighter in pursuit had jettisoned its remaining cargo; a bomb had hit his home. They had lost everything, but had survived themselves, unhurt.

The outside staff and the roster of firewatchers for that week had a very busy time, trying to avoid fire on the Installation. Even though we had our own fire brigade, a lot of help was needed to watch for incendiaries, or unexploded bombs or shells, falling amid the tanks. It was while on fire-duty during this week that a member of the outside staff won the George Cross for his outstanding bravery.

One night, the end of the Installation's jetty was blown off. Here, American tankers were tied up and their contents pumped through pipelines running the length of the jetty, straight into the storage tanks. When the river end of the pipes was damaged, oil spewed into the water before the flow could be stemmed, and the Mersey suddenly became a deadly menace.

Wardens ran from house to house, and the news was spread by telephone from dock to dock along the river, not to so much as strike a match for twenty-four hours, while two tides swept up and down the river and cleared the spill.

As the week progressed, the national newspapers reported nonchalantly that there had been a raid on a North West town. But by word of mouth, ominous stories reached us, even in our rather isolated workplace. We could see the heavy pall of smoke over the city centre, and on the wind came the smell of burning rubber, roasting wheat and peculiar chemical odours, and over all, and lasting the longest, the smell of wet ruins of plastered walls.

Officially, the city was not under martial law. The Board's lorry drivers reported, however, that soldiers were on guard in a number of places and were helping with the rescue work. They said, also, that the roads into the city were jammed with fire engines, caterpillar tractors and lorries, and buses full of workmen.

After several nights, I stopped in the yard one morning to ask a group of drivers waiting for their tanker lorries to be filled whether any of them had been to Bootle.

One took his cap off to me and said he had.

'What's it like?' I inquired. 'Is the damage very great?'

'It's bad. Very bad. Supposed to be eighty per cent of the houses flat or damaged. Have you got friends there, Miss?'

I sighed, as, in my mind's eye, I saw the packed waiting room and the weary, ragged queue on the staircase. 'Yes,' I replied. 'I have a lot of friends there.'

'Sorry, Miss.'

I smiled up at his deeply lined face, eyes almost lost in wrinkles with much driving. 'Thank you.'

Considering how great even its normal need of help was, there were very few social workers in Bootle. Now, the inhabitants must be desperate. So often, after being rescued from their smashed homes, it was middle-aged women who had to trail about on foot, children clinging to their hands, to find a place to live, to get new documentation – like ration cards, or pension books for the elderly, visit those members of the family in hospital or arrange burial for those who had died. And frequently they had no money whatever.

I knew that, at first, they would be defiantly cheerful, though shaking with shock. Their sorrow and despair would strike them a few days later.

As the week progressed, I thought of the fatigue of

the police, the firemen, the wardens, the Women's Voluntary Service, the First Aid and the rescue squads. During that week, most of them never had a proper wash or took their clothes off, and they had, of course, no knowledge that the seventh consecutive raid would be the last of the series. The Germans afterwards turned their attention to London and Glasgow. The Luftwaffe was also being regrouped for the invasion of Russia – a piece of news which left us speechless when we were faced with it about six weeks later.

Meanwhile, not only Bootle, but the whole city was constantly showered by the ash of the records of hundreds of offices, their burning files drawn upwards by the draught of the fires to make a dismal pall for a considerable time, until finally it was washed out of the air by rain, and the residue dusted up by housewives and street cleaning crews.

On the seventh day, I was so quiet as I prepared my payroll, that one of the male clerks asked me what was the matter.

I was near to tears, as I responded heavily, 'I feel I've left Bootle when they needed people like me the most. They'll be in an awful mess after this. I should never have left.'

Although I must have sounded a little pompous, he was sympathetic. 'You might be able to get leave from here for a week or two,' he suggested, and after a second's thought, he added, 'without pay.'

'You think I could? I'll ask Miss Hughes at lunchtime.'

Like everyone else, I was so tired simply from lack of sleep, that all I wanted to do was put my head down on the desk and nap off. Everybody tried to keep going, however, and, for myself, I often felt that if for one moment I let go of my usual routine, I would collapse, simply fall apart mentally with fear and fatigue.

By lunch time, my courage began to fail. The old fear of being dismissed for absence engulfed me, of being without a job and kept at home by a triumphant mother. I thought with growing dread of asking a favour of the rude man in the bowler hat, of his wandering gaze and coarse speech, or, even worse having to go to see the manager of the entire installation, a vague authoritarian figure, of whom the girls spoke in whispers, a personage who in five years I saw only once.

After eating my bread and margarine, I went for a little walk along the single paved road of the Installation. The smell of petrol spoiled the lovely day, and I could understand why many of the older employees suffered from ulcers.

Near the main gate guarded by the police, I met

the Head Stenographer, Miss Hughes, a lady who, like the regular staff in my little office, usually kept a little apart from the wartime temporary employees. She stopped, however, and beamed and asked if everything was all right.

I replied with genuine feeling, 'Oh, yes. Everybody is very nice.' I wanted to say to her that, to me, it was like having a new, extra family to love and admire. But she would have thought I was mad. It was unlikely that she had ever been quite so lonely, so isolated, torn from her natural roots, as I had been.

She seemed in no hurry to leave me, so I asked her what she thought about my taking leave of absence for a couple of weeks, to work among the bombed-out in Bootle.

She pursed her lips while she considered the question. Then she said in a doubtful voice. 'You might get it – as long as you don't expect to be paid – I can't imagine them paying you while you were away. Do you *really* want to go?'

I sighed. 'Well, I know Bootle so well, and they wouldn't have to teach me anything – as they would an inexperienced person. I could get on with a lot of work for them.'

She looked me up and down, and cleared her throat. Then she said decisively, 'I don't think you should worry about it. Somebody will have taken over your job, I expect – and there's a lot of outside help coming into the town now. For the moment, they'll need brawn rather than brains out there – to clear it up.'

I smiled at the implied compliment – I had already discovered that approbation from Miss Hughes was unusual. 'Do you really think so?'

'Yes, I do.' She looked round her as if to encompass the whole Installation; and, though there was a hint of disparagement in her voice, she sounded convincing when she went on, 'We're working hard enough here – we've got to have petrol, after all.'

My smile became a grin. I could not say to her that I had never in my life done so little for so much money. After my loaded desk in Bootle, and the earlier five years of ruthless hounding I had endured in the Head Office of the same Charity, it took me some time to realise that most people did not work themselves to a standstill in their jobs, that many employers were thankful if they got a fair day's work for a fair day's pay.

I thanked her, and then added brusquely, 'I can't afford not to be paid at all – and I doubt if the charity in Bootle could pay me, in addition to my successor.'

'All the more reason to stay here – and stop worrying about it.'

CHAPTER SEVENTEEN

The premises of the chemical company for which Sylvia Poole worked had been totally destroyed during the Christmas blitz. The staff was lucky that the raid occurred at night when the building was empty. As Sylvia told me, 'The only perpendicular object in a devastated landscape was the strong-room – where the cash and ledgers were kept.'

Sylvia was my oldest friend, my theatre-going companion, a fountain of common sense which, through many discussions, sobered my passionate, idealistic interpretations of life. I was very concerned about her. Her company, however, continued to employ her for some weeks, while they re-organised. But her future seemed uncertain. When an opening occurred for a clerk in another department of the Petroleum Board, I recommended her and, since she had excellent references, she got the position. Though she worked there for the duration of the war, I saw little of her during the day. She was quick-witted and cheerful and became very popular.

She was always a little late for work, and I can remember her flashing past the policeman at the gate, blue skirts lifted in the breeze, short, blonde curls glinting in the sunlight. She would rush up the steps of the main office as fast as her high heels would allow, in order to sign the attendance book before the clock struck nine. At the stroke of nine, the Senior Clerk drew a red line across the page. If her signature was below that line, the Manager would demand to see her, and she would have to give him a good reason for her tardiness.

If the Senior Clerk happened to hear her rapid steps on the stairs, he would wait with pen dripping red ink, ruler at the ready. As she shot up to him, blue eyes wide with impish hope, he would slowly lower the pen to the paper.

'Oh, no,' she would shriek, much to the glee of the watching staff. 'I'm not *really* late, am I?'

The Senior Clerk would grin, look at her slyly, and slip the ruler one line down the page, so that she could sign above the red mark.

Sylvia would thankfully scribble her signature,

fling off her coat and, still puffing, slip into her seat.

Though Sylvia did not seem to care about being late, I was always very scared of not being on time. The old scars, the old fears of unemployment, were always with me. In this respect, living within a mile of my workplace was very comforting; I was not dependent upon the hard-pressed bus and tram services, of which every air raid took its toll.

On the eighth of May, the whole city was prepared for further destruction. So that Father and Tony could sleep, I helped Mother drag a double mattress downstairs again, and lay it on the cellar floor.

The underground railway stations were packed with people lying on the platforms as tightly as sausages in a frying-pan. Others walked out of the city and into surrounding fields, their bedding and younger children piled into prams. Many children were put to bed in damp Anderson shelters buried in back gardens, and some curled up in the chicken-wire bunks of street shelters, regardless of the foul smell of them. Though used in the daytime by most families as dining room tables, cagelike Morrison shelters were crammed. Many families, like us, dragged a mattress down to the cellar, to lie beside the fine slack left over from last winter's coal.

Father and Tony, both completely worn out, slept as soon as they lay down, and only wakened when Brian returned from his messenger service at the end of the raid. Brian had had a quiet night. The raid was short and scattered, though Bootle had been bombed again, a final eradication of slums built in the 19th century. The gasworks of the suffering little town had also blown up.

Father went off to work on his bicycle, looking much better after practically a full night's sleep.

At the office, I heard that it had been confirmed officially that thousands of workmen had been drafted into the city, to help to repair the damage. The bad news was that much of dockland lay in ruins and huge fires still blazed. The city centre was a smouldering pyre. Rescue workers were still moling their way into acres of rubble that had once been houses. In the river and docks, fifty-seven ships lay sunk. Out at Bootle, a huge communal grave was being dug in which were laid together the remains of Roman Catholic and Protestant victims, united in death after a lifetime of communal strife.

Grimly the people – and a city is nothing but a mass of individuals – struggled to rebuild, repair, tidy up. Wrecked homes were combed for prized possessions, the dead were buried and the injured doctored. Somehow, shelter was found for the homeless. Companies, too, rescued safes, filing cabinets and precious machinery from the rubble and performed miracles of re-organisation. The Government did well in keeping up the flow of food and repair material into the ravaged port. Marvellously inventive, skilled workmen – the types with whom I had danced at the Club in Toxteth – found ways to hook up telephones, lay water pipes and electric cables and mend the huge sewers. Truckloads of rubble were removed from the streets, to be used as landfill, wherever possible, and as ballast in empty ships going to the United States.

The lives of survivors were not so easily repaired. In many cases, they had literally to start life anew; they had no possessions, no work, no money, no family, and no home.

As I walked home from work that Saturday afternoon, I remember being humbly thankful that, up to then at least, our house had lost only a few slates, its gutters and down-spouts and a kitchen window blown out. If the water supply was still functioning, Mother and I would soon clear the house of dust and soot, during the weekend. Probably the agent of the Earl of Sefton, who was our landlord, would be able to arrange the replacement of the missing window and the slates. All this, of course, provided we were not faced with another raid that night.

The terror of the concentrated raids had pushed my own sorrows to the back of my mind. Like everyone else, I dreaded further bombing.

As I approached our front door, crunching across the pavement through a mass of small detritus, my eyes felt like burning coals from lack of sleep. I put my fingers through the letter box and pulled the piece of string which activated the latch. The door swung open.

Mother and Brian were in the hallway putting on their jackets. Mother looked like a small thundercloud. I could almost smell her suppressed anger.

'Don't bother to take your things off,' she ordered huffily. 'We're leaving.'

I stood in the narrow hall, my zipper bag dangling in my hand, and gaped at her. To move was the last thing I expected.

'What do you mean?'

'We're going over the water.'

'Over the Mersey? Why?'

Mother jabbed a hatpin into her pink straw hat and glared at me from under its brim. 'I told you that we are moving. Do you want to face another raid?'

'Of course not. But – but I think you might have told me, talked it over with me. Where are we going?' I glanced through the open doors of our tiny sitting-room and living-room. The furniture still sat there, filmed with soot. 'What about the furniture?'

I was indignant at being so unceremoniously uprooted again, as if I was of no consequence. It was a repeat performance of the unconsidered, ill-advised move which had catapulted us into a Liverpool slum ten years earlier, and I wondered what kind of hell we might be heading for this time.

Mother jabbed another pin into her hat, and ignored my questions. 'Come along,' she ordered, as she picked up her handbag. 'We'll take a tram to Central Station. Come along, Brian.'

Brian, who probably did not remember much of our earlier life or the panic which had brought us originally to Liverpool, had stood grinning at me, enjoying my mystification. Now he buttoned his blazer and made ready to go.

I stood my ground.

'Where's Father?' I asked, trying to keep a tremor out of my voice. 'And where *are* we going?' What had Mother done?

Mother, who could not get out of the front door

until I moved, looked as if she would explode at any moment, so Brian hastily interjected, 'Mum's found a house out at Moreton. It's an army officer's house, and it's furnished – he's in Scotland. And Daddy and Tony have already gone there.'

I was reminded of Father's set face during the attacks; he had looked on Thursday as if he had reached the end of his endurance. At breakfast time, however, after managing to snatch a night's sleep, he had looked much better.

'OK,' I acceded reluctantly. 'Give me a minute to put my clothes into my zipper.' I had so few clothes that they would easily fit into the small bag. 'I'll be quick.'

I eased past Brian and started up the stairs.

'For goodness' sake,' shouted Mother angrily. 'Never mind about packing. Hurry up and come. We don't want to be caught in another raid.'

As if I were still six years old, I felt frightened by the loudness of her voice and her intimidating expression – I guessed that she had already had a fight with father, a fight he must have lost.

'Five minutes won't make any difference, Mother,' I managed to say.

She stamped her foot, and began to shout again, 'I insist . . .' when Brian announced suddenly, 'I've got to go to the bathroom.' He turned and trotted through the living-room, to go to the lavatory at the far end of the back yard.

'Oh, really, Brian!' Mother spat at him exasperatedly. Then she said more soberly, 'Perhaps I should go myself.' She looked up at me poised on the third stair, 'You just come downstairs, girl, and let's have no nonsense about clothes. There isn't time.'

As she followed Brian out, I flew upstairs. I was once more a child bent on thwarting her. In the bedroom, I tore off my coat and slipped over the dress I was wearing the two other dresses given me by Harry, heaved a skirt over that, and put my coat back on again; it fitted very snugly! Into the zipper bag, I shoved two blouses and my other set of underwear, a spare pair of stockings and a pair of old shoes I wore at home. My night school books, which I prized and still sometimes studied, together with a diary I had begun to keep in an old account book, had to be left on the shelf. They were too big to hide in the bag. Makeup and newly bought comb – my only other possessions – were carried at all times in my handbag. I was thankful that I had transferred Harry's few letters from my desk in the Bootle office to the back of the bottom drawer of my current desk. They were as safe as I could keep them.

When Mother and Brian returned from the back

yard, I was sitting quietly on the bottom stair, seething with resentment.

It was fortunate, perhaps, that the family still had some clothing in pawn, because, when the removers collected the furniture, there was no clothing, crockery or utensils left in the house. A looter must have climbed through the broken kitchen window and removed them. The thief must have been very poor, or perhaps bombed out himself, to have been interested in such a shabby collection.

During the following week, Mother crossly retrieved some bundles from the pawnbroker's loft, which had miraculously remained undamaged.

CHAPTER EIGHTEEN

In the dim electric light of Central Underground Station, we picked our way carefully through families sitting or lying on the dusty platform – people were easily incensed at passengers who brushed them when passing, or who trod on the blankets they had spread to mark their space. The reek of urine, of babies who needed their nappies changing, of old sweat, and musty clothing, was mixed with the peculiar, clammy odour of underground railways, and the sound of a myriad conversations rose and fell around us like the sea washing up on a shore. I thought with misgiving of the disease and vermin which could run through such a tightly packed crowd sleeping together, with inadequate lavatories and no water supply. It was only a very few years since we had ourselves finally got rid of body vermin, and I remembered how body lice could carry typhus, and how quickly influenza and typhoid could plague such a gathering.

Two feet from the edge of the platform had been kept clear by the station staff, for the use of passengers, and we waited there.

On the tram bringing us to the station, Mother had maintained a forbidding silence, and she continued frigidly silent, as we sat in the unlighted train, surrounded by an Air Force contingent. For servicemen, they were unusually quiet. They clutched bumpy-sided kit-bags and seemed to be festooned with other canvas bags hanging from their shoulders. I did not know then that close to Moreton was a Royal Air Force transit camp where men were collected prior to being sent overseas, and that the thought of being overseas was not always greeted with excited anticipation.

Looking down at my hands tightly clasped in my lap, I began to worry about how I was to get to work each day. There would be train fares from Moreton to Liverpool, I fretted, and then tram fares out to the Installation. I remembered the unbearable effort I had made to reach my work in Bootle. Would I have the same difficulties all over again?

There had been a time when I had looked out

over the Mersey river and prayed to God to send me twopence, so that I could take the ferryboat across it and escape to my grandmother's house. Now, it seemed a cruel joke that I should be passing underneath the river and was worrying about getting back into Liverpool.

With eyes cast shyly down I sat tightly wedged between two tall servicemen carrying on a desultory conversation over my head. I began to tremble, and one of them looked down at me and asked if I was all right. Mother scowled at him from the opposite seat, and, after a sheepish grin at me, he resumed his conversation with the other airman.

The little train rattled out of the tunnel into fading daylight. Birkenhead Park and Birkenhead North. Memories of childhood journeys to Grandma's house overwhelmed me for a moment. Then Bidston, a country station, and Leasowe, a clean waste of fields. Moreton was the next red brick station, eight miles from the Birkenhead ferry. The airmen began to stir and haul their kitbags closer.

I had never been to Moreton. I had merely passed through it on the train. I knew that much of it was twenty feet below sea level and was, in those days, protected by a sea wall which was much admired by Dutch experts when they visited the village. As a child, I had viewed with disgust the shanty town built between the railway and the sea wall, just after the First World War, by people who could find no other cheap place to live. I had been told that there was only one source of water there, to serve several hundred people, and I had seen that when there was heavy rain or a very high tide these miserable shelters were flooded.

Immediately adjacent to the station a neat village of council housing had been built, but some people still lived in the old shanties. The original village of Moreton was clustered round Moreton Cross about a quarter of a mile away.

As we trudged silently towards the Cross that mild May evening, a familiar odour was borne on the clean breeze. I could smell the sea!

How wonderful it would be to run along the shore, dance in and out of the oncoming waves, and look for sea-shells again. Despite my worries, I took a big breath to savour the familiar odour, and my spirits rose.

We turned into a road lined with fairly new houses. Each had a front garden. In some there were more weeds than flowers – those would be the houses where the menfolk had gone to war – but in others, spring flowers were in full bloom. I could not remember when I had last seen tulips growing in a front garden.

We turned into a garden where the weeds were beginning to choke out the smaller plants. We crowded on to the porch.

Before Mother could get the key out of her handbag, the door was opened by a stout, white-haired lady. I stared at her, utterly confused.

In a soft Irish accent, she welcomed me effusively. 'Come in, come in.' Then she realised my surprise, as I stepped over the doorstep, and said, with a note of puzzlement in her voice, 'Your Mam must've told you? I'm going to share the house with you. I was bombed out.' She ushered me into the modern little hallway.

'I didn't know,' I replied, as I shook her hand, and Mother, wearing her best society smile followed me in.

'Well, I'm Mrs Callaghan,' she told me. 'I met your Mam in the butcher's queue the other day, and we got talkin'.'

As we took off our hats, and Mother hung her coat up, all kinds of unwelcome thoughts spun in my head. How long would these two ladies get along together, I wondered bitterly. Mrs Callaghan appeared to be a very kind and charming woman, however, so I swallowed my growing sense of panic, and said, 'I'll put my coat in whichever bedroom I am to be in.' I was anxious that Mother should not see how I had transported my small wardrobe, in spite of her instructions.

'You'll share the hall bedroom with me,' Mother told me. 'Brian, Tony and your father will have the back bedroom, and Mrs Callaghan will have the front bedroom.'

Apparently the living-rooms, kitchen and bathroom would be held in common, and, as I went up the well-carpeted staircase, I thought of the clashes of personality that would indubitably occur as a result of this.

It was a very pleasant house, newly decorated, and furnished with modern, shiny pieces. The owner was a childless army officer, and his wife was currently staying near to his camp. I guessed that they had not been long married.

Down in the white-tiled kitchen, I helped Mother cut bread and spread it with margarine, while Mrs Callaghan got out six plates and put a slice of cold meat on each. When she carried some of these into the dining room, I asked Mother in a whisper why we were sharing the house.

'We have to share the rent. We can't afford it alone.'

As I went to help Mrs Callaghan find the knives

and forks, my thoughts turned to Father. Perhaps the move would truly benefit him and thus be worthwhile.

'We're all going to eat together,' Mrs Callaghan explained to me, as I took cups and saucers out of a sideboard and set them on the table. 'And I might as well do the shopping, being as I don't have to go to work as early as your Mam has to.'

It took about forty-eight hours for a sharp difference of opinion to arise between Mother and Mrs Callaghan. Mrs Callaghan had a much more generous idea of how much food to buy for six people than Mother had, and she was discovering that she was paying in part to feed us, as well as herself. As well as doing all the standing in queues, she seemed to do most of the cooking.

Aggrieved, she protested politely.

Mother told her icily that she could cater separately.

Our furniture arrived and was stowed in the attached garage, except for one or two pieces for which room was found in the house.

Ten days later, while everybody was still at work, except for Mrs Callaghan, a woman friend of our new landlord called, on his behalf, to complain that no rent had been paid, though it was due every Friday.

Mrs Callaghan asked the lady into the sitting-room, and assured her that she had paid her half of the rent to Mother. She insisted that the rent must have been sent by Mother, by post, to the landlord.

'What about the first week's?' inquired the visitor coldly. 'That was promised for the day you came in. It has not arrived.'

Mrs Callaghan, as she told me later, was so worried that she was stricken with palpitations in her heart. 'I was sure your Mam must have the receipt for it stowed away somewhere,' she said. 'And I cast about as to where it could be. Then I realised that your Father's bureau had been moved into the sitting-room, and I thought it was sure to be in that. In the circumstances, I didn't think your Mam would mind if I had a look.'

Apparently, she opened the unlocked bureau and began to sift through the papers in it, and, at that moment, Mother, having returned early from Liverpool, heard a stranger's voice and walked into the room, to see who it was.

'What are you doing in there?' she shot at the hapless Mrs Callaghan.

'And then, my dear,' Mrs Callaghan told me, 'there was a dreadful row, and the lady who came went away nearly crying. When your Mam come in I was that flustered I didn't know what to say.'

On returning from work, I had found the poor woman standing on the front garden path, surrounded by her luggage, while the next door neighbour's young son went to the village to get a taxi for her. She answered my inquiries as to what had happened, by saying, with a hint of awe in her voice, 'Your Mam was that angry she was nearly in hysterics. I couldn't believe it. I explained that I was just looking for the rent receipt – but she just went for me. There was naught I could say except that I would leave immediately. I reckoned she must have paid something in advance. But she hadn't paid nothin'. Just talked her way into the house.'

'I'm so sorry, Mrs Callaghan. Where will you go?'

'I'll go to me son in Liverpool. I'll be all right, luv.' She patted my shoulder, 'It's not your fault.'

As far as I know, Father went blithely on, glad to be out of the raids, and never questioned the sudden departure of our sub-tenant. The next morning, Mother simply announced to him that, now she was rid of 'that woman', she would go down to Shropshire that very day and bring the children back home. 'It's safe enough here,' she added.

Father gave a vague nod of his head, and I wondered if he cared. Without being asked, I gave

Mother a pound note towards the fares, and, when I returned that evening, Avril and Baby Edward, both looking thin and wan, were back with us for good. They were pitifully thankful, and, rent or no rent, I was very glad that they did not have to continue as evacuees.

We survived more than a month in that house without paying a cent of rent, though Mother collected the usual contributions from Father and me. The poor owners, not being used to dealing with recalcitrant tenants, never did manage to collect the money owing. Twice, Mother managed to squeeze money out of me to pay it, until my little savings account had nothing more in it, but, as usual, the money was largely frittered. The rent was never paid.

Finally, the young, pink-cheeked Captain came down to Moreton, on his first leave, and simply ordered us out within a week. He said, 'Get out, or I'll have you thrown into the street.' As a silent and saddened spectator of the scene, I felt he was much too kind, though I was glad, for the sake of the children, that he gave us another week.

Father had begun to look much better. His hands had stopped shaking and regular sleep had eased the strain on his face. In the fresh air of Moreton, his smoker's cough had also lessened.

After the Captain had swept out of the house, Father said nervously that we should remain in Moreton. For once, Mother agreed with him. She took a day off and went house-hunting. She found, in a small back road, a jerry-built bungalow of incredible shabbiness. It looked as if only the brambles hugging its walls kept it upright. It was, however, to my mind much better than our Liverpool house. It stood in a garden, if a rough piece of fenced field could be called that. Someone, years before, must have planted roses round it, because we had hardly been in it a week when its thorny thicket became a great cascade of creamy rosebuds.

It had a dark kitchen, thick with grime, but big enough to hold a table for eating, and an even darker sitting-room. There were two tiny bedrooms and an indoor bathroom – which seemed a wonderful luxury to me, after years of washing at the kitchen sink. Moreover, the kitchen fireplace also heated a hot water boiler behind it, so, whenever we had coal, we could have baths. It was partially furnished with the poorest and grubbiest of pieces, but when our furniture was added to it, it looked quite full. We were, however, chronically short of bedding and towels and china until long after the war was finished.

Because the cottage was so damp, it had lain empty

for many years and had been badly neglected. Not even a refugee from bombed Merseyside had been willing to rent it. We soon discovered that clothes left in a cupboard for more than a week or two became covered with mould. But it did have two advantages – the rent was extremely low, and it was only a mile from the sea. So modest were my ideas that I thought it was paradise.

CHAPTER NINETEEN

Though Moreton provided a wonderful escape from the slums of Liverpool, residence there engendered the horrendous financial problem which I had anticipated. How were we going to pay the heavy train and bus fares to Liverpool?

Father paid his own without comment. Mother had to find money for her own and Tony's fares, and part of Brian's, and the housekeeping money had to provide these. Though Mother complained bitterly about this, she still seemed to be able to smoke and go to the cinema two or three times a week.

The drain on my own pocket left me with almost nothing. I was back again to working simply for food and roof.

Mother's magpie habits were much enhanced by

her own dire need, and I had the utmost difficulty protecting from her my handbag containing the precious fares. Living in Moreton, there was no hope of my being able to walk to a job across the river at the south end of Liverpool, though many times I walked from Central Station to the Dingle Bank Installation.

One morning, while running along the cinder track that followed the railway lines to Moreton Station, a girl of my own age came panting up behind me. She was very smartly dressed, and smiled at me as we ran together for the train, already signalled.

She fumbled in her handbag and produced a season ticket to show the porter at the entrance, while I went to buy a day ticket and, consequently, missed the train.

A season ticket, that was it! I felt like Paul enlightened on the road to Damascus. Every time I was paid thereafter, I bought a season ticket before I went home. This ensured that I could, at least, get as far as Liverpool.

The hike which I so often did out to the Installation was not a pleasant one. The way lay through badly bombed slum districts, and I must, in some way, have looked peculiar to the inhabitants, because whey-faced women in black shawls would stare after me and snigger; and men, hanging around the street corners with as little to do as they had had in the 1930s, would eye me curiously. Perhaps, with my extreme neatness and old-fashioned spectacles, I looked too prim.

Mother used to borrow the season ticket in the evening, so that she could go to the cinemas in the city. Although this was illegal, I did not mind. She would often, however, try to hold on to it for use herself the next day, and on several occasions the fight to get it returned to me was so bitter that I nearly came to blows with her. She still had the fixed idea that she owned not only her daughters, but everything they had as well.

Shedding hot, angry tears, I would threaten to leave home immediately, but since I had no money, even for a night's lodging, and could not go to join Fiona without the season ticket, it was an empty threat. She knew it, and once or twice I missed a day at the office, simply because she would not part with my train ticket. When Father once intervened, she said calmly that her work was more important to the war effort than mine was. I could have the ticket the next day because I could then collect my wages, it being pay day. Once, when I was particularly distraught, after Mother had left, he lent me the day's fare, and

I arrived late at work, to sign my name below the red line.

I was so used to being bullied that even at twenty-two years of age, I could be crushed. A lifetime of giving in to a strong and ruthless personality is not easily shaken off, as any beaten wife will testify.

I wondered frantically if I could be transferred to a job in Moreton, and I inquired at the Employment Exchange, but they would not even consider it. I was lucky to be where I was, I was told, and I agreed with them. Though the work was the most boring I was ever to do in my life, I truly loved each one of my colleagues in the office. The good nature which prevailed there was a revelation to me.

I had been to see Fiona, and had spent a happy evening with her. I considered asking her if I could share her flatlet.

I was quite worried about her. Although she liked her little apartment and the money she was earning, she hated the factory and the merciless sexual harassment which she was enduring. She was also not popular with the other women on her assembly line, because she worked so fast. Her output had drawn the attention of the management, because she produced two and a half times as many components as the other women did. Their game was to idle as much as possible during the day, aided and abetted by their immediate male supervisors, so that overtime became necessary. Overtime was payable at one and a half times the daily wage, double time on Sundays and public holidays. Fiona felt that this was cheating, and said so.

She soon found her overalls torn, her tools stolen, and she was verbally threatened. One day, she sat down on her chair and it collapsed under her, bruising her badly; the bolts holding it together had been loosened. She ate alone in the canteen, because nobody would sit with her.

When she went to the office to ask to be moved to another line, the Manager fondled her and told her she could work in his office if she became his mistress.

She took a day off and went to the Employment Exchange to ask to be transferred to other employment.

The male clerk who interviewed her, asked, 'Don't you know there's a war on?' Then he looked her over insolently, and added, 'You probably brought it on yourself – painting your face and showing yourself off.'

The idea of the wicked, painted woman still lingered in the lower middle class, but poor Fiona was speechless. She burst into tears and stormed out of the building.

A couple of days later, before I could ask her if she would like to share her flatlet, Father received an urgent telephone call at his office.

Fiona's young watchmaker had plucked up courage to telephone him, because he was so concerned about her. 'She's at home with the flu. And the people she's working with aren't human – she's having a dreadful time,' he told him. 'She'd be better in the Forces – but she'd never pass the medical.'

He gave Father Fiona's address, and Father took leave from his office and went straight over to see her. She answered the door in her nightgown, and it was obvious that she had been weeping. When she saw him she burst into tears again and threw herself into his arms. He told me she was burning with temperature, so he got her back into the bed, and then collected a set of clothes for her and brought them to the bedside.

While she lay and sobbed, he packed everything he could find, and then persuaded her to get dressed while he went to see the landlady. She demanded a week's rent in lieu of notice, but he told her flatly that he could not pay it and that his daugher was so sick that he must take her home. Reluctantly, she allowed him to take out her luggage and agreed to forego the extra rent.

He had hardly exchanged a word with Fiona, except to tell her that he was taking her home, and she sat passively, occasionally sobbing, while he went to the nearest telephone box to call a taxi, and, afterwards, they waited in the hall of the building for it to arrive.

By the time Mother and I returned from work, they were both at home. Father had put a hot water bottle into my bed and persuaded his distraught daughter to get undressed and get into it. He had then left her, to go to the telephone box nearby to phone for the doctor.

'Fi, darling, whatever happened?' I asked, as I rushed into the bedroom, followed closely by Mother. Father pattered after us in his carpet slippers, explaining what he had done.

We might, as a family, quarrel like caged cats, but we all loved Fiona, and we grouped round her to protect her like a solid phalanx of Roman soldiers.

She lay with eyes closed in exhaustion, and did not answer me. Instead, tears welled again from under the sweeping, black lashes.

So, on either side of the bed, Mother and I patted and cooed comfortingly that the doctor was coming. 'And Daddy will make some tea and bring the aspirins, in the meantime,' Mother said pointedly, glancing at Father, who was himself beginning to look rather haggard.

The doctor arrived in his usual rush. He was already half way across the living-room, having let himself in, before Father had eased himself out of the tiny bedroom in order to answer the bell.

'Now, what's to do?' he asked, as he charged into the wrong bedroom, did a fast reverse and came out into the living-room again. 'Where is she?' he barked.

He was hastily ushered to Fiona's bedside. 'Now, young leddy,' he addressed her, as he snapped open his black bag and took out a thermometer. 'Let's have your temperature first.' She opened half-glazed eyes, as in the poor light, he leaned forward and thrust the thermometer between her lips. Then he leaned closer and ran a finger gently over one eyelid. 'My goodness!' he exclaimed. 'That's going to be quite a black eye. Have you had an accident?' He turned to Mother and inquired, 'What happened?'

Mother looked at him, quite shocked, 'We don't know – that is, she has been living on her own. I thought that swelling was from crying too much.'

'No. That's a blow.' He took the thermometer from Fiona's lips, and she gave a huge, shuddering sigh.

'One hundred and two,' he announced, and then pursed his lips. 'I want to listen to your chest, and then you can tell me about the black eye,' he said very gently to Fiona.

Mother undid the buttons of the ancient, Victorian nightgown, culled from a second-hand shop, to expose, as she thought, the creamy whiteness of Fiona's breasts. 'My God, whatever happened?' she exclaimed in horror. I gasped.

Most of Fiona's chest was scarlet and purple.

The doctor's eyes widened. He whipped a pair of scissors out of his bag, and without asking permission flipped the bedding off Fiona and cut down the length of her nightgown and of its sleeves. Her arms matched her chest. Very carefully, the doctor rolled her on to her side. Her back and buttocks were likewise covered with bruises.

He eased her legs apart. There was no sign of bleeding, but he sat down on the bed by her and, with extraordinary gentleness for such a belligerent, little man, he took her hand and stroked it. 'Fiona,' and when she did not reply, he said again, more urgently, 'Fiona, listen. You must tell me what happened, so that I can help you. Did someone try to rape you?'

'No.' We could hardly hear the whisper.

'Well, what happened to you?'

'They caught me in the lavatory – and beat me – the women did. And when I ran out the men were laughing outside, and one tripped me up and I fell.' Sobs burst from her, as Mother and I gasped at her explanation. 'Then the women caught me again and kicked me and hit me with a broom.'

She was weeping loudly now, and could not go on. The doctor, obviously as shocked as we were, let her cry for a minute, and then asked, 'What did you do?'

'Well, one of the men protested that they were going too far, so they let me crawl away. Then I got up and ran to the assembly line, took my handbag, and ran out of the factory. The man at the gate shouted after me, but I just ran. Then I got the bus home to my flat.'

She began to shiver, and the doctor hastily lifted the blanket over her. 'You shouldn't have gone to work, anyway,' he said almost crossly. 'You've got influenza.'

Fiona moved restlessly on the bed, and then winced with the pain of it. 'I thought I ought to go if I could. They need aeroplanes,' she said simply. 'But I did try to persuade the Employment Exchange to transfer me.' She gave a deep shuddering sigh, and then went on, haltingly, to describe to the doctor what the counter clerk had said to her.

'Humph,' the doctor grunted. 'Well, it'll be a few weeks before you're fit for anything, young leddy. I'm going to check that no bones are broken, and then I'll give you something for the bruises and the temperature. Aspirin should help the pain for a few days.'

Father got up from the old settee as we came out of the tiny bedroom. The doctor was furious at Fiona's state, and Father was horrified when he was told. 'We must tell the police,' he said. 'She can't go back there.'

'If you are agreeable,' replied the doctor, 'she certainly shall not. I'm outraged that the Employment Exchange wouldn't do anything to help her. Wartime restrictions – Registration for Employment Orders – or whatever – don't mean that an Employment Exchange clerk can behave like a little tin god.' He handed Mother a prescription form which he had scribbled out, and a second form saying that Fiona was unfit for work.

'What shall we do?' asked Father.

'Oh, I'll just keep signing her off, until you can get the Employment Exchange to transfer her. I'll talk to them if you like. I'd like to raise hell for that clerk.'

'Thank you,' Father replied. 'It would help if you could talk to them. It would carry more weight.'

Neither Fiona nor I ever knew if the doctor's complaint ever got back to the factory. We consulted our local policeman, who said Fiona could certainly lay a charge of assault. But she would need a lawyer – and lawyers cost money and we had none. The policeman recommended leaving it to the doctor and the Employment Exchange, unless Fiona wanted to claim damages.

Fiona was terrified at the idea of laying charges. 'They were shouting after me that if I told anyone, they'd murder me,' she shuddered. 'No! No charges.'

The doctor kept Fiona on the sick list for six weeks. She sat in our wilderness of garden, when she was a little better, and enjoyed the fresh air and sunshine, while occasional fighter planes zoomed overhead. Then, one day, a letter came for her from the Employment Exchange, saying that as soon as she was fit, she was to report for an interview, to the Income Tax Department, recently evacuated from Liverpool to a Moreton hotel.

Fiona's recovery was immediate, and she served as a tax clerk for the duration of the war. Her mathematics were even worse than mine, and she would often say, with a gale of laughter, that the Department of National Revenue never quite recovered from her ministrations.

CHAPTER TWENTY

It was customary during the war, particularly amongst middle-class people, to volunteer one's services to organisations connected with the war effort. Because of the long hours of work and the difficulties of travel to Bootle, I had never done this. Sylvia Poole had, however, undertaken to do the secretarial work for a unit of the Air Training Corps, and she now asked me to share these duties with her, partly because she was not a shorthand typist.

Before I went to live in Moreton, I had been filled with delight at my new-found freedom in the first six weeks of my time with the Petroleum Board, so I had agreed. For the first time, I could afford extra tram fares, and I had a little leisure during the early hours of the evening to do something useful towards winning the war.

I had no idea what the Air Training Corps was, but during a lunch hour Sylvia gave me a fast course on the subject.

The Corps had been formed to upgrade the education of boys who hoped to join the Royal Air Force when they were called up at the age of seventeen. All the uniformed officers were themselves volunteers. Many of them had served in the Air Force during World War I; others were middle-aged school teachers, not yet called up.

Amongst young boys, to be in the Royal Air Force carried considerable prestige, so all of them strove to improve the mathematics and English which they had neglected during their school days. They learned the theory of flight and the mechanical makeup of the planes of the day. A considerable time was spent learning to recognise, under all conditions, the silhouettes of both the Allies' planes and those of the enemy; if the boys became aircrew, their lives could depend upon this acquired knowledge. They learned from flash cards, some of them cigarette cards, to recognise in an instant the make of a plane from any angle. To test their skill, they constantly played games with each other or made up contests between teams. When finally they were called up, most of them could guarantee a perfect score.

Another skill many of them acquired, with much practice, was how to read and signal in Morse code.

So that they would be able to navigate a plane from the positions of the stars, they studied the basics of astronomy. On clear nights a lot of time was spent in the school yard, gazing at the heavens, which were much clearer in the blackout than they had been in peacetime. They made small telescopes out of cardboard cylinders, and drew star maps. Small groups tried to lose themselves in the city, so that they could find their way home again by the stars. They had a lot of fun. It is saddening to recall that most of them were dead before the war ended.

A dentist voluntarily examined the boys' teeth and encouraged them to use a toothbrush and to have fillings attended to. Many of the youngsters had rotten teeth from poor diet or plain neglect; people did not usually go to the dentist unless toothache became unbearable.

Civilian doctors were extremely hard-pressed, because all their younger colleagues had been called into the Forces. But one of them managed to find the time to help by examining the boys physically. He taught them to keep themselves clean and other simple rules to improve their health. I can remember the boys' skinny white chests glistening under the dim electric light, as they took off their shirts and jackets to have their heart and lungs listened to. There was not a fat boy amongst them.

The boys were issued with a uniform, which often did not fit very well. More than one mother whom I met was persuaded to unpick the garments and restitch them, so that they looked smarter. Then the boys would parade themselves before the local girls, like young cockerels in a barnyard.

Dressed in their uniforms, they drilled in the school yard, sometimes bumping into each other because in the long winter evenings it was almost too dark to see. They also went in a long ragged procession on route marches about the city. When it was too cold outside, they doffed their shirts and jackets, and did physical exercises inside. Many of them had never done such exercises in their lives, and there was a lot of good-natured jostling and joking, as they fell off climbing ropes or balked at vaulting the old wooden horse in the gym. Perhaps, because they were instinctively aware that they *must* learn to bear pain, they endured their bumps and bruises very stoically.

I was painfully shy amongst these youngsters and their sober, middle-aged instructors. I do not remember opening my mouth there, except to say, 'Yes, sir' or 'No, sir'. Yet I would have dearly loved, on evenings when I had not too many letters to type, to have asked if I might sit in on the mathematics and astronomy lessons. But I could not bring myself to own up to my own ignorance. I was surprised and touched when, absent with my usual dose of winter flu, the officers sent me a wonderful box of chocolates, which must have used up all their rations for at least a month. The box had a ribbon bow across one corner and a bright picture of an Elizabethan cottage. I shared the contents with the family. Then I pierced two holes in the lid, threaded them with string and hung it up over the tiny, empty fireplace in the bedroom I shared with Fiona and Avril. It was the first ornament we had had in our room, and we all thought it was very pretty.

The officers were, of course, in close touch with their counterparts in the Royal Air Force, and so I heard at secondhand some of the gossip of the men who had fought the Battle of Britain and were now defending our cities, or going out to bomb German cities. According to the gossip, an alarming number of men lost their lives not from enemy action but from well-known faults in the construction or design of the aircraft they had to fly. No wonder RAF men referred to planes as crates. It was expensive to lose an aircraft's crew, but it was much more expensive to abandon the production or design of a particular aircraft, or to inspire the kind of people Fiona worked with in the aircraft factory to greater care in manufacture. So young men, in the prime of life, became expendable.

This realisation appalled me. I could accept that people died in wars, but not that they should be sent to their deaths because of considerations of money.

Though moving to Moreton made it a little more difficult, I continued with the voluntary work at the Air Training Corps.

I was always a little heavy-hearted that I was assisting in sending the youngsters surging round me out to die unnecessarily. The idea weighed on me – and yet we had to have an Air Force. Perhaps these ideas increased my normal reserve, and, in consequence, I did not make a single new friend. I thought my plainness and dullness, as compared to Sylvia's sparkling personality and bright blondeness, were the causes. But looking back, I realise that the longer the war went on, the more sickened I became by the decimation of my generation, and I began to understand how my parents must have felt, when they remembered their friends lost unnecessarily in the ghastly trench warfare of the First World War. This attitude of mine was, I realised, not a popular one, and so I never spoke about it.

CHAPTER TWENTY-ONE

Moreton and Leasowe were famous for their market gardens. Huge crops of cabbage, kale, carrots, potatoes, onions and brussels sprouts had, for a century, been raised to feed the cities of Liverpool and Birkenhead. During the war, all this produce had to pass through the wholesale market, so that the cities were plentifully supplied. It was not difficult, however, to buy a single cabbage or a few potatoes straight from the field, if one knew the owner, and, as we became acquainted with our new neighbours, we sometimes did this, to augment what we could buy in the greengrocery shops.

Though, like many people of that period, we did not cook our vegetables very well, they did help to put the roses back into little Avril's cheeks. Edward was always pale, but he grew like a weed. Both of them trotted off each morning to the village school, a small stone building in the centre of the village.

The children in the school were quite as tough as those in the Toxteth school, in Liverpool, that they had attended. Since their numbers were small, however, they were better supervised, and in due course, Edward won a scholarship to Wallasey Grammar School. Avril, equally bright and with the same sticking power as Edward, did not win one. She certainly received no encouragement from her parents, and unless a girl was absolutely outstanding teachers tended to push the boys rather than the girls. In any case, girls were not supposed to be brainy – men did not like brainy women.

Tony continued his education at the Liverpool Institute. When he matriculated, he got a job in the Mercantile Marine Office in the old Customs House, to fill in time until he was seventeen and a quarter and would be called up. His hilarious stories of the seamen he met there often enlivened our evenings at home.

Living out at Moreton meant that it was difficult for me to visit several old friends, like the Spanish lady, who, long ago, had given me the Chariot, an ancient pram, in which I had trundled Baby Edward through Liverpool's depression-ridden streets. The pram was still with us in our first days at Moreton.

As coal became scarce, we used it to carry our small ration from the railway depot to our home. Under such harsh treatment, it finally fell apart and was sold for scrap.

At the Petroleum Board, our little staff in the Wages and Personnel Department occasionally lost a member. The girl so like my childhood nanny married a farmer in the south of England and left to help him run the farm. Her place was taken by a quiet, grief-stricken young widow with ulcers. She had to eat frequently, to assuage the pain of the ulcers, and was rather unfeelingly teased by some members of the staff. She soon left, and I hoped that she found more gentle and understanding companions elsewhere. Another girl, transferred to us, became pregnant with an illegitimate child. It was her second illegitimate child, and she was dismissed because of this; one child could be forgiven, but not two.

About this time, our whole department was moved from the isolated building by the gate of the Herculaneum Dock, to the main office opposite the policeman's hut at the entrance to the Installation. We were now all in one big room. One of the men went upstairs to another department, and an elderly gentleman joined us. This man sat silently through the days of the war at a desk facing a wall, with his back to the rest of us, and I often wondered how he endured the wall and our noisy, vulgar gossip. I liked him very much, and sometimes when the room was otherwise empty, we would talk about the war together. Like Father, he had a map on which he would pinpoint our retreating front lines.

Because offices of management were now immediately above our heads, we were rather more prone to unexpected managerial invasions, despite the Purple Warning system. In consequence, it was our department which took the first blows of the Stocking War.

In June, 1941, all clothes were rationed, and with our usual ration books we were given a number of 'points'. The ration was not generous – it took six months of these tiny coupons to buy a coat, and to be shabby became fashionable. Hats were replaced by head scarves and stockings by slacks. Before the war the wearing of slacks marked a woman as fast, and, though women doing men's jobs in factories had been encouraged to wear them, most women still regarded them as not quite nice.

Many people had at the beginning of the war a good wardrobe which could be mended or renovated, but our family had nothing to fall back upon, nor could we afford to buy with our coupons quality clothing which would last.

Very, very few women owned enough stockings to last for the duration, and it became apparent to all of us that we would rarely have enough clothing points to buy them. There was a brisk trade in clothing coupons at the rate of two shillings and sixpence per point, many of these coming from the rations of working men, who had ten points more than the ordinary citizen. But to buy these black market points would make stockings so expensive that they would be reserved for special occasions only.

Over several lunches, the girls in the office discussed the situation, and agreed that stockings were out.

We shaved our legs and went barelegged. Our skin looked horribly white, and all wrong with heavy shoes. So we experimented with painting the part that showed. Liquid makeup was the most effective. But cosmetics were expensive and increasingly difficult to obtain; it took nearly a bottle of liquid makeup to paint two legs. One girl swore by gravy browning, and even went as far as drawing a careful line up the backs of her legs with her eyebrow pencil, to give a resemblance to a stocking seam. But most mothers objected to losing their carefully hoarded gravy browning!

This problem was solved by enterprising firms

who made up large bottles of what felt like tinted whitewash. It was difficult to get it on smoothly, but the general effect satisfied us, and we all went to work triumphantly, with painted legs. I was particularly thankful for this piece of entrepreneurship, because Mother, as housewife, held my ration book and, consequently, the clothing coupons in it. I suspected I would be lucky if I ever saw one of them, and, indeed, this proved to be the case. No amount of cajoling would make her part with one.

'The children must come first,' she told me loftily. But she herself never went outside the door without stockings. Throughout the war, I continued to buy second-hand clothing and shoes.

Bare, well-shaven, white legs called forth many ribald remarks from the male staff, and, sometimes, from men in the street. I remember a group of aged Chinese, waiting with me at a tram stop, being convulsed with giggles and pointing at my bare legs. Nobody had any sympathy for the cold that we suffered once the winter came. The skin of my legs was ruined forever by being constantly chapped.

Because the Installation Manager's secretary, Miss Hughes, wore strong, old-fashioned lisle stockings, she was still able to cover her legs. He was, therefore, unaware for some time that the younger females on his staff were stockingless. It was the man in the bowler hat who first told us loudly and coarsely to cover ourselves decently.

We bowed our heads and remained silent. What were we to do?

The next morning, two enterprising girls arrived neatly clad in slacks. The man in the bowler hat regarded this as an impertinent affront. The girls were subsequently sent for by the Installation Manager, who must have been informed of their impudence. They returned from the interview in tears. Either they dressed decently or they would be dismissed. Since they were young, dismissal implied that they would be either called up for the Forces or be transferred to another part of the country, possibly to a factory.

While they bemoaned the unreasonableness of the edict and wondered how they were going to tell their fathers that they faced dismissal, great waves of indignation rose up in me. This was the kind of unreasonable bullying that I had been subjected to all my life at home, and here it was again surfacing, in the workplace.

'We should all go to see him together,' I said. 'He must have *some* common sense and should be able to see the point, if it's explained carefully to him.' I turned to the girls, and asked, 'What did you say to him?'

The girls looked at me bewilderedly through watery eyes, and answered, 'We didn't say anything!' They shrugged their shoulders slightly and looked helplessly round at us, and we all understood. People simply did not answer an employer back, if they wanted to keep their jobs.

The men in the offices thought it was tremendously funny, and came up with some more vulgar jokes about our naked legs. Behind my spectacles, behind my quiet mien, I was furious.

'Let's talk to Miss Hughes,' I suggested, and the girls began to gather round me, as if I were their leader. This frightened me, and yet the situation was so difficult that I felt that we had to do something about it.

At lunch time, four of us asked the advice of Miss Hughes. Could she speak for us?

Middle-aged and with a pensionable job at stake, Miss Hughes was flustered. She suggested that we should buy thick stockings like her own.

'But they don't last *that* long, and they do cost coupons,' I protested, painfully aware of Mother having my ration book in her handbag.

The other girls looked at each other, and I could read their agreement that bare legs were better than lisle stockings, even if one could afford them.

'Could we see the Manager?' I asked Miss Hughes. 'Could you arrange it?'

'I'll speak to him,' she promised bravely.

Written in stone, the edict came down once more. All ladies on the staff would in future wear stockings.

Those girls with brothers talked uneasily of begging a few of their coupons from them. 'After all, men's clothes last a lot longer,' they argued. This did not help me; Mother held *all* the family's coupons.

In company with two other girls, I went to Miss Hughes and told her that it was impossible for the girls to comply with the order.

'I've already told him that,' she said. 'But he can't see it – he said you should learn to darn.'

'It looks as if every one of us will have to resign,' I suggested, stammering with nerves.

'You can't do that,' Miss Hughes responded, unexpectedly sharply. 'You'll disrupt the whole Installation.'

My stance hardened. 'It won't be our fault,' I retorted.

'Don't forget that you're frozen into your jobs. You can't move that easily.'

'We can volunteer,' responded one of my companions, overcoming her timidity at last.

'At least we'll get stockings in the ATS, even if they're awful, woolly ones,' the other girl chimed in.

The first girl added, a little smugly, 'As an officer in the Wrens, I'd get nice silky ones.'

Lucky girl, I thought. She had been at a private girls' school until she was eighteen, and would stand a good chance of becoming an officer.

Miss Hughes turned a little more towards us on her swivel chair, and looked down at our pretty, neatly painted legs. She sighed, and said glumly, 'I'll try again – but it's difficult to shift a Yorkshireman!'

We all smiled at each other, a secret society of women. Yorkshire was going to have to have his mind changed.

At lunch time, Miss Hughes announced that the Manager would see the female employees, for five minutes, the next morning at eleven o'clock. 'You can't all go,' she told us. 'You won't be able to get into his office. There are too many of you.'

A few of the older women and one or two of the younger ones refused to go. Most of them had had the foresight and the money to buy four or five dozen pairs of stockings when first the rumour of clothes rationing was circulating. Judging by the dresses they wore to the office, some of them had so great a variety of other clothing that they could have lasted through five or six years before having to buy anything but the more perishable stockings.

One of the younger, more desperate ones said, 'If, say, five of us went, and Helen did the talking . . .'

Helen was immediately petrified with fear. The reputation of our Yorkshire, Purple Warning, Manager was enough to strike fear into the heart of the toughest barge deckhand, never mind a crushed coward like me.

'I'm not very clever . . .' I wavered.

'Oh, come on, Helen, you know how to put things nicely. I'll come and back you up – only, if I do the talking, I'll lose my temper, and that'll put us in the soup.' This from one of my colleagues in the Wages Department, and she looked rather contemptuously round our nervous little group.

I smiled at her. And then something of the courage which had sustained me in Bootle came back to me. There, we had done nothing else but battle against the stupidities and the neglect of Government, the rapacity of business, or the cruelty or bigotry of individuals. Many times, when my sweet, over-worked colleague out there had been away, I had had to cope with all kinds of threats.

And here I was now, caught between male pig-headedness and dire necessity. Except possibly on the black market, which I could not afford, there was no way in which I could obtain stockings. If I lost my job for impudence, I could not help it. I mentally resigned myself to scrubbing saucepans in Army kitchens, and agreed to be the leader.

The next morning, five frightened shrimps were washed into a very bare office, where sat a stout, elderly Yorkshireman, blinking at us over heavy horn-rimmed spectacles. His slightly grubby beige suit was creased across him, as if he had put on weight since he bought it. The expression on his face made me cringe.

'Well?' Scorn was in that single word and in the glance he gave us, as he looked up from a pile of papers.

'Sir, we have come to see you, because we cannot afford to buy stockings now that they are rationed,' I squeaked. Miss Hughes stood quietly by her employer, her facial expression a carefully controlled blank. She had done her best for us. She would do no more.

The small eyes seemed smaller behind the thick glasses.

'Why not? Are you telling me that you are not paid enough? You get coupons for them. Bare legs are not respectable, you know that.'

I swallowed. My throat was so dry that I thought I would not be able to reply. Then I said rather hoarsely, 'It would take all our coupons to keep us in stockings. There would be none left for anything else.'

'You'll 'ave to learn to darn, won't you?'

I thought of my carefully mended stockings, the ladders rehooked with the aid of a fine crochet hook, an eye-destroying task. I forgot my fear in a burst of anger.

'Sir, none of us wastes our stockings. We can't afford to.'

'And are you telling me you're not paid enough?' He leaned back in his chair and tapped its wooden arm with the end of a pencil. 'When I were in 'ull, the female staff was paid the same rates, and I never 'ad one complaint.' He looked us over with such an air of self-satisfied complacency that I wanted to kick his shins. Mercifully, his desk lay between us.

'No, sir. None of us is complaining about our wages.'

One of the other girls interjected, 'Sir, we could wear slacks, like the women labourers on the Installation.'

His mouth fell open. He was genuinely shocked. 'Not in my office,' he replied frigidly.

'It seems to be the only alternative, Sir,' I added. 'Slacks would last, they would be neat, and they would be warm in winter.'

Another girl, who had not up to then said a single word, suddenly spoke up. 'If you insist about stockings, we shall all have to find other jobs,' she said baldly.

I could have clapped my hands in relief that I had not had to make this threat. The man in front of us had had all his fit male staff under the age of thirty called up. He had just got his offices nicely re-organised with female staff; he would not want to start the whole operation again.

Encouraged by the Manager's silence, the girl went on, 'Our legs don't look too bad.' She stepped round his desk and lifted her calf length skirt slightly and stretched out a pretty foot. Her legs were evenly stained a light brown, giving the effect of a fine silk stocking. 'Oxo,' she announced simply.

He glanced embarrassedly at the proffered leg, took off his glasses and began to polish them furiously with a crumpled handkerchief. Angry frustration was written all over his plump, pasty face.

'I'll talk to the Office Manager. You can go,' he almost snarled, as he clapped his glasses back on again and scowled at us.

'Thank you, Sir,' I replied for the group.

Herded by Miss Hughes, we shuffled out of the room.

As soon as Miss Hughes had gone back to her own desk, we all began to giggle helplessly, holding on to the stair rail so that we should not fall. One of the girls who wore glasses pushed them down to the tip of her nose, and blinked at us. 'I'll send you all to 'ull to work, if you're not good,' she announced, and we broke into helpless laughter, and fled back to our respective offices.

After I had regaled the Wages Department with the story of our adventures, I asked, 'What does he mean by, when I was in 'ull?'

'He means Hull, you idiot. That's where he came from. Everybody was perfect there, didn't you know?'

After that, 'when I was in 'ull' became a catch phrase on the Installation, guaranteed to make even the most solemn person break into a grin.

I spent a whole week worrying myself sick that I, at least, would be dismissed because I had led the delegation.

Nothing happened. Not a word came down from on high. Gradually, we all began to breathe more easily. None of us wanted to wear slacks – they were too daring – and common. So we continued to paint our legs. In the winter, our legs sometimes bled, because they were so chapped, and cold cream, to put on them at nights, was so scarce.

Though we had won our little war, I had an uneasy feeling that the Purple Warning Manager had not forgotten the name of the leader of the malcontents, and in this I was right.

Later on, the Minister of Labour decided that the young women employed by the oil companies could easily be replaced by older women. The indignant oil companies, faced with training yet another new office staff, fought back. I became the test case, a most uncomfortable position to be in.

CHAPTER TWENTY-TWO

Moreton with its clean, sea air, combined with a much less demanding job and regular hours, improved my health. Despite the long journey to work, the help I gave in the house and the endless queueing for the basic materials of life, I also had more time.

As with everyone else, at the back of my mind the war was a continuous, scarifying threat to me and mine. Alan was still in Kent, an area constantly threatened by German air raids. At the age of seventeen and a quarter, Brian was called up into the Navy, which was a great disappointment to him; he had hoped to follow his brother into the Air Force. Once he was at sea, we worried constantly about him.

The news was dreadful. In North Africa, the siege

of Tobruk was an ongoing litany of losses. In East Africa, there was bitter fighting – a facet of the war that not many remember now.

In Greece, an infantryman, together with his unit, slowly retreated through its harsh mountains, to Crete, only to be bombed and attacked there, and to arrive eventually, with bare and damaged feet, in threatened Egypt. His unit was regrouped and he fought his way across North Africa. He still goes each year to the El Alamein reunion, where the survivors of this bloody battle meet to touch hands and relive for a moment their shared trauma. During those dreadful days, he might have felt a little better if he had known that the most beautiful girl in his native Moreton would one day be his wife. But Fiona's future husband, a gentle, peaceful person, was a very long march away from home.

The Battle of the Atlantic was a continuous running sore, and an even more destructive battle for the Mediterranean, including the besieged and battered little island of Malta, GC, took a frightful toll of both the Royal Navy and the Merchant Navy. I was no longer dealing with the relations of the men lost, but through the gossip of the port I heard the names of innumerable sunken ships. I cried in sympathy with more than one acquaintance who lost husband, son or lover.

As I tried to build a new life for myself, like a willowherb precariously rooted in the ruins of a bombsite, I clung to a rigid routine of daily catching the same train, concentrating on the boring payrolls, cooking, standing in queues on Saturdays, cleaning and mending for the family, and, of course, doing my voluntary work for the Air Training Corps, a welcome change. Occasionally, late in the evening, I went to a village dance. My partners were the men from the Royal Air Force transit camp or from the nearby gun sites. I sometimes accepted a date, but there was not much time to get to know any of them before they were sent overseas. One or two of them wrote to me for several years, and I always replied. I hoped that my letters were comforting, and fun to read.

To the astonishment of many who had not had time to read in the newspapers the reports of the preliminary build-up, on the 22nd June, 1941, the Germans attacked Russia. Three million German soldiers rolled like floodwater into an ill-prepared country.

Though the famous German Panzer Divisions must have seemed terrifying in their immensity, the Germans themselves had certain weaknesses in other areas, to which they had not given sufficient attention. They lacked general transport. Also, they had not fully appreciated the problems raised by the fact that Soviet railways are of a different gauge from the rest of Europe, and this complicated the use of German rolling stock in occupied Russian territory. To help to shift the vast number of men and the amount of materials they needed, they employed 625,000 horses in the invasion. Horses do not need petrol, but they do have to be fed.

As they followed the retreating Russians deeper and deeper into their huge country, the Russians' scorched earth policy, that is, burning everything in the path of the enemy, must have made the feeding of the animals progressively more difficult.

Suddenly, we all became knowledgeable about Russian cities and rivers. The names of Russian generals, at first tongue-twisters to the British, became fashionable as the names of household cats. The voyage from Britain to Murmansk in Northern Russia created another graveyard for our seamen, as the Allies sent aid to a nation which had suddenly become one of us, instead of one of them. Hot water bottles and fur coats, already hard to get, vanished from the marketplace; and we were told that they had been sent to Russia.

Father did not need a map of Russia to follow this latest invasion. He leaned back in his greasy

easy chair and said with quiet satisfaction, 'The Germans have lost the war.'

Considering that the Germans were rolling up the Russian army as if it were a carpet about to be discarded, this seemed a very optimistic remark. But Father knew at first hand something of Russia, of its tough peasantry, its horrendous winter, and when I demurred at his remark, he merely said, with a grin, 'Remember Napoleon.'

Particularly amongst the working class, there was considerable sympathy for the Russian people. As goods from factories began to arrive in Liverpool for shipping to Russia, it was common to see boxes, tanks and planes scrawled with messages, like, 'Another for Stalin' or 'Long live Russia'.

I simply hoped that Father was right.

At this period of the war, although I had such endearing colleagues at the office, once out at Moreton I was quite lonely. Edward and Avril soon made friends at school. Brian and Tony began to put down roots in their new village. Before being called up, Brian joined the Home Guard, and spent Saturday and Sunday, and occasional nights, guarding the coast, or practising repelling imaginary invaders amid the grass-tufted sandhills of our seashore. Fiona forgot her watchmaker and enjoyed herself at local Church dances. I always went to different dances, because I felt overshadowed by her. Besides, I was shy and abrupt and, until I established myself as a very good dancer, I frequently sat depressedly watching the other couples jitterbugging to the big band music.

The shoulder flashes of the airmen on the floor were those of a myriad countries, from Australia to Czechoslovakia. A sailor of any kind was a rarity – seamen were more common in Liverpool and Birkenhead, where lay the docks.

Many of these young men wanted to meet a girl who would take them home. There, by a civilian fireplace, at no cost to themselves, they could be warmer than in the freezing camp sites and could share what there was of homecooked food. They also often got their socks darned and buttons stitched on.

The rank and file of the Forces were paid only twenty-one shillings per week. If they wished their wife or mother to receive a family allowance from the Government, they were obliged to make an allotment for her of seven shillings a week from their pay. The remaining fourteen shillings bought them very little, though I came across one or two men in Bootle who, out of this miserable pittance, sent their wives additional money, because the wife's allowance was only twenty-five shillings a week, including their allotment. As they often said, 'She's got to pay the rent *and* the hire purchase man.'

Bearing in mind that a man in a reserved occupation in a factory could earn a basic wage of one pound per day, plus boundless overtime at one and a half times or double that rate, British servicemen were ridiculously badly paid. It was no wonder that, when American servicemen arrived with their much better pay, uniforms and food, there was considerable jealousy. However, many a mother with sons in the Forces did welcome into her home someone else's boy, particularly for short leaves of twenty-four or forty-eight hours. Occasionally, the language barriers were formidable and yet friendships were cemented that lasted a lifetime, and many a girl married and went to Europe, after the war, to share the hardships of a continent which had been wrecked by the conflict. There were even a few brave souls who married German and Italian prisoners of war.

Many of the Polish, French, Dutch and Czech dancers whom I watched had already lost home and family to the Germans. Some of them were bags of rattling nerves, who should have been allowed to leave the Forces to become civilians in Britain. Instead, they had yet to face the great and bloody battles of North Africa, Sicily, Italy, and the Normandy invasion.

Mother discovered the cinema in Hoylake, and she went there frequently. Later in the war, she complained sourly, 'It's simply packed with American soldiers, and they are with the most utterly vulgar blondes. I don't know where they pick them up – I really don't.'

Though many of the girls were perfectly respectable local residents, army camps, especially American ones, drew to them professional prostitutes from all quarters; and, despite work orders and the general regimentation of civilian life, these ladies flourished mightily.

As long as the beer allocation lasted, Father found the village pubs, also full of servicemen, lively and interesting. He spent most of his evenings in them.

At times, I could find myself sitting in the evening with a cat on my lap to keep me warm, because the coal ration had run out, and wondering once more what I was living for. Sometimes, I would try to make plans about what I should do after the war, or I would toy afresh with the idea of going into the Forces and would shrink yet again from it, because I dreaded more physical hardship – I felt I had had enough.

Even worse than being alone, I could find myself sitting opposite an extremely irritable mother who had run out of money for the cinema or cigarettes and had finished her library book. If she happened to be in a good mood, however, and if I were careful to tread my way gingerly through all the verbal minefields, we were able to talk about books that we had read or about our old home of so very long ago, a whole lifestyle which I suspect Mother never really appreciated until she lost it. I was the only child who really remembered much detail of that more affluent life and could share in her recollection of it.

In the early days of her marriage, she had collected Georgian silver, and she was still interested in antiques. We would tell each other of pretty examples of silver still occasionally displayed, at usurious prices, in antique shops.

She had been brought up in a Roman Catholic convent school, and she would occasionally recount experiences she had had in this rarefied environment. She had retained her Anglican denomination, though she carried with her, from the First World War and its senseless carnage, the same doubts and bitterness that Father did. While the Second World War whirled around us, we would sit in our cold, still very comfortless sitting-room under a dim, single electric light bulb which flickered occasionally, and stir our colourless tea, while we discussed whether the Body and Blood of Christ was, indeed, made real in the bread and wine of the Communion Service. Mother tended to believe, and also discussed, the idea that it was probably all right to address prayers to the Virgin Mary. I once responded that, to me, she always seemed to be only a plaster statue. This irreverent remark brought a storm down about my ears, and she was only placated by a promise to take her to the cinema the following evening.

Of course, any leisure which any of us had was quite late in the evening. Even if I had the necessary fares, I had to allow an hour and a half to get to work and an hour and a half to return, because the transport timings were uncertain, and, to begin with, I had a twenty-minute walk to Moreton station each day. Some buses ran from the end of the road to an intermediary station, but to take one would have added to my already expensive fares. Nobody in the family travelled as far as I did to work. Apparently, many of the neighbours never knew I existed, until nearly the end of the war, because I left home so early and returned so late – and yet it was an improvement upon the struggle I had had to get to and from Bootle. As buses and trains grew older and were not replaced or properly serviced, the whole nation suffered from difficulty in getting about, and the Government's slogan, 'Is your journey really necessary?' became a joke. Few would want to travel for pleasure in dark, close-packed vehicles whose timing was uncertain; except those with a little leave, who battled to get home to their families for a brief reunion.

Sometimes it is the small irritations of a war which irk the most; the blackout, the inability to fight one's way down a packed corridor of a long distance train, simply to get off or go to the lavatory; the problem of obtaining even a cup of tea on a long journey; trying to find a cobbler to mend shoes; or an electrician, or a plumber; or a washer or a switch in order to do a repair oneself. But gradually we got so used to people looking grey, shabby and unmended, to buildings left unpainted, to taps that dripped and appliances which did not work, to furniture with seats worn thin, to shopkeepers like bullyboys, that we did not even notice them.

CHAPTER TWENTY-THREE

The coming of clothes rationing on 1st June, 1941, laid the foundation of a huge black market. Everybody knew somebody who knew somebody who could obtain articles of clothing, particularly dress lengths. In order to serve this market, theft must have been wholesale.

Women who had never owned a decent dress in their lives except, perhaps, their wedding dress, were now earning good wages. Naturally, after buying food, their first desire was for pretty clothes – at any price.

A very handsome girl, Betty, who lived not far from our quaint mustard pot of a bungalow, heard from her mother that I could sew. She arrived on our doorstep one evening with a fine length of blue woollen material in her arms.

I did not know her, but without preamble, she said, 'Me Mam says you can sew – she saw a frock you made for your sister. Could you sew this for me? I got a pattern.'

Flattered by her trust, I invited her in. I fingered the beautiful material wistfully. Then I said, 'I'd be afraid to cut it. I'm not a professional dress-maker.'

She laughed. 'Go on with you. All the dress-makers is in factories and things. Me Mam says you can do a nice enough job.' She eyed me hopefully, and then carefully laid the bundle of cloth down on the kitchen table. I hastily moved an abandoned pot of tea out of the way, and carefully eased the material away from the ring of cold tea it had left on the table's battered surface. 'Go on. Take a chance,' she urged. 'I can't sew for toffee.'

'Well.' I paused. 'If you like, I'll cut it and I can tack it up. But I don't have time to stitch it. I sewed Fiona's frock by hand, and it took me ages – we don't have a sewing machine.'

Betty's face fell, her full red lips pouting. 'Oh, blow! Me Mam's got a machine she mends on. But she won't tackle a dress for me.' She giggled unexpectedly, 'Says I'm too hard to please!'

I took a big breath. Mentally I saw the girl, with her exquisite figure shown to its best advantage in a completely plain blue dress with, perhaps, a string of pearls as the only ornament. She would look lovely.

'Show me the pattern,' I commanded. 'And let's cut it. I'll tack the darts which have to be machined first. Perhaps your mother could then machine them. You could bring the pieces back to me, and I'll continue the tacking. Bit by bit, we could do it. And, finally, I'll fit it very carefully on you.' My voice gained in confidence, as I outlined the plan.

Happily she drew the pattern out from the folds of the cloth. It was not at all suitable for the material, and my heart sank. 'I thought we could trim it with blue satin ribbon, if I can find some,' she said eagerly. 'And I'd like a proper low sweetheart neckline, if you know what I mean. Do you think you could make panties to match? Like, when you jitterbug, they whirl you round so much your panties show, don't they?'

I persuaded her that the material would not be suitable for frills, as shown in the pattern, and that blue ribbon to match would be hard to find. We compromised on a full, gathered skirt and a tightly fitting bodice with a sweetheart neckline. I sighed. It seemed sacrilege to make such a vulgar dress out of such fine stuff, and I suggested that she might dye an existing pair of knickers blue – wool ones would be too warm, wouldn't they?

It was her turn to sigh, as she reluctantly agreed that they would be too warm.

When I took some pieces to her mother to show her how to machine them, I asked idly, 'Where did Betty get such lovely material?'

Her stout mother laughed. 'A lad in the village had it. And our Betty's got money to spend. She asked no questions and she got told no lies.'

Betty was delighted with her dress and went gaily to show it off at the next village dance. I thought no more about it.

About a week later, in the evening, an elderly man in crumpled work clothes came to the door and asked to see me. Mother allowed him to step into the living-room, but did not offer him a chair. She hovered in the background, while I came hastily out of the kitchen, wiping my hands on my apron.

He said gruffly, 'I'm Betty's grandpa. Her Ma sent this for you. Our Betty's that pleased with the frock.' He handed me an envelope.

I took the envelope, thanked him, and, then as he seemed in no hurry to depart, I invited him to sit down.

He slowly lowered himself into an easy chair, and

said, 'You'd better open t' envelope. I told 'em it weren't enough.'

Standing in front of him in my damp apron, I did as I was bidden. Inside was a clean pound note. I looked at it in amazement.

'For me? For the dress?' I exclaimed.

'Yes, you worked hard on it, Betty's Mam said.'

'It was a pleasure. Betty's mother did practically all the sewing. Betty was very welcome to the help.' I made to hand the money back to him, but he waved it away. He had been looking round our dreadfully shabby living-room, its walls darkened by years of coal fires, its upholstered furniture threadbare and grey with age, the carpet with but a shadow left of its original pattern. He said stolidly, 'Don't be foolish, love. You keep it – you earned it.'

He stared past me at my mother, still fidgeting by the kitchen door. Then the bloodshot blue eyes came back to me. He twiddled the ends of his big grey moustache. It was evident that he had more to say, and I waited politely, the opened envelope still in my hand.

He cleared his throat. 'Our Betty told me you couldn't sew her frock 'cos you haven't got no sewing machine?'

I nodded. 'That's true, unfortunately. And to sew it by hand seemed too much work.'

'Well, you know, I've got a secondhand shop, and I got a good Singer sewing machine in it. I oiled it and tried it this morning, and it runs well. You could have it for five pounds, if you like.'

Five pounds was a lot of money – it seemed excessive, even bearing in mind that new machines were almost impossible to get. Yet suddenly I longed for it. There was always mending to be done, and I could sew so much better with a machine.

'I couldn't pay it all at once,' I burst out. In the background, Mother exclaimed, 'Tush!' in a derogatory way.

'That's all right. You could pay me two shillings a week.' He smiled at me, watchful old eyes nearly vanishing amid wrinkles.

I guessed that he had probably bought the machine for a few shillings years before and had forgotten about it until Betty reminded him.

I was not sure how I would find even two shillings a week, but I did have a pound note in my hand that very minute.

'I could put Betty's pound down on it, if that would be all right, and I could drop two shillings into your letterbox every Friday.'

He got up from the chair quite briskly, took the

proffered pound and slipped it into his trouser pocket. 'Done,' he agreed. 'I'll bring it over tomorrow night.'

As soon as the door closed behind him, Mother berated me for giving him the pound note. 'He would have let you have it without a deposit,' she stormed. 'I could have used that money, even if you're so well off that you could part with it.'

I refused to answer.

The machine paid for itself dozens of times over. All of Betty's friends seemed to have dress lengths obtained from anonymous sources, and not one of the girls could sew. Betty was right that local seamstresses had all got wartime jobs, so I had the field to myself.

Though the work was hard – I sewed far into the night and most of the weekends – it solved my financial worries. I often made the wildest looking dresses, especially when the country was flooded with American soldiers, fond of over-dressed blondes. The decolletages sank ever lower, the waists became breathtakingly tight, the panties ever more gorgeously frilled or embroidered; I collected second-hand clothes with lace and ribbons on them, and recycled the trimmings. Buttons, too, became something to be ardently sought for. And I remember pouncing on a packet of hooks and eyes in a haberdashery department, as if I had found a gold sovereign.

Periodically I made dresses for Fiona, Avril and myself, though the material we had was either paid for with coupons or culled from second-hand garments, like old evening gowns or men's evening shirts. A frilled evening shirt was soon adapted into a pretty blouse.

A sailor sold me a uniform he did not want. The material was rough navy serge, but it made a fine warm skirt and jacket for me. I bought an almost unworn blue georgette evening gown from a neighbour, and made two blouses to wear with the serge suit.

Clothes rationing unexpectedly changed my whole existence, but the foundation for my sudden success had been laid years before. Sylvia's mother was a dressmaker and she had showed me how to cut out and fit ladies' clothes, though I was not able, of course, to emulate her fine finishing techniques.

Mother put her usual pressure upon me to share in my hard-earned monies. I refused. I was already paying her more for my keep than I would have paid a landlady. A number of times, however, when she was threatened with Court proceedings by local shopkeepers, I paid the bills. I was always afraid that she might pawn or even sell the machine. Fortunately for me, there were no pawnbrokers nearby, and the machine was too heavy to carry far. Every night, when I returned home, my first thought was to look to see that it was still on its kitchen shelf.

With the money I earned I was able to buy a good lunch, because the Installation unexpectedly acquired an excellent canteen.

During the May blitz of 1941, the Germans had not only destroyed ships, docks, warehouses, homes and the core of the city, they had burned out most of the frowsy little dockside cafes in which the dockers customarily ate. These minute eating places were usually run by one woman. They had provided good plain breakfasts and snacks for a few pennies. I remember seeing a pencilled cardboard notice in a steamy window which announced that for twopence the cafe would provide a large bowl of porridge with sugar and milk and buttered toast to follow. Now, the ever recalcitrant dockers began to complain bitterly that they had nowhere to eat.

Strikes were, and still are, endemic in the Liverpool docks. With remarkable alacrity, the Government built subsidised canteens, to placate this vital work force. The petrol installation at which I worked counted as a dock, so a canteen was established there.

Though the canteen was allowed a certain amount of rationed food, we would have fared poorly had the Manageress not been such a good cook. She produced large plates of good, plain food every lunchtime, by using much-despised and unrationed offal, and cooking it well. The office staff and the outside workers paid a small sum for these meals, and lamented loudly about how awful the food was.

I ate everything put in front of me. I rejoiced at the sight of roast heart, fried cow's udders, devilled kidneys, and liver in a thick gravy. Steamed puddings, lacking both eggs and sugar, vanished from my plate. I thanked God heartily that my dressmaking money had come along just in time to enable me to pay for these meals. I thought all morning about the joys of lunch.

Despite the long hours of work and travel, I put on weight and my figure rounded out a little. At work, I began to laugh and sometimes to be happy, though the terrors of the war lay over all of us.

The Wages Department was responsible, through the payrolls, for collecting employees' contributions towards War Savings Bonds. Through all kinds of special promotions, such as *Buy a Spitfire*, the

Government encouraged this siphoning off of the increased earnings of the civilian population – money saved was money not spent on the few consumer goods available, which otherwise would have increased in price even more than they did. It also raised much-needed revenue.

One of my colleagues, with all a Yorkshireman's care of money, suggested that I too should save a little each week in this way. Feeling very daring, and hoping that my dressmaking would continue, I committed five shillings a week to this. I wanted to buy for Mother a set of artificial teeth. She had lost every tooth, as a result of the hunger we had endured when first we came to Liverpool, and I really pitied her. It was quite common in those days for people to manage without teeth. But Mother had been a very beautiful woman and I felt for her. Though I had lost several teeth from the same cause, the devastation had not been so great, perhaps because I was so much younger.

I knew that I would need at least twelve pounds, and thought I should save thirteen, to be certain that I could meet the Dental Hospital's bill. If I did not do this for her, I knew that nobody would.

I have always been grateful to my colleague for this suggestion, because it taught me to save methodically. He also talked one coffee time, when all of us were discussing money, about the idea of keeping a personal account of our spending.

Father's favourite complaint to Mother had always been, 'I don't know what you do with the money!' So I took my colleague's advice, and have all my life kept an account of my spending.

CHAPTER TWENTY-FOUR

Autumn rain was thrashing across the office window-panes when one of the payroll clerks said, 'Eddie Parry's on leave. Saw him just now.' She slipped into her seat and began to spread out a paysheet, similar to the one that I had laid out on my desk.

We were much busier nowadays than we had been, and I sighed, as I looked down at the neatly ruled columns. What a boring job it was, to fill it in, week in and week out. I was always thankful when it was done, and I could revert to shorthand and typing. Figures never obeyed me; they seemed to jump about on the page and they never added up to the same total twice. Being a shorthand typist was not exactly mind-stretching, but it did offer a little more variety.

The regular employees of the oil companies

often spoke of their male colleagues now serving in the Forces, and, gradually, mental pictures grew up in my mind of these absent friends. When one was killed or taken prisoner, I felt almost as sad as the other girls did, and, like them, I contributed to a fund to provide the prisoners with parcels of food. The virtues of the dead were extolled; the stories of the living, like those of Eddie Parry and his brother, had a tendency to become legends.

'Eddie Parry and his brother – they're both in the same regiment – are as tough as old Nick,' I was assured by one of the girls, who had worked with Eddie. 'They go on pub crawls and they get wildly drunk.'

Eddie had been seen with a known prostitute.

Bully for him, I thought. A decent business deal, rather than the importuning for favours that went on amongst the staff. Most of the girls were able, with a laugh, to brush the men off, but a few were indignant and upset. Nobody ever bothered me – I suppose I was too prim.

Eddie's father had died when the boys were young, and their mother, so went the story, had never been able to control them.

'Never been to church since they were christened,' I was informed. 'If there's a fight anywhere, they'll be at the bottom of the scrum.'

I smiled to myself. Quite a reputation.

About mid-morning, a tall, red-faced man passed rapidly through our office, without any greeting to the girls and – dreadful sin in those days – without removing his cap. He went straight into the little room occupied by the male staff members, and shut the door behind him. There was a rumble of hearty greetings from behind the partition.

I was left with an impression of a man without an ounce of spare fat on him, a man who walked lightly and swiftly, despite clumsy army boots. An infantry private's battledress certainly did nothing for him, with its ridiculous forage cap perched on top of fair hair cut extremely short. To me, he seemed too old to be wearing a Forces' cap.

'How old is he?' I whispered idly to my nearest neighbour.

She grimaced. 'All of thirty, I should think.'

'Humph.' That made him younger than Harry had been.

I laboriously filled out my payroll, while, through the partition, we could hear Eddie discussing the problems of military life. Though many of the incidents sounded very funny, the stories were couched in language so bad that even I, exposed to every kind of humanity in the streets of the slums of Liverpool, was not sure of the meaning of some of the words. We made faces of disgust at each other, as we listened.

We went out for lunch and, when we returned, he had gone.

A few days later on in his leave, he came again, and had afternoon tea with his male friends. I happened to be typing at a table right up against the partition beyond which he was sitting, and I became very annoyed at having to endure listening to such bad language.

I stopped typing, and for five minutes I kept on a piece of paper a running count of the words of which I disapproved. Then, seething with indignation, I marched into the other room.

The three men had their heads together, as they leaned over the same desk. At my entry, they looked up in surprise.

I addressed Eddie.

'Excuse me,' I said firmly. 'I'm working on the other side of the partition, and I want to ask you that, when you are speaking, you remember that there are ladies present.' I put down my list in front of him.

A subdued hurrah came from the girls in the other room.

Eddie looked at it, and then slowly rose from

his chair. I found myself looking up at hazel-green eyes, astonishingly like my own. He was silent for a moment as he looked first at the paper in his hand and then at me. His red face went a deep plum colour, and then he said in a mildly Liverpool accent, 'I'm very sorry.'

'That's all right,' I responded, feeling suddenly shy. 'You probably forgot we were here.'

As I went out of the door, the other men sniggered. I felt that they were sniggering at him and not at me, and I was suddenly sorry for him.

Half an hour later, when I had moved over to my payroll desk, he came out, this time cap in hand. He asked one of the girls, who knew him, how she was, and after a minute or two's polite talk, she introduced him to the newcomers.

I was the last one to be made known to him, and he paused to look down at the payroll. 'Hm,' he grunted. He looked along the lines of crabbed figures, and then remarked, 'You know, this is a very slow way of doing it. Didn't anybody show you how to do these payrolls?'

'No,' I replied with a small shrug, 'except for the headings of the various columns – they told me what those should be.'

'Good gracious,' he exclaimed, with a grin. 'What's this office coming to?' He turned, and pulled a chair close to mine. 'Move over. I'll show you how to do it in half the time.'

He did the entire payroll for me in a very short time.

I was very grateful. His instruction improved my accuracy a little, as well as my speed.

He leaned back in his chair, letting it rock perilously on its two back legs, and began to talk as if we had been co-workers for years. He was amusing, as he told tales of when he was himself a very ignorant junior clerk and had been the butt of the jokes of the other men on the Installation. He made all of us laugh at his youthful predicaments, and not much work got done.

I began to put away the papers on my desk, and the other girls slipped on their coats and took out their powder compacts to powder their noses, before going home.

'Is it that time already?' he asked, and looked at his watch.

'Yes,' I said. 'Time to go home.'

'Where do you live?'

'Across the water.'

He got up from his complaining chair and helped me on with my coat. 'I have to go down town, to get a tram for Orrell Park,' he announced, 'I'll take you down.'

Behind his back, our two male clerks pulled wondering clown faces at me, and I hastily looked away from them. A spurt of anger went through me. They were his *friends*, weren't they?

Blow them, I thought. I looked up at Eddie and said, 'Thanks. It will be nice to have company.'

In a steady drizzle of rain, I was most politely shepherded on and off the tram. He insisted on paying my fare, and chatted away about nothing in particular. Then, after a little while, he slowly drew out of me how I came to be working at the Installation.

At the station, he inquired, 'Have you got a ticket?'

'Yes, thank you.'

'Wait here a minute, then. I have to buy one.'

'But you said you lived in Orrell Park,' I protested. 'That's this side of the river.'

'Oh, I'll see you home,' he announced airily, 'I've nothing on this evening.'

'Our house is quite a long walk from Moreton station,' I warned him.'

His eyes twinkled. 'Do me good,' he assured me. 'Need exercise.'

I was embarrassed, and fell silent as we approached Moreton. Since he had come so far, I would have to ask him in, give him tea at least. I hoped fervently that we had some tea in the caddy – and some milk and sugar.

It had rained most of the day, and as we walked out of the station it was pelting down. The darkness was almost absolute once we had left the dim lights of the railway. I had on a coat and hat, but Eddie had only his battledress and his absurd little forage cap.

I expressed concern for him. 'It's nothing,' he said cheerfully. 'I won't melt.'

To make the walk short, I started down a muddy back lane. We had not gone far before we were splashing through deep, unseen puddles. I apologised. 'There's only one house in this whole lane, and we've passed it,' I added gloomily. 'There's absolutely nowhere to shelter.'

'Press on regardless,' he shouted over the pummelling rain.

The water was up to my ankles, and I wondered how much deeper it would become. If the tide were in, the water would not drain until it turned and the little River Birket and its tributary, the Arrowe Brook, could once more flow seaward. I stopped, and said to my almost invisible companion, 'Look, I can't drag you through this. You must go back. I'll be all right.'

'Good God! I'm not leaving you in this. I'm

glad I came.' A comforting arm came round my waist.

I was sneakingly thankful that he was there. I was quite frightened.

'I'm going to carry you,' he announced, and before I could protest, I was swung up into his arms. 'Put your arms round my neck,' he ordered.

I obeyed, and suddenly the world became less scary, though wind and rain lashed us. I did not weigh much, but I was surprised that he could carry me so easily. I had not then heard of Commando training; after a course of that a man was either nearly dead or could carry anything.

He made a joke of the whole episode, as he struggled along in the water, which rapidly became knee-deep before we reached the rise on which our decrepit bungalow was built.

He slid me down on to the doorstep, and I could hear him breathing deeply in the darkness, while I fumbled for my key.

It was obvious that nobody else had arrived home yet, and I was trembling a little. I shivered, not so much with the cold, but with feelings that I thought I had conquered in the long dark days after Harry's death. I did not dare look up at Eddie, as I ushered him over the doorstep into our sitting-room, and switched on the light. We had forgotten to draw back the blackout curtains before leaving in the morning, and I was thankful that I did not have to switch the light off again and pad round in the pitch black to draw them.

The bungalow was clammy and unwelcoming. Eddie took his forage cap off and shook it. Like his jacket, it was sodden, as were his trousers up to the knees. His feet squelched in his boots when he moved. I kicked off my own ruined shoes, and took off my coat and hat and shook them, regardless of our aged carpet.

'Take off your jacket and boots, and I'll get a towel for you,' I told him.

Though our single towel was not very clean, it was dry. I took his socks from him and wrung them out over the kitchen sink, and wiped his huge boots inside and out with the floor-cloth. I put the kitchen bowl on the floor and he wrung his trouser ends out in that.

I persuaded him to go back into the sitting-room and sit in an easy chair, while he rubbed some life back into his feet.

The coal was kept in a lean-to hut outside, and I snatched up the coal bucket and plunged through the back door. My dress was damp already, and it was thoroughly wet by the time I had felt through our small store of fuel for some decent sized lumps.

Back in the kitchen, I was thankful to see a bundle of wood chips under the sink; at least, for once, we had kindling. I snatched up yesterday's newspaper from the table where it had been abandoned, and went back to my unexpected guest.

For all his size, Eddie looked strangely young and vulnerable, sitting by the empty hearth, in a khaki shirt with dark, wet patches across the shoulders and army braces keeping up his ill-cut trousers, from under which peeped large red toes.

I knelt down by the fireplace and began to rake out the ashes.

'Here, I'll do that,' he said quite gently. 'You go and change your frock, and put your hair back up.' My hair was straggling down my back because I had lost half my precious hairpins in the wind.

I protested. 'I can't let you.'

'Oh, go on now. Don't be silly.'

I went. On my way to the bedroom, which led off the kitchen, I stopped to fill the kettle and put it on the gas stove.

When Mother, equally wet, burst in through the front door, railing against the weather, bringing with her gusts of wind and a dripping dog, who had, somehow, got left out all day, we were kneeling close together on the rug, steaming gently.

I was shaking out my hair, to dry it, while Eddie

slowly added coal to the blaze, piece by piece, to obtain the maximum heat quickly. Beside each of us, on the rug, lay half-drunk cups of tea.

The dog shook himself and then ran across the room, to nose in between us, accepting Eddie as if he were part of the family.

As we turned to look at Mother, she stopped half way across the room, her coat slipping off one arm.

She ignored me. 'Who are you?' she asked rudely of Eddie.

In one movement, Eddie unfolded his six feet of height from the rug and looked down at her warily. Then he turned to me. I pushed back the hair from my face and scrambled to my feet. I introduced him as a colleague now called up.

'Oh,' said Mother. She neither offered her hand nor smiled, but turned and shook out her coat.

I flushed crimson. 'Do sit down again,' I begged Eddie, as he watched Mother vanish into the front bedroom, which led off the room we were in. 'You must get dry; otherwise you'll get a chill.'

His face suddenly had a hard, guarded look.

'I think I should be going,' he said. 'I told Mother I'd be back before eight.'

My mother came back into the room. She had changed her dress and shoes and combed her hair.

'Will you stay to tea?' she inquired of Eddie.

It was polite, but most unwelcoming, as if some strange aura was exuded by both of them, to clash and form an instant dislike of each other.

'No, thank you. Mother is expecting me.'

He reached for his steaming socks on the fender, sat down and put them on without looking at Mother again. Nickie, the dog, climbed over the fender and into the hearth. He was shivering and his wet coat smelled strongly.

Mother said stiffly, 'Since your trousers are so wet, I presume you came through the lane. The front road and the main road are clear of water. It was foolish of Helen to bring you out here on such a night.'

'I was happy to see her home.' He slipped on the sopping jacket, which I handed to him, took his cap and boots from beside Nickie in the hearth, and moved to the front door. He put the still muddy boots on the tiny doormat and carefully laced them up without stepping on to the threadbare carpet. As I watched him, I was near to tears. Yet I was afraid that if I said anything Mother would be ruder still.

'You can get a bus at the end of the road, straight to Birkenhead Park,' I whispered, as I opened the front door for him. 'Turn left at the gate and then left again.'

He must have seen my distress, because, unseen by Mother, he gave me a careful wink. Then he said goodnight to Mother, and she nodded acknowledgment.

As he went out into the continuing storm, I said, 'I am so sorry.' I felt his humiliation as much as my own. To send anyone out into such weather was unforgivable, but I knew Mother. If once she lost her temper, she could be unprintable.

'Don't worry, luv,' he muttered, 'I'll be all right.'

The storm inside the bungalow broke immediately. Picking up a strange soldier and bringing him home, without first asking, was shocking. Such a common man, too.

The tirade was still going strong when Father and Fiona came home, complaining that Moreton Cross, the centre of the village, was also flooded. They were so wet and miserable, however, that they could not have cared less if the entire British Army had surrounded the house. They were followed by Avril and Edward who had been playing in the homes of friends down the road.

As I lay sleepless in bed that night, with Avril and Fiona tucked in beside me, I burned with shame that anyone could be so discourteously treated. I was thankful that I had kept all knowledge of Harry, my lost fiancé, from Mother; I could not have endured such a good man being insulted by her.

In the office the next day, I was the object of many jokes and inquiries about Eddie. I replied shortly that he had very kindly seen me to the station.

That made matters worse. The male clerks looked knowingly at each other and suggested, with gusts of laughter, that I had probably had to fight the man off. I was so depressed that I did not answer them.

CHAPTER TWENTY-FIVE

The next day, my Yorkshire colleague announced, 'I'm having a few people in on Sunday, mostly from the Installation, and you're invited.'

My second grownup party! After much thought, I chose to wear a black dirndl dress which Harry had brought me. Though its black material was becoming a little shiny with wear, it had a pretty gathered waistline emphasised by lines of tiny embroidery stitches, a pattern repeated round the little collar and the edges of its puffed sleeves.

I was tremendously excited, as I entered my friend's beautifully kept home and was greeted by him and by his quiet, friendly parents. I think I envied him his father and mother more than I have ever envied anybody anything. They seemed so calm and stable.

As I went into the crowded sitting-room, I glimpsed on the other side of it a familiar red face. A scarlet blush suffused my own face and neck. Eddie nodded, and grinned at me, so I summoned up a smile, while the other guests swarmed between us.

My busy host pushed a chair forward for me, so I sat down between two girls I did not know and whose names I did not catch when I was introduced, and tried to join in their conversation. But I had little small talk, and was soon lost. They blithely continued their conversation across me. I offered to change places with one of them and the girl accepted effusively. This put me in a corner, where I sat dumbly, except to thank my host when he proffered food and tea. I was a most hopeless guest.

People were standing talking between Eddie and me, but I caught an occasional glimpse of him. He too seemed rather quiet. On his best behaviour, I thought, and wanted to giggle at the idea. He was being amiable to the many people he obviously knew.

He slipped away early, I was told by my host, because he had to return to barracks the next morning.

I must learn how to gossip, make light conversation, I thought in despair, as I went home in the train. Perhaps if I could find some film reviews and read them, it would be possible to talk about films and film stars with reasonable intelligence. And I must listen to the radio – a lot of the conversation had been about programmes I did not hear. I listened only late at night when everyone had gone to bed, a time when one could pick up all kinds of strange radio stations – one of my favourites was Schenectady in the United States – and to this day I do not know by what quirk of the air waves I was able to hear them.

Despite my lacklustre performance as a guest, I had, nevertheless, enjoyed being asked to the party. I compared the hospitable welcome to Mother's snubbing of Eddie – and felt sad, because Mother could be a very good hostess when she pleased to be. She was, for example, very pleasant to Sylvia whenever she visited me. I wondered if, perhaps, Eddie really was an incorrigible rogue, and she sensed it.

I was most surprised, a week later, to receive a letter from Dover Castle.

From behind the thick walls of the castle, Eddie wrote, he was supposed to be guarding the White Cliffs of England. In fact, he felt that he was the centre of the bullseye for target practice by the Germans, twenty-one miles away on the other side of the English Channel. The boredom, he assured me, was excruciating, relieved only by the occasional hits and misses of the enemy. He was sure he would be drawing his Old Age Pension by the time the British got down to tackling the German army.

Though pets were strictly forbidden in the Castle, two friends and he had, to alleviate the dreariness of their days, adopted a family of three kittens born in a local pub.

Most armies have an enormous capacity for collecting pets of every kind, and Dover Castle would indubitably have resembled a zoo, had the ban not been in force.

The problem, wrote Eddie gravely, was to smuggle their newly adopted family into the castle. This required careful study.

The three soldiers went to town to shop. They returned with a paper bag and two boxes from the bakery – a uniform usually beguiled under-the-counter goods from a shopkeeper, and they had been successful. As they went through the guard room, a lovely smell of newly baked buns issued from the bag, and a mild scuffling from the baker's cake boxes went unnoticed by the bored guards.

It was the first time, said Eddie, that he had ever owned a mewing spongecake!

Feeding the little family had its own difficulties. 'It is not easy to smuggle rice pudding – or fish,' he informed me. 'Even if you can find a piece of greaseproof paper to wrap it in. My pockets are a disgrace to the British Army. However, Timoshenko and Voroshilov are both gaining weight. We are a little worried about Zhukov.'

There were, of course, inspections to be avoided. The Corporals or the Sergeant would roar through the damp, stone rooms, swearing that the whole place smelled as if every randy tom in Dover was prowling the place. The kittens, hastily deposited in a long-forgotten dungeon, howled unheard.

Once, when he had gone down to retrieve the little prisoners, he found only two. Trying to find them by the light of matches was not easy, because they scampered about so fast, and one had apparently escaped when he opened the door.

After a frantic hunt, it was eventually found in the kitchen, the centre of a circle of admirers, as it cleaned up a saucer of food.

Eddie and his friends decided against demanding the cat back, because they did not want to draw attention to themselves or to the other two members of the family. He justified their desertion of their small friend by saying, 'The cooks could always say that they needed a cat down there, because of the rats and mice. He's found himself a job!'

I had never before received such an amusing letter. In a quiet spell in the office, I concocted as lively a reply as I could, and thus a sporadic correspondence grew up between us. At first, so low an opinion did I have of myself, that I assumed the letters were not for me alone, but to be shared with his friends in the office. Then, though still very light-hearted, the letters became more personal and I kept them to myself. The adventures and narrow escapes of the kittens and their owners kept us going through most of the winter of 1941–42, and helped to divert me during the hardships of coal shortages, failing electricity, autumn air raids, illness in the family, and very depressing war news.

By spring, Eddie was voicing in his letters the general frustration felt by the British Army at the lack of action. He wrote about the frayed nerves and irritability of his friends, and, as the Germans continued to use the Castle as a target, their depression at being holed up in such a cold, damp place.

I knew what cold, damp and frustration could do to a person, and I was able to commiserate.

In the early spring, he came, unheralded, to see me while on leave. We spent several hours drinking half-cold coffee in an unheated cafe in Hoylake, while I listened sympathetically to his woes.

At one point, he said, 'I'm worried about my mother. She's not very strong, and she's living alone. Our house is fairly large and it needs more heating than the coal ration will stretch to. I'm trying to get a new electric fire for her.'

This was very different from the man who strode round the Installation, swearing like an infuriated Arab or even the soldier who kept cats and, at the same time, wanted to cut the throats of German gunners.

Afterwards, when I had seen him off on the train, a little comforted, I hoped, I walked slowly home.

I thought of two little boys being brought up fatherless, by a mother trying to keep some sense of discipline in them. As they grew up, I ruminated, they would assert their independence, endeavour to untie themselves from her apron strings. And they might easily do it by over-emphasising their masculinity. Put one of those boys into the world of oil companies, where toughness is all, and you would have Eddie, determined to show that nobody was going to kick him about. I wondered suddenly what his mother was like.

CHAPTER TWENTY-SIX

Late in the same autumn that I became acquainted with Eddie, I arrived home one evening in time to hear Edward, now a tall, thin ten-year-old, complaining of a sore throat.

'You're probably getting a cold,' replied Mother, and then added, with some exasperation, 'If you *will* go out in the rain without a mackintosh, you can expect to get a chill.'

The next morning the throat seemed worse, and, over breakfast, he complained of weakness and said he did not want to go to school. He was, however, bustled off by Mother, with the assurance that it was indeed only a cold. She had to get to work.

By the next day it was obvious that he was ill. He was feverish, and when Mother thrust a spoon handle down his throat to see if his tonsils were swollen, white patches were clearly visible. 'Tonsillitis,' announced Mother. 'Perhaps we should go to the doctor.'

He was, however, too weak to walk and was near to tears. Mother put him back to bed, and walked down to the telephone box at the corner to call our explosive, overworked general practitioner.

According to Mother the doctor, after examining Edward, was very rude.

'Good God, woman!' he shouted. 'Why didn't you call me before? The child has diphtheria – and badly, too.'

The ambulance arrived within half an hour, and a very scared youngster was whisked off to the isolation hospital.

'Who would think of diphtheria?' Mother asked me plaintively. She had not been allowed to accompany Edward to the isolation hospital, and she was naturally upset. I had made her a cup of tea, Merseyside's cure-all, and was feeling very sorry for her.

'Well, I must say that I didn't,' I assured her. Frail, underfed Edward! I was sick with fear.

When he heard the news, Father, too, was genuinely distressed and, armed with a new subject of conversation, he went down to the local hotel for his usual rounds of beer.

When he mentioned diphtheria to his fellow gossips nodding over their glasses of thin wartime beer, he was surprised to be told, 'Aye, there's quite a lot of it around. Three kids in a family by us have got it. They've started to vaccinate them in the schools.'

From house to house the infection spread. Deaths began to be reported. In the next road to us a family of six died, and we felt the same helpless fear that Londoners must have suffered when visited by the plague.

'There's a carrier somewhere in the village,' people whispered, and they eyed each other speculatively.

All the teachers and children in the local schools had their throats swabbed, and by this method several cases were caught in their early stages.

The headmaster of one school worked unceasingly amongst his stricken charges and their families. He hardly slept while he supervised the examination and swabbing of every child in his school, and then had the school specially cleaned, in case the infection lay there. The only person in the school whose throat was not swabbed in the frantic haste was his own, until very late in the epidemic.

He proved to be a carrier of the disease, and it was heart-breaking to see the man's distress. Friends and parents and family, fearing that he might commit suicide, closed around him to comfort him. But I think it was a long time before he stopped blaming himself for the death of some of his pupils.

Mother took days off in order to visit poor Edward, who was, of course, kept isolated. As I remember, she was allowed to look at him through a pane of glass, so that she did not pick up the dreaded disease.

About ten days later, Father came home from work unusually silent. Instead of standing his umbrella in the kitchen sink to drip, he propped it in a corner by the door, where the water slowly ran down its shiny blackness to form a puddle. He took off his mack and draped it over the kitchen door to dry. Then he said heavily to Mother, who was herself still arranging her wet coat over the back of a chair, having only just come in, 'My throat feels very odd. I think I'd better see the doctor when his surgery opens.'

By the time I got home, he had already gone, and Mother was optimistically assuring Avril and Tony that it was nothing serious.

I had hardly washed the dishes stacked up on the kitchen draining-board after tea, when he was back.

He sank down on a kitchen chair, his face drained of its usual redness, to the point where he looked yellow. 'The ambulance will be here shortly. Have I got any clean pyjamas?'

We looked at him appalled, while something akin to terror ran through us. Fear for him, fear for ourselves.

'Doctor said I probably caught it from a dirty glass in the pub,' he told us.

With his bad heart and his generally undernourished condition, we knew and he knew that he had received a death warrant.

As with Edward, no one was allowed to go with him in the ambulance, and it seemed so cruel to me that he was going away to die alone, without family round him. We dared not even kiss him. Even Mother was silent and deflated.

Mother usually took a bus from Moreton to Birkenhead Park, and then caught a train to Liverpool. While she was waiting at the bus stop the following morning, the doctor passed her as he hurried from his car to a patient's house. She ran after him and asked him, in despair, if there was anything she could do to save the rest of her family from infection. 'Where does the germ come from? Is it only from other people?'

'It could be anywhere,' she was told. 'In the

drains, in the dust in the house, the curtains. You could try boiling all your dishes and linen – all the clothing. Wash down the entire interior of the house with strong disinfectant. Sluice every drain with more disinfectant. Wash down the furniture.'

'Thank you.'

'And don't forget to have all your throats swabbed,' he called after her, as she got on the bus.

The next day, a Saturday, was clear and warm. A flawless blue sky looked so peaceful that it seemed impossible that it could ever be the stage of ruthless aerial combat. But Mother and I were bent on another battle. Neither of us now worked on Saturdays, so, with the aid of Tony, we moved every stick of furniture, except the bedframes, out of the tiny bungalow. Avril went back and forth with small items.

On the aged gas stove we boiled all the dishes. Into a gas boiler, which Mother had recently bought on the hire purchase system, went our scant supply of clothing and bedding, to bubble like some ancient cauldron until everything looked cleaner than it had ever done before.

We brushed the mattresses and then wiped them with clothes steeped in undiluted pine disinfectant. The settee and easy chairs, which belonged to the landlord, got the same treatment. Then we scrubbed them with soapsuds and a scrubbing brush, removing years of grime. A week later, when they were thoroughly dry, they looked very much nicer, though very frayed around the arms, and very sunken of seat. Standing on the yellow grass of autumn, we washed down all the wooden furniture and left it to dry in the sun.

Then we started on the bungalow itself. Disinfectant, followed by kettles and saucepans full of boiling water, went down every drain. The revoltingly clogged outside drains, still a feature of most English homes, were prised clean with the aid of a stick from the garden, and were then given a dose of undiluted disinfectant.

Standing on wooden chairs brought back in from the garden, we attacked the walls and ceilings, and with swollen red hands we scoured them with hot water, Vim and more disinfectant. The result, while wet, was grey and streaked, but by the time they had dried something of the original colours of paint and wallpaper had emerged.

Every so often, Tony was dispatched to the tiny shop at the bottom of the road for yet another bottle of pine disinfectant, for which I had to produce the money, since Mother did not have any.

We washed door handles and tap handles and the lavatory chain with particular care. We wiped picture frames and the wires and shades of the single light in the centre of the ceiling of each room, and we scrubbed the front and back doorsteps and a couple of feet of concrete in front of each. We cleaned the shoes and washed their soles.

By late afternoon we were exhausted. Everything that we could think of had been washed, except the clothes we stood up in, and as soon as a change of garment was dry, we would wash those, too.

While I pegged the clothes and linen out on the line or spread them to bleach on bushes, Mother went indoors and made tea and brought it into the garden, with bread and cheese and the newly boiled cups and jam jars we used for drinking purposes.

We sat down thankfully on the grass, still damp from the downpours earlier in the week. The back garden looked as if an auction were in progress. The front garden was almost covered by the sitting-room rug, which had been beaten and then scrubbed on both sides. It belonged to the landlord, and I was surprised to find, as it dried, that a faded flower pattern had emerged and that it looked quite presentable, except in the middle where it was worn through to the backing.

'Heavens,' Mother groaned. 'We've still got to lift everything back into the house.' Her hands, like mine, were scarlet and wrinkled from hot water and the strong cleansers we had used, her face was haggard, and her hair, damp with perspiration, straggled round her face. The front of her cotton dress was soaked where it had been splashed. I was in no better state of repair.

I sipped my tea gratefully. 'Where's Fiona?' I asked suddenly. I had seen her at breakfast. I had not thought of her since. She worked in the morning on a Saturday, but she should have been home soon after noon.

'She had a date this afternoon, straight after work.'

Smart Fiona, I thought unkindly, as I stretched my aching back and arms.

Mother looked as if she would collapse if she did much more, so I suggested to her, 'What about lying on the grass for a bit, to rest, while I do these dishes. They can go straight back into the kitchen cupboard now.'

Without demur, Mother lay down on the warm, rough grass, regardless of its inherent dampness, and I took the dishes into the kitchen. Despite their poor, white china, our cups were very precious. Mother had found them in a shop in Hoylake, and I washed them carefully. With a bit of luck, we might acquire one or two more secondhand, and thus be able to discard the rest of the jam jars.

I put the dishes into the cupboard and closed its doors slowly. Like every other door in the house, it was warped, and liable to spring open again. I leaned my head against it. God, how I ached.

From the direction of the front door came a cheery inquiry, 'Anybody home?'

'Eddie,' I yelled, fatigue forgotten, as I flew to the open door. 'Come in. Come in. How are you?'

As he entered and took off his forage cap, he grinned down at me. Then he looked round the empty room. 'What's happened? First time I've ever seen a carpeted front garden. Are you moving?'

I was suddenly sobered. 'Eddie, you must turn round and go straight home. All Moreton is rotten with diphtheria, and that includes us. We've been disinfecting everything.' I went on to explain about Edward and Father. 'And we might give it to you,' I finished up, realising that I cared very much that he should not be endangered, though all of us in going to work or to school probably endangered others.

'You OK?'

'Yes, I think so.'

'Humph, I've never been sick in my life, to speak of.' He moved further into the room, swinging his cap between his fingers, as he looked up at the streaked ceiling.

'It's dangerous, Eddie. I wouldn't like you to catch it.'

His ruddy face broke into a grin again, the hazel eyes dancing. 'Not to worry. I doubt I'll catch it.'

'Come through then. Mother's in the back garden, taking a little rest. We've been on this job since seven this morning.'

'I'll give you a hand,' he offered, as he strode after me, through the little bungalow. 'Got nothing to do for several hours.'

'How did you get leave?' I asked.

'I'm not on leave. I brought a prisoner up. Got to go back at first light tomorrow.'

It was clear, as Mother rose gracefully from her grassy couch, that she still did not like this big, ugly man. But he was over six feet tall and well-built, so he was the best sight she had seen all day, and she shook his hand as he offered to help us.

'Sit down,' she ordered, gesturing vaguely towards the grass. 'I'm sorry we are in such a state. Helen, go and put the kettle on again. Let's have some more tea.'

Tony and Avril had wandered off to play somewhere, so we drank our way through another pot of tea. The sun seemed brighter to me, as Eddie's witty tongue soon made a joke of our predicament and made us both laugh. 'They know how to deal with diphtheria nowadays,' he assured us. 'You'll soon have your husband and son home.'

He put down his cup on the grass and heaved himself to his feet. 'Now, where do we start?' he asked.

While Mother went to call Tony and Avril from their game of catch in the front street, Eddie and I folded the carpet up and hauled it indoors. Like the rest of the house it reeked of disinfectant and it had no little mud on its underside. We surveyed the untidy pile of it, after we had dumped it on to the living-room floor.

'Out here, the damp is so great it'll take weeks to dry properly,' I said, with a sigh.

'Once you get a fire going in here, it won't take so long,' Eddie comforted, and then gave his attention to heaving it into place.

While Mother put back the contents of the kitchen cupboard, Eddie, Tony and I brought in the mattresses and laid them on the beds, which we had not attempted to move out on to the grass before washing. I was ashamed of the grubby, stained striped covers of the thin palliasse-type mattresses, and was relieved that the bed linen was still drying on the bushes, so that he would not see that at close range.

When we went back into the living-room, the

sun was streaming in through the curtainless windows. The windowpanes glittered with newfound cleanliness and the papered walls and whitewashed ceiling looked quite spruce, now that they were dry. Feeling more cheerful, I helped Eddie and Tony bring in the settee and easy chairs and place them on the damp carpet. Then we moved in the remainder of the furniture.

Mother looked up from poking the living-room fire, which she had just persuaded to burn. 'Would you like to stay to tea?' she inquired. The invitation was much more civil than on the first occasion.

'No, thanks. Promised my Mam I'd be back for tea.'

I said, 'Take a seat for a moment, and I'll just tidy myself and walk with you down to the bus stop.' He turned, with a nod, to one of the easy chairs, and I shrieked, 'Not on one of those – you'll be wet through!' I lifted a wooden chair towards him, and he laughed and plonked himself on to the scratched bentwood chair that I gave him.

I hurriedly washed my face and hands and put on a clean dress, thankful that Fiona had not borrowed it – Saturday was a great borrowing day, as far as she was concerned, because she usually had a date and wanted to look nice. I hastily rubbed vanishing cream into my face, from a little silver-grey tin labelled Snowfire, and then powdered it, combed my long hair carefully and tied it up, rolled over a shoestring round my head. I was ready to further my acquaintance with Eddie, and I felt elated that he and Mother had got on together a little better.

We wandered slowly down to the bus stop. The sun was warm on our backs and we were so relaxed that it did not seem necessary to talk much.

As we waited for the bus and watched the sparse traffic pass – mostly women going home on bicycles, with a shopping basket on the front piled perilously with groceries – I apologised for putting him to work during his visit.

'It was nothin'. First useful thing I've done for weeks.'

The bus came in. It was early and the driver and conductor got down and stood in the sunshine to smoke, while we looked at each other shyly.

'Hope your Dad and your brother get better,' he said.

I sighed. 'Yes. We're really worried about Daddy.'

'Goddamned awful thing to happen.'

The driver, fat and red-faced, was slowly climbing into his seat again. The conductor threw away his cigarette end, swung on to the platform and up the stairs to the upper deck.

I held out my hand and he took it and held it for a moment, looking down at me with piercingly shrewd eyes. I smiled at him, and the rather forbidding face became quite gentle. 'Take care of yourself,' he said. 'See you next leave.'

I watched the bus out of sight, and then turned homeward.

A very washed out Edward was returned to us by the Isolation Hospital. Physically, he recovered from his ordeal quickly, though I often wondered what scars this narrow escape from death must have left upon his mind. The isolation itself must have been terrifying to a youngest child used to being petted by a large family.

The fear of Father's dying lay heavy upon us all. Though we were far from being a happy family, faced with death we tended to huddle together. Unlike most families, we had no real circle of friends who knew us all and who would support us with their presence and sympathy, and the loss of Father would leave a frightening gap in our small ranks. I do not know if any of the younger children truly loved their father. He was kinder to them than he had been to Alan and me when we were little, though he never played with them and he lived a social life completely separate from all of us. There was, however, genuine relief when Mother announced that Father had passed the crisis point and would return home in a week's time.

After a few days at home, he was strong enough to walk slowly down to see our doctor to have his sick note renewed so that he could send it to his office to justify his absence.

When he entered the surgery, the doughty Scottish doctor gazed at him in astonishment, and then rushed round his desk, to wring his hand and say, 'Good God, old man! I never hoped to see you again.'

Poor Father did not get much care at home, but he went to bed early and walked by the sea, and gradually he was restored to his old self.

Eddie wrote to inquire how he was, and this pleased both Father and me. At the sight of the familiar handwriting, I remember thinking wistfully that I seemed to be quite rich in men friends – as a good dancer, I met quite a number of pleasant men – and yet the emptiness in my heart was often hard to bear. As I lay in bed, I would still occasionally burst into tears, and have to swallow the grief, because I might wake Fiona or Avril.

I had begun to be great friends with the girl who ran along the cinder track beside the railway, bent on catching the same train to town as me. This fast sprint together every morning, often through fog or rain, the pair of us panting rueful jokes about seven league boots being a necessity in Moreton, or better still, a skiff to take us over the floods, formed the basis of a lifelong friendship. She had a great zest for life and I enjoyed listening to her eager chatter. She was engaged, so she did not often accompany me to dances – despite all the stories to the contrary, most women stayed faithful to husband or fiancé to a touching degree. Her daily company was, however, something to which I looked forward.

CHAPTER TWENTY-SEVEN

One early June evening, in 1942, I was alone in the bungalow. I washed up the dishes left from the evening meal, and then stood in the middle of the shabby little kitchen, wondering what to do. I was restless, and though there was always cleaning or mending to be attended to, I revolted at getting out either buckets or brooms or sewing needles and cotton. For once, I did not have a dress on hand to be finished.

I put on a cardigan and went out for a walk with the dog, who bounded along ahead of me, sniffing hopefully at every pig bin we passed. I thought ruefully, as I went by, that the sickly smell of the area's collection of potato peelings and other kitchen waste in these bins would have put off even the pigs it was intended for!

I took the main road to the next village, Meols. Though it was a fine summer evening, there was little traffic, except for a few army lorries. Petrol rationing made people nervous of taking their cars out in the evening, when they might be accused of using petrol for unnecessary journeys. If stopped by the police, they would be asked the source of their petrol, and if they had bought it on the black market they could be in serious trouble.

On either side of the road lay fields of young vegetables or pastureland, and the air smelled salty and fresh. Hedge birds chirruped sleepily, while gulls shrieked in a pearly sky.

At Meols, I turned down a deserted side road, lined by ancient stone walls. It led to the sand dunes on which I had, as a child, often played hide-and-seek with a patient maiden aunt, who later took care of Tony and Edward when they were first evacuated.

Beyond the grass-spiked dunes, the tide was out and wet sand stretched to the horizon. I took off my sandals and splashed through the water left by the tide, going towards Hoylake. In the distance the coast of North Wales was a purple line on the horizon.

At Hoylake, I passed the tall red brick house where I had been born. All its windows reflected the great whirls of colour from the setting sun; no wonder Turner sometimes came here to paint sunsets. I trod lightly and cautiously through slippery seaweed at the foot of the gardens of the prestigious houses of Meols Drive. Many of the houses had recently been requisitioned, and were now used as convalescent homes for the services or as government offices. I had often played in those houses when, as a child, I had come to visit Grandma in Hoylake, and I wondered if their fine furnishings had been removed before the onslaught of careless servicemen and civil servants spoiled them.

As the dog and I splashed along, the sound of our squelching feet was the only noise; even the gulls were quiet. I wondered idly if the beach was really mined. I had not noticed any sign warning of it, though, with a fine carelessness, I had walked over the flattened barbed wire protecting the sand dunes from invasion by sea.

I was getting tired. 'I'll go through to the Red Rocks, and then I'll be extravagant and take the bus back to Moreton,' I promised myself.

As I clambered up the familiar sandstone rocks, the sun was slipping below the horizon, but despite the lateness of the hour, I sat down contentedly on the topmost rock. The afterglow made the damp sand shine like a dance floor and cast deep shadows in the hollows between the great humps of stone. A shadowy Nickie lay panting at my feet, his pink tongue lolling out, his bright eyes glittering up at me.

The peace was so great that I was suddenly truly thankful that Mother had moved us out of Liverpool. My dressmaking had solved the problem of how to pay the fares to work, though the long evenings of sewing were very confining. This huge beach was home to me. On this high chunk of sandstone I had sat so often as a child. It was a refuge, when I had been naughty, on which I could sit and cry. Here, I had sat and wept out many small disappointments, had come and cried again when I knew my beloved Grandma was coming to the end of her life. It had always been, to me, my crying rock.

Despite my name for the lonely rock, I was not prepared for the sound of muffled sobbing which rose suddenly from the darkness below me. Nickie bristled and gave a warning bark.

I had believed myself alone and the sound was uncanny.

The sobs came again.

I stood up. 'Hello,' I called nervously. 'Hello.'

Had someone slipped down between the treacherous seaweed covered rocks? Too hurt, perhaps, to get up?

I peered downwards, trying to see into the shadowy corners below me. Yes, someone was there. I could see what looked like a humped back. Was it blue? I squinted behind my new spectacles. It was.

Air Force blue. How odd.

I moved lightly and carefully downwards from rock to rock. Below me, a nose was blown very forcibly.

I paused uncertainly. 'Are you all right down there?'

A very weepy male voice replied that he was all right, thank you.

A male voice? Men did not cry easily, I thought, as I picked my way more slowly towards the blue back. Something must be badly wrong.

As I stood poised on a patch of sand accumulated between the rocks, my shoes swinging from my fingertips, and looked down at a crouched figure, a tear-sodden face was turned towards me. It would have been a handsome face if it had not carried such a desolate expression. A very long handlebar moustache, such as the Royal Air Force pilots often cultivated, drooped sadly. Wavy, golden hair caught the light of the after rays of the sunset. A handkerchief was being hastily stuffed into a breast pocket.

The man began to rise, winced, and then straightened himself. He was very tall with wide shoulders and slender waist. In his finely cut uniform, he was good-looking enough to be a film star.

He looked up at me, as I inquired, 'You're hurt? Did you fall? These rocks are awfully treacherous.'

'No. I'm all right, thank you.'

The voice had the polish of a good public school, the dignified dismissal was that of a trained officer. The lips had clamped tightly. The breath came in short, small gasps, like someone trying to stifle pain. Nickie whined and then scrambled down to him, to snuffle round his feet. The airman ignored him, and the dog trotted off to sniff at some interesting bits of seaweed.

I hesitated. The airman did not attempt to move. He stood rigidly, politely, staring seaward, like a bored guest waiting for a lady to say her goodbyes from a tea-party.

Then I remembered the convalescent home for airmen, on Meols Drive; it was full of flight crews with leg injuries. One often saw shoals of them gravely cycling along the drive, to exercise damaged legs and get them to work again. Some of the men could cycle before they could walk. They would laugh and joke with each other as they glided along, but none of them seemed to whistle after the local girls, like the men from the transit camp did. They seemed like a secret brotherhood, bound together by their shared experiences and their pain.

'You *are* hurt,' I said impetuously. 'You're from the Convalescent Home, aren't you?'

Wells of pity for him rose in me. But go carefully, I warned myself; many of these men are close to nervous breakdowns, too. Don't show too much pity. He'll resent it.

He had turned his face upwards, to look at me. But it was as if he did not actually see me, rather that he had turned inward mentally and cut himself off from his surroundings.

'I'm coming down,' I told him very softly. 'Do sit down again on the rock, for a minute; and then we'll help each other climb the whole pile. I have rheumatism in my knees; I can get down these rocks quite well, but it's awfully difficult for me to get up them again. I shall need to rest myself for a little while. I'll be glad of help.'

My knees, which had pained me greatly after a series of throat infections had caused rheumatism in them, were now nearly well, but, to save his pride, perhaps he could be persuaded to help me.

The blank face came slowly back to life. 'Really?

Let me help you down.' He held up a hand to me, and I grasped it, and jumped the couple of feet on to the patch of sand between the rocks, where he had been sitting. The jump hurt me unexpectedly, and I groaned.

'I say!' he exclaimed in a surprisingly concerned voice.

I took in a quick breath. 'I'll be all right in a minute,' I assured him.

I sat down on a rock. He picked up a walking stick propped up by him, and with its aid, eased himself down beside me.

We sat soberly looking at each other, and then he smiled slightly under the drooping moustache. I grinned back, trying not to give any further hint of the throbbing in my outraged knees.

He was easily the most handsome man I had ever met. Yet, as we sat quietly sizing each other up, it was like looking at some beautiful gift of nature, a perfect Arab pony, for example. No jump of desire suggested a sexual attraction.

I wanted to break the silence.

'Convalescent Home?' I inquired again.

He nodded. 'Yes.'

I could clearly see his insignia on his tunic, but to open up communication, I asked, 'Air crew?'

'Bomber pilot.' He was young enough to be

unable to conceal his pride, as he touched the wings on his uniform with one finger.

'What kind of aeroplane?'

'Lancaster.'

'Really? I've never heard of them. Are they something new?'

'Yes. They are.' A hint of enthusiasm entered his voice, as he added, 'They're great.'

'Did you get shot up during a raid?'

'Not exactly. The old lady was beginning to look like a colander; and Alf, the rear gunner, had bought it. I managed to nurse her back home – but the landing gear was jammed. Had to crash land – pancaked her. And I broke my thigh.'

'How about the rest of your crew?'

'Well . . . Alf was killed, as I mentioned.' He paused, and then said, 'We'd been together a long time . . .' He rubbed his hand over his face, and I feared he would begin to weep again.

'You must be feeling dreadful about it . . .' I began.

'He was dead before I landed. One of the others was badly wounded, and he got pretty shaken up, but he'll be all right. The others were bruised. I think I made the best landing I could.' Though his lips were trembling, there was a defiant pride in his voice as he spoke of his good landing.

'I'm sure you did. It must be absolutely terrifying to have to land like that, particularly after a raid. No wonder you were cry . . .' I stopped.

'Crying? Sorry about that. They say my nerves are shot, but it's nothing a good holiday wouldn't put right.' He stared moodily out to sea, a view that was practically invisible now, except for the faint glint of the afterglow on stray puddles left by the tide. 'I get fed up at times, and it's been a bad day. The everlasting orders – the quacks are worse than the regular COs – and the everlasting company milling round you – never any peace.' The quiet, cultivated voice trailed off.

'It must be very difficult,' I sympathised.

'I'm fine when I'm with the Squadron, but when you're stuck in a place like this . . .'

I bristled immediately. What was wrong with my favourite rocks?

He was close enough to me to have felt me stiffen, because he added quickly, 'It is a nice district, but it seems miles away from the war I'm supposed to be doing something about.'

'About eight miles,' I said. 'Have you seen Liverpool and Birkenhead?'

'No.'

'I'll take you one day, if you like. Believe me, you are very close to the war.'

I saw his teeth flash in the darkness, as he smiled. 'Really?' He sounded irritatingly supercilious.

'Yes, you are. You should see what is happening to civilians. It's no joke.'

Though he had regained his self-control, he did not answer me. Instead, he again pulled out his handkerchief and wiped his face.

The handkerchief brought with it a folded piece of paper, which fell on to my sandy feet. I bent and picked it up. It was obviously a letter. 'You've dropped this,' I said, and handed it to him.

'Oh! Thanks.'

He took it from me and looked down at the well-thumbed, folded sheets, and suddenly I sensed by his expression that the missive was the basic cause of his grief.

'Bad news?' I asked impertinently.

'Just a last straw,' he admitted, after a moment's silence. He sighed, as he returned the letter to his pocket. 'My best friend has been posted to Egypt. We've been together ever since our first day in the RAF – always managed to manoeuvre our postings – somehow or other. We went to the same school, actually.'

The news from Egypt was daily getting worse. I said gently, 'The Allies may have managed to turn the tide by the time he arrives.'

He said without hope, 'Humph. He has to get there first.'

The news regarding sinkings and downed aircraft in the Mediterranean was even worse than the news from North Africa, so I did not try to counter his pessimism.

We sat for a little while longer and talked about the convalescent home and what a long time it took to mend a bone. I inquired where he came from and discovered he was a Yorkshireman, something not apparent from his accent. 'I'm hoping for a spot of leave soon,' he remarked wistfully.

Finally, I said I had to catch a bus back to Moreton, and pointed out that the same bus would pass his convalescent home. He immediately got to his feet. His face contorted with pain. Then he said, when his face had acquired again its curious blankness, 'I am sorry to have taken your time like this.'

'It's been my pleasure,' I assured him. 'Now, I'm going to guide you up the easiest path to the road, because it seems to me that we have both walked too far this evening. Just give me your arm.'

He took my proffered arm without demur, which surprised me. The walk to the main road and the bus stop seemed very long. I was tired and he was in obvious pain.

'When your leg is better,' I said, as we crawled along, 'you must let me show you Liverpool and especially Bootle. People forget that London isn't the only target.'

My continued indignation at his not appreciating that the war was on his doorstep, amused him, and he smiled faintly. He did not reply immediately, and then he said, 'I am not sure that it is a good idea for me to know precisely what bombs do to civilians.'

This remark stopped the conversation in its tracks. It had not occurred to me that our bomber pilots might not get much satisfaction from wreaking havoc in German cities. I did not care if German cities were reduced to ashes. Yet here was a modern knight, popularly regarded as nearly as much a hero as a Spitfire pilot, who questioned it – or did he?

I was hooked. I was interested. One could have a lively debate with a man like this.

He broke into my thoughts by asking suddenly what my name was.

We solemnly exchanged names. His was Derek Hampson.

As we waited for the bus, he asked me diffidently if I would like to go to the cinema with him the next evening. 'That is, if you're not engaged?' he added.

I misunderstood. 'My fiancé died at sea,' I replied stiffly.

'I am so sorry. I did not mean that. I only meant if you had nothing else arranged for tomorrow evening.' He looked at me carefully, much more searchingly than he had done up till then. 'Tough luck,' he said.

'Yes.'

'Do you feel all right about going to the cinema?'

I smiled. 'Yes,' I said. 'I do.'

And so began what proved to be a most unusual friendship, which lasted a good many months, while doctors and physiotherapists argued about how to treat his poorly healed thigh.

CHAPTER TWENTY-EIGHT

As Derek Hampson's leg began, at last, to respond to the efforts of the doctors and physiotherapists, he was encouraged to try to dance. We had been to the local cinema together a couple of times and to a concert in Liverpool. It was, therefore, natural that we should begin to go to the local Red Cross dances together.

He proved to be great fun, as his spirits improved and his pain became less.

One day I refused to go to a dance because I had promised to finish a dress for a girl.

'Really?' he queried in a sudden interest. 'Do you often make clothes?'

I told him about my dressmaking efforts, and it was obvious from his responses that he knew a great deal about women's clothes, particularly dresses.

'Some of the patterns the girls bring me are awful,' I confided. 'They can't get the right size – and I have to adapt them.'

'Don't you know how to make a pattern?'

'No.'

We had been for a walk and were sitting in a shelter on Hoylake Promenade, watching the tide come in, while he rested his leg. He continued to watch the whitecaps breaking over the sandbar. Then he said, 'I could show you.'

'Could you?' I queried in surprise.

His face went pink, and he turned towards me, as he said, 'You see, I'm in the rag trade.'

'What's that?' I immediately thought of rag-and-bone men. But an educated man like Derek could not really deal in rags and bones, could he?

'I sell clothes – ladies' dresses, mostly.'

'Oh!' I laughed.

He went even pinker. 'Look, you absolutely must not tell anybody, particularly the RAF types. I would be ribbed to death, if they knew.'

'Of course, I won't, if you don't want me to,' I promised. 'I had thought, when you told me that you were a shop manager, that perhaps you were a factory shop manager – working for your father, or something. I didn't like to inquire exactly what you did.'

'No. You never ask personal questions, do you? That's why I like you – you're not in the least nosey. You never seem to pry.' He grinned at me.

'Thanks, friend. I try not to invade people's privacy.'

He looked back at the foaming tide, and sighed. 'Well, I'll teach you how to make a pattern,' he promised. 'I own eight dress shops scattered around Yorkshire under different names. Normally I do my own buying. And I was beginning to do a bit of designing. I've an elderly woman who can cut and sew very well.

'Father left me two biggish shops when I was only twenty. I'd been working with him since I was eighteen, and in the holidays long before that, and I really enjoyed it. Mother hates anything to do with the business, though she is holding the fort at the moment. Fortunately, I've got excellent management – older women who were with Father for years.'

'How did you come by the other six shops?'

'Looked for well-placed little shops that were out of fashion or going out of business, and put a smart woman in charge of each. Nearly drove Mother mad by saving every cent I could and reinvesting it. Most of the shops I got for a song – times were so bad.'

'How exciting,' I exclaimed.

He smiled shyly. 'It's a kind of game,' he said. 'I'm doing a roaring trade now – can never get enough stock. The hat departments are dead, of course. But dresses and suits go like hot cakes, because we alter and fit the garments properly – not many department stores do a good job of that.' He turned back again to me. 'You won't tell anybody, will you?'

'Silly boy. Of course, I won't.'

I began to think a great deal more about this extraordinarily handsome young man, as we discussed the history of fashion, its craziness, the present government interference in the trade, and its future. Occasionally, he talked about his bombers, the eccentricities of his crew or the pranks and wild games of the mess.

He would also talk sometimes about his friend and fellow pilot who had gone to Egypt. He heard from him quite regularly, and it was as if he pined for his company. As he grew more sure of my friendship, it became obvious that he loved the man. And then I understood why Derek presented no physical temptation to me and why he never touched me – it was not that he was being forebearing because, not too long before, I had lost a fiancé. It was that he was not sexually interested in women. He was truly and faithfully in love with a man he had known since boyhood.

Anybody who has lived in a port, at least in my day and earlier, tended to accept tacitly that sailors away from home on long voyages often turned to their own sex for consolation, and the women left alone certainly frequently had good women friends, whom they referred to as 'me mate'. Publicly such goings on were condemned; they were illegal and punishment could be heavy. But I was not so shocked as I might have been. Derek was a charming, comfortable person to know and I enjoyed his company. It was pleasant to dance with a well-educated and cultivated man, who offered no threat to me whatever.

A trust rose up between us, as he got to know me better. Finally, he realised that I knew *why* I did not get so much as a goodnight kiss from him.

He was frightened.

We were, as usual, walking to exercise his leg, and I cannot remember how it dawned on him that I knew. But he stopped and turned to look at me. He was so tense that I thought he might take flight like a hare from a furrow.

'It's all right, Derek. I can keep my mouth shut. I've kept secrets before and kept them well.'

I heard him swallow in the gloom of the blackout.

'Yes,' he replied slowly. 'Yes, I believe you.'

Later, I found that his greatest fear was of blackmail, if he were ever betrayed.

'Don't be daft, Derek,' I said roundly. 'I wouldn't harm a friend like you. I think we're true friends, aren't we?'

And he said, with feeling, 'Yes, I think you are the best *friend* I've ever had.'

On my way home, I thought about this beautiful person with considerable pity. With what mental agility he would have to face the close life he led amongst the air crews. Or did they know, and not care? I wondered what Eddie would think of him if he knew what he was; and decided that *his* language on the subject would not be fit to print.

CHAPTER TWENTY-NINE

The fact that I never asked personal questions did not stop Derek slowly worming out of me the history of my family and myself, and he became very curious about my parents.

When he was feeling stronger and it was apparent that his stay at the Convalescent Home was coming to an end, he offered to call for me at our bungalow, one Sunday afternoon, and take me for a walk.

Though I was ashamed of our intolerably shabby home, I agreed. I was also very nervous about the kind of reception he might get, so I began to prepare Mother for his arrival.

I was ironing Father's handkerchiefs when I announced to Mother, sitting reading by the fire, 'If it's fine, a friend of mine is calling for me about three o'clock.' I licked my dry lips, as she looked up from her book. 'I've been dancing with him quite a lot.'

Mother put down her novel on her knee, and asked mildly, 'Who is he?'

'He's an RAF officer – a bomber pilot.'

'Humph.'

'He's a public school man,' I told her, seizing on one point which might give him standing in her eyes.

'Really?' I had captured Mother's interest. 'What does he do as a civilian?'

'He owns eight dress shops. He's interested in dress design – he hopes to expand this part of his business when the war's over.' I felt it would not hurt Derek if Mother knew this; a solid financial background might endear him to her.

'He must be too young to own such a large business.'

'He's about twenty-eight or twenty-nine. The first two shops were left him by his father when he was twenty. He still helps to run them – he's always writing to his manageresses and to his mother – she's helping out at present. When he's on leave he rushes round checking stocks and books.' I folded a handkerchief neatly, and then continued, 'It's surprising, actually, how many men I've met, who are in the Forces and who are still trying to keep a hold on businesses they have had to leave to others. There's an old chap I see on the train. I'm told he is past ninety, and yet he's managing a law practice for his two sons, who were called up from the Naval Reserve. I bet *his* sons worry at times that he won't last the war out!'

Mother smiled, and, encouraged, I said, 'The other morning he was trotting steadily up the steps of Central Station, singing "Put another penny in, in the nickelodeon. All I want is loving you and music, music, music."'

This made mother really laugh, an unusual thing for her, and she asked, quite good-naturedly, 'Would you like to ask this young man of yours to tea?' She closed her book.

'If we could manage it, Mum.'

'All right. I'll make some scones.'

Hooray for a public school education, I thought a little cynically, as I swept the iron round the corners of Father's hankies. Old school ties, and all that.

As soon as I had put away the ironing, I went into our wild, unkempt back garden, where flowers continued to spring unexpectedly from amid the brambles and the knee-high grass, a reminder of another time when there was no war. I returned to the house with a huge bunch of creamy roses, and some long spurs of blue lupins.

Later, in one of his letters, Derek told me that one of the happiest memories of his life was that of sitting in our sitting-room, with the sun pouring in, and seeing vase after vase of flowers, and bright, interested faces. Perhaps, as a homosexual he had avoided contact with families. Immersed in his business, he would, anyway, not have time for much social life.

He understood how to please older women, probably from dealing with his customers, and Mother fell in love with him immediately, as he bowed and shook her hand, and then waited for her to be seated before taking the chair indicated to him. My still convalescent father was delighted to talk about the exploits of the Air Force, and the boys were visibly impressed by his uniform and his limp, which made him something of a hero to them. In bed that night, Fiona and Avril both said, with a sigh, 'He's gorgeous!'

Derek was quite smart enough to know the impression he was making. His twinkling eyes, for a second, met mine across the tea table, and I ached to laugh.

This was the first social event I could remember

in our family, in which everything seemed to go well, and in which I was not tied up with fear that Mother would be rude or Father would be patronising.

I could just imagine Derek, as he pinned and tucked and fitted in his fitting rooms, soothing, flattering valued customers, customers like my mother might have been in her heyday. While he concentrated on getting the best effect for slightly bulging figures, his handsome face would pucker up earnestly, just as it was doing as he explained to Father the tactics of night bombing. They would love him. No wonder he had been so successful so fast.

We were launched on our walk by the waving hands of the family. Though it was a beautiful day, we did not get very far because Derek's leg was aching savagely. To rest him, we sat on top of the sea wall which protected Moreton from the inroads of the tide.

We ignored the barbed wire which was supposed to protect us from invasion, and talked longingly about what would happen to us after the war was over.

Derek did most of the talking, as he lazily picked loose pebbles out of the concrete of the wall and threw them into the waves gnawing restlessly at the foot of the dike. I said simply that I had no idea what I would do when the war ended.

After a while, Derek fell silent. He smoked steadily, taking the cigarettes from a beautifully chased gold cigarette case, which I knew his lover in Egypt had given him. That man must have money, too, I had thought, when first I had learned of its origins.

With his cigarette held between his fingers, he rubbed the case gently with his thumb, as he looked down at it.

'What does your friend do for a living – in Civvie Street?' I inquired.

'He's in the Foreign Office.'

'In London?'

'Yes.' He put the case back into his inside pocket. 'I was planning to open a shop in London and he was going to put up some of the capital, when the war came. We thought we might share a house or a flat – have a real home. But it's difficult. People gossip.'

He did not need to tell me that. The neighbours would be biting about them, even in a good district.

He turned to me. 'I wondered, Helen . . .'

'Yes?'

'Helen, you've never given any indication of

wanting to marry, now your fiancé is dead.' He paused awkwardly, then he said, 'And we get along very well together. What I'm trying to say is that, well, what about marrying me? My friend is as pleasant a person as you're likely to meet,' he rushed on, 'and, you know, we'd make a good family together. And, Helen, it would offer some protection to my friend and me – having a woman in the house.'

'Derek!' I was more surprised than shocked.

He put his hand on my arm. 'Now, wait a minute, and listen to what I have in mind. I would take you into the business with me, as an equal partner. Mother has a third share, so we would be about equal in that respect. She'll be thankful not to have to do anything in regard to the business. And you're good with clothes, and it's an interesting thing for a woman to be in . . . I'll show you the books and you could have an accountant check everything.' The wide blue eyes looked at me hopefully.

I was lost for words. I gaped at him. This was where drifting along without thought had landed me.

He shook my arm. 'Helen, think about it. You'll have a good house, I promise you, and a lifetime career in the rag trade – between us we could make it flourish like the old green bay tree.' He was as red as a McIntosh apple by this time, as he struggled to express his need. 'It could suit you very well, Helen. And we'd never question your comings and goings – I mean, if you found, well – a lover.'

After a moment, I found my voice. If the suggestion had come from anyone else, he would have had his face sharply slapped for the impertinence. But Derek *was* good, as honest a man as a critical world allowed him to be. And he was trying to make an honest deal which would benefit both of us, while getting some cover for a proclivity which, though it harmed no one, was illegal and heavily punishable.

'I couldn't, Derek. I just could not do it. I am a normal woman with a normal set of desires and hopes. I am just very, very tired at present; yet, sometime, I hope to marry.' His face had fallen, the stubby golden eyelashes covered the eyes, and I felt very sorry for him. I put one arm round his shoulder. 'Thanks for being so frank with me, Derek, and for such a generous offer in its way. Believe me, I understand your predicament. But I could not live such a lie. I just couldn't.'

The huge, waxed moustache quivered, as he grinned slyly at me. 'I was afraid you'd say that – no harm in asking, though.' He stopped, picked up another stone and shot it straight out over the sea. 'Are we still friends?'

'Of course, you idiot.'

Just before he returned to his unit, he asked me if I would like to reconsider his offer. Again, I refused.

He bent, and kissed me goodbye.

CHAPTER THIRTY

With her usual lack of preparation, Mother announced a few days later that we would be moving to another bungalow, the following week. The rent was double that which we were at present paying.

I was filled with alarm. 'Where is it?' I asked.

'Just down the road.'

'Phew, I thought we were going to be faced with more travelling costs.'

'I shall expect half the increase in rent from you. It's useless trying to get any more out of your father or Fiona. We shall have to share the extra rent between us.' Thus Mother, laying down the law of the Medes and Persians, which cannot be altered.

I argued that we were better off to keep our overheads low and spend any extra money on food.

It was a waste of time.

With the aid of a handcart, we moved into a decent three-bedroom brick bungalow. Appearances were, however, deceptive. The back garden, we soon discovered, had never been cultivated because it was so frequently under water. The Arrowe Brook, a tributary of the River Birket from which Birkenhead got its name, formed the boundary of the back of the lot. Every time there was a high tide, the little river backed up and spilled over its banks. The house was, consequently, just as damp as the one we had left and was certainly the coldest house I have ever lived in. As far as chill was concerned, I was back in the attic rooms of our first home in Liverpool. When we could get coal, we burned only one tiny fire and this never dispelled the damp. As in our previous bungalow, shoes and clothes left in a cupboard for more than a few days gathered mildew. Bones ached, as I shivered with my sisters under inadequate bedcovers. It seemed as if we always had colds or influenza.

There was an air raid warning during the first night we spent in our new abode. A lone enemy plane, chased by the Air Force from its dockside target, jettisoned its bombs over the countryside around us. One demolished a nearby farm and one shot aslant our roof, taking slates and beams with it, and exploded in the marshy garden, shattering the back windows.

We tumbled out of bed, and huddled together in the centre hall, there being no stairs or cellar in which to shelter. We were petrified at the unexpected attack.

After a few moments of frightened uncertainty, Father tried the electric light.

It worked, and we surveyed cracked ceilings and walls. Not much plaster had fallen. We assumed, quite wrongly, that the roof had just lost a few tiles, and, when silence reigned, we went back to bed.

Early the next morning, a Saturday, we all tiptoed through the back door to look at the rough piece of field which constituted the garden.

Looming through the mist we could see a large hump of earth, and as we approached it, we found our feet crunching on a litter of broken slates. I tripped and nearly fell over a big chunk of clay thrown up by the explosion.

'Be careful,' warned Father, suddenly uneasy. 'It could be an unexploded mine.' He gestured to us to keep back, while he slowly clambered up the heap of muddy earth. Steadying himself with his hands, he stretched himself near the top and peered over the top.

He shouted quite cheerfully. 'That hole's from an explosion all right.'

We were covered with mud, by the time we had all scrambled up to have a look, and exclaimed over our lucky escape. We were less cheerful when we turned back towards the bungalow and saw that a large piece of the back roof was missing.

After breakfast, Mother went to see our landlady who lived next door. She, too, of course, had been shaken by the blast and had already been into our garden to assess the damage. She asked us to send someone up into the attic to make sure that the water tank and its attendant pipes had not been cracked, while she found someone in the village to bring a tarpaulin to cover the gaping roof.

One of the advantages of living all one's life in a small village is that one knows everybody. Our landlady was no exception. That same day a withered old man with a large white moustache arrived, with his ladder on a handcart. By night, he had replaced a couple of beams and covered the hole with tarpaulin. The next day he rehung the slates. When I asked him how he managed to get new slates, his face wrinkled up in a knowing smile. 'Never you mind, young lady,' he said. 'Be thankful.'

While the boys had a great time scrambling

round the attic and exclaiming over piles of old sheet music scattered in it, Fiona and I went to have another look at our bomb crater.

'Look, Helen,' Fiona held up what looked like a ball of mud. 'It's china. How extraordinary.'

She ran her hands round the object and cleared the mud, to reveal a Crown Derby egg cup without a single chip.

Eagerly we prodded around with sticks and came up with another one. A further search unearthed a metal plate, but nothing else, except dead worms.

Very intrigued with our finds, we took them indoors and washed them under the kitchen tap.

Since it was the weekend, Mother had decided to paint the sitting-room of the house, and she was levering the lid off a tin of paint, while we examined the plate we had found.

'This isn't tin,' I said. 'I think it's silver.'

Mother glanced at it. 'Rubbish.'

'But look, Mum. It has such pretty fretwork, and I'm sure this is a silver mark on the bottom.' I held out the blackened dish for her to see. 'I'd like to keep it, if you don't want it.'

'I do want it. I can put it under the paint tin to catch the drips.'

'But it would be so pretty if it were polished,' I protested. In a world where anything dainty or charming had long since vanished, I really wanted to keep my find.

'Well, I'm going to keep the egg cups,' Fiona said firmly, as she gave them a final rub with the teacloth, and she marched out of the room with them.

'Come along. Give me that,' Mother held out her hand, and she laid the paint lid down on a piece of newspaper.

'It's a shame, Mum.' I held on to the plate.

Mother snatched it off me, put it on the draining board and heaved the heavy tin of paint on to it.

'Really, Mother. We could put the paint on a wad of newspaper.'

All that afternoon, as I painted, I simmered with rage, and the drips plopped slowly down the sides of the paint tin to form a thick encrustation cementing the tin to the plate. In the middle of my resentment, I wondered suddenly where Mother had raised the money to buy the paint, and as soon as the room was finished and my hands washed – a washing which left great scabs of dried paint all over them – I ran into the bedroom I shared with Fiona and Avril and checked my handbag, which I had tucked under the side of the bed against the wall. It was inviolate, and I heaved a sigh of relief. I guessed that she had got the paint on credit, and I was right. Later, I helped to pay the bill.

On Monday, instead of staying on the Installation during the lunch hour, I walked briskly up to Mill Street, where despite the bombing, there were still some shops. There, after a very fast hunt, I managed to buy an enamel kitchen plate.

That evening I passed it over the table to Mother and asked if the paint tin, with its dregs of paint, could be set on it and I could have the little plate I had found. 'I really would like to have it, just as a memento of the bomb coming down.'

I thought Mother would burst with rage. She lifted the enamel plate and threw it straight at me. It skimmed past my face and crashed against the wall.

'I'll decide what happens in this house,' she screamed, 'Get on with the sewing you're so keen about, and mind your own business.' She jumped up and began to collect the dishes off the table. She dumped them on the drain board, and they rattled in protest. She was shaking with anger, and muttered under her breath.

I had been familiar, since childhood, with Mother's irrational rages, and I became afraid that she might throw some of the crockery at me, so I quickly left my cup of tea on the table and went into the bedroom. Fiona was there, contentedly rooting through the contents of a battered suitcase, in which she kept her small treasures. I wanted to cry.

'Why does she blow up like that?' I asked Fiona helplessly.

Fiona clicked the suitcase shut and locked it, then pushed it under the bed. Still kneeling on the cold linoleumed floor, she looked up at me. 'I don't know. She only does it with you and Father – most of the time.' She must have seen the tears in my eyes, because she got up and put her arms round me, and said, 'Don't take it to heart. Perhaps it's because you look so like Father.'

It was no compliment to say I looked like my father. He was a plain, large-nosed man with red-rimmed blue eyes. His nose was made more prominent because it was plum red. According to Mother this was because he drank so much, but he actually suffered from a form of acne.

I sighed, and smiled waterily down at my classically beautiful sister. She was right. To look at, I was like my father. And I, too, suffered from the scourge of acne, except that in my case it took the form of septic spots on my chin.

Later on, when Mother had gone to the cinema, I rescued the enamel plate, which now had a large chip in its rim, and hid it under the mattress of the bed I shared with Fiona and Avril.

Some weeks later, when the painting of our new sitting-room had long been finished and forgotten and the residual paint had been stored in the lean-to shed at the back of the bungalow, I came across the plate while making the bed.

I stood for a moment with the ugly utilitarian dish in my hand. Then, since Mother was out shopping, I took it out to the shed.

The paint tin, well bonded to the silver platter by its drips of paint, still stood on the shelf. The paint in the tin had dried out.

With the aid of a screwdriver, I prised the tin off its stand, and put it on the enamel plate. I dipped my fingers in the dust on the shelves and rubbed them over the shiny whiteness of the new plate. It dulled its newness very satisfactorily, and, years later, it was still sitting there, undisturbed.

I spent a very satisfying hour scraping the heavy ring of paint off the old plate, and then scouring it with a newspaper dipped in earth. A silver-plated serving dish was revealed. I dried it and put it under the mattress.

I have it still and use it often. It is a reminder of an extraordinary escape from injury or death during the war – and of a mother with a temper sufficient to supply a whole opera company.

The enamel plate was not the only dish thrown by Mother that summer, but she threw the second one with much more justification.

CHAPTER THIRTY-ONE

Derek wrote to me once a month quite regularly, and I replied. It was easy to write to him, because we had much in common.

'Killing off civilians is not much joy,' he wrote bitterly in one letter.

'You go for military targets,' I reminded him in my reply.

'We often miss,' he responded drily. 'This game of tit-for-tat won't solve anything.'

It was evident that Government propaganda was not getting through to everybody. The horrors of Nazi genocide had not yet burst upon us; our collective rage had not yet peaked.

Suddenly, he missed writing. I sent extra letters, feeling that he might be going through a bad attack of conscience.

No response. I was worried about this charming, gentle person who had been washed up at my feet by accident of war.

Came a letter from Yorkshire in a strange hand. I opened it with unaccountable nervousness. His mother had found a letter from me in the papers returned to her after her son's death. She said she was happy to discover that he had found a girl friend. He had been too lonely in civilian life.

Killed in action. Those awful words every mother and wife dreaded.

I took a long time to write the most comforting letter I could, and I grieved myself, not only for Derek, but for the slaughter of my generation. And this, I knew, even when added to the losses at sea, was only the beginning.

Life can deal out other kinds of grief, and, for once, I was sorry for my mother. Feeling pity for Mother was like pitying the scorpion which has bitten you. A fair amount of personal pain has to be overcome first.

Father had a long convalescence after his battle with diphtheria, partly because our doctor was concerned about the strain on his heart. For several weeks, he took little walks and stayed late in bed and had an afternoon nap.

The City continued to pay him. Each week his

wages were delivered in cash to the house by one of his colleagues, with whom, normally, he went to the theatre or on pub crawls in Liverpool. Mother was delighted to have for her own use the money Father normally spent on fares and lunches. Poor Father got no pocket money, though he still seemed to be able to stand a round at the village pub.

Father's colleague himself fell ill, and another employee, who lived in the next village, kindly undertook the delivery.

The man came for the first time in the early evening, when Father had gone down to the village for a drink.

According to Mother, he was a sober, quiet person, obviously ill at ease, who sat making small talk, before he produced Father's wages in a sealed wages envelope. This surprised Mother because the earlier messenger had always counted the cash into her hand.

As he handed the envelope to her, he said, 'Your husband telephoned me, to ask me to open the envelope and put half the money on one side for him. I reluctantly agreed. Then, I felt so conscience-stricken that I talked the matter over with my wife. We both feel that your *husband* should divide the money – it is dishonest for me to open the envelope containing another employee's wages.'

It was obvious to Mother that he was very embarrassed.

Mother said she looked at the amount of the net salary written on the outside of the envelope. It was over double what Father had told her he was earning, and she did not know how to reply. She felt both angry and bewildered.

The man went on, 'I know it is not really any of my business, but my wife says that you bear much of the financial burden, that you go to work in spite of having three children still at home. Forrester earns enough to make this unnecessary – I wouldn't treat my wife like that,' he finished roundly.

He had voiced his disapproval very honestly, and now he paused for breath. She thanked him for coming and then showed him out.

In the days when few homes had any labour-saving devices, there was plenty of work for a housewife to do, and added to the normal load were all the problems of the war, of queueing, trying to cook with little fuel, and making meals out of very few ingredients. It was still the custom for the husband to be the breadwinner, and many men objected strongly to their wives working outside the home.

I was always home much later than the rest of the family. On this night, Mother sat down on the other side of the table, as I began my solitary dinner, which was always kept for me in the oven at the side of the kitchen fireplace – whether it was dried out with heat or absolutely cold depended on whether or not we had any coal.

Suddenly, she put her head down on the table and began to weep, sobbing hopelessly as if she would never stop.

I put down my knife and fork with a clatter, and shot from my chair.

'Oh, Mum! Whatever is the matter? Please don't cry.' I put my arm round her heaving shoulders. 'What happened?'

Resting her head against me, she told me.

'Every word hit me like a blow,' she sobbed. 'I was so mortified that all I could think of to say was that it was a heavy load. He must have seen I was upset, because he repeated that it wasn't honest to open someone else's pay packet, and I agreed.'

I could not think how to reply, I stroked her ruffled hair and made soothing noises, and mentally cursed Father.

Finally, I said, 'I thought you enjoyed going to work, having money of your own.' I thought of all the cigarettes, the cinema seats, the Marks and Spencer's clothes that she was able to buy. Surely she was doing what she liked.

She did not reply, so I added, 'Of course, the strain on you is great, I know that. And I do try to help you, Mum.'

Totally unexpectedly, she agreed. 'Yes, you do. You are the only one I can depend upon.' And she sobbed on.

Though it was scant reward for my going without things Mother took for granted herself, it was nice to know that she had at least noted that, of all her sons and daughters, I was the one who had helped her.

She sobbed on. 'I'm so tired. And if your father paid me proper housekeeping, I could stay at home. There is no real need any more for me to go out to work.'

The crumpled pay packet on the table told me that what she said was true.

There was also the fact that there were no longer young children in the home – even baby Edward was old enough to be studying for a scholarship to Wallasey Grammar School. The house, peacefully empty from half past seven in the morning until half past four in the afternoon, when Edward and Avril returned from school, must have appeared a much more attractive place to Mother than in years gone by. And Mother herself had aged. The line of hair along her parting, where the dye had grown out, was grey, with silver threads in it.

'It's been harder for me since we came to live in Moreton,' she said, her words muffled against my side. 'Travelling is so tiring, and it takes so long.'

She did not need to tell me that. Strap-hanging in packed, overworked trains and trams for a couple of hours a day was wearing. One was often surrounded by troops travelling with kitbags, suitcases and bulging haversacks, enveloped in a cloud of cigarette smoke, and one could end a journey to and from work bruised and exhausted. Father fared better than most of us. He had been transferred to an office in Birkenhead, and the bus from the end of the road delivered him to its door.

It had always mystified me that Father could go out so often and come home nearly drunk, on what I had assumed was a very limited amount of pocket money. I had imagined that he earned a little more than he divulged, and I had hoped that he saved some for his old age. Though men gave little enough to their wives for maintaining the home, they did sometimes save, so that if they were unemployed or on strike, they could still keep up the amount of housekeeping. Father once said flatly that he had never saved a penny in his life – money was meant to be spent.

I held my mother until she stopped weeping. I was nearly in tears myself.

'Don't go to work tomorrow, Mum. Have it out with Father. He must realise his responsibilities – Tony, Avril, Edward, yourself, *are* his responsibilities.'

'I've already had it out with him,' Mother replied sulkily, as she blew her nose.

'Where is he?'

'In bed.'

That was reasonable. If he had had a fight with Mother, the resultant constrictions in his chest would have sent him to lie down.

I sighed heavily. I did not know what, if anything, I could say to him that would make matters any better.

While I scraped my cold dinner into the rubbish bin and washed up the dishes, Mother went into long, haranguing detail about wanting to stay at home.

'I'm over forty,' she said, 'and I've still got three children under fourteen, so they won't call me up.'

I agreed that she was not likely to be bothered by the Ministry of Labour.

Mother had opened her handbag and taken out her powder compact. In between lingering sobs, she powdered her nose. I dried my hands and went over to her. I put my arm round her shoulders and kissed her for the first time for years. I pitied her.

'I'm going down to visit Mrs Brown,' she said in a shaky voice, 'I *must* get out of the house.'

Mrs Brown was a gossipy elderly lady, a widow, who lived in the same road as we did. Mother would, I knew, pour out the whole story to her, and the next day the entire village would know about it. Nevertheless, she was the nearest thing Mother had to a friend, and a sympathetic listener might diffuse the strain in the family which this upset would cause. So I helped Mother into her coat and saw her out of the back door. Then, with a heavy heart, I went to see Father in my parents' bedroom. The bed was empty.

I found him lying on top of Edward's bed. Though the curtains were closed across the window, I could see in the dim light from the hall that his eyes were shut. Along the line of his chin was a dark mark. My heart jumped in apprehension. I quickly switched on the light.

Against the pallor of his face, a long weal oozed blood. His nose also had been bleeding. There was more blood on the pillow under his head. Despite the light, he had not opened his eyes.

I was shocked.

'Daddy! Whatever happened?'

He made a deprecating gesture with one hand, and then let it drop.

I went close to him and smoothed the pillow back, so that I could see better the cut along his jaw. Beneath the shadow of the day's growth of beard, there were signs of heavy bruising, as if from more than one blow.

'Good heavens, Daddy! Whatever did you do? I'll get some water and a compress. Just a minute.'

I fled to the bathroom. Where the devil were the children? Why was Fiona never there when help was needed?

I ran the tap until the water was ice-cold. Then I wrung the family face flannel out under it. It was an old piece of towelling, but probably as clean as anything else I could find.

Back in the bedroom, I saw that Father had not moved or opened his eyes. I gently took off his spectacles and laid them on the bed. Then I looked closely at the cut and at the bruises. I pressed the flannel hard against the bleeding cut. He winced, and turned his head slightly. When I realised how white he was, apart from the bruises, I asked anxiously, 'Shall I get the doctor, Daddy?'

'No,' he whispered from between swollen lips.

'Well, this will stop the bleeding,' I assured him.

Though he was certainly conscious, he did not answer.

After a minute or two, I turned the bloody flannel over, took one of his icy hands, and told him to press the rag over the cut himself. He did so.

'I'm going to get a blanket to put over you,' I told him. In my bedroom, I tore one from the bed I shared with my sisters, and hurried back to him.

'How's it doing?' I asked, as I tucked the blanket round him. Gingerly he loosed the pressure, and I peeled back the cloth. 'I think it's stopped,' I told him. 'I'll wipe round your nose.'

When his face was cleansed, I asked him, 'Can you lift your head a bit, if I help you; and I'll turn the pillow clean side up?' I slipped a hand under his neck and eased the pillow over.

'I'll wring the flannel out under the tap again. The cold may stop the bruise from spreading. Whatever did you do?'

Still he did not answer, and after I had replaced the flannel over the bruises, I straightened up, and sighed. 'I'll make a cup of tea with lots of sugar.'

I went back to the deserted kitchen to boil a couple of cups of water for tea. Why had not Mother helped him? I thought angrily. They certainly had had a row, but that was no excuse for not helping a man who was so hurt.

The gas pressure suddenly failed, and I ran into the hall to get my handbag, to find a shilling to put in the gas meter.

I brought the scalding tea and put it on the chair by the bed, to give it time to cool a little.

Father had discarded the flannel. It lay on the chair by the teacup. His eyes were open and he looked dully at me.

'Daddy, tell me, please, what happened?'

At first he would not reply. Then he said bitterly, 'She threw a plate at me, and I fell, and then she came at me with another and hit me across the chin with it.' He closed his eyes again, and muttered, 'She might have killed me, if I hadn't rolled over.'

She might indeed have killed him. He could have had a heart attack.

He was continuing. 'I think I've got bruises on my back where she kicked me.'

'Good God!' I looked down at this wreck of a man, and then I asked, 'Did you hit her back?'

'One does not strike a woman,' he said primly.

Father's sense of honour sometimes surfaced in curious ways, and suddenly I wanted to smile. Instead, I sighed again. 'I'm going to get the pillows from my bed, to prop you up, so that you can drink your tea more comfortably.' I had been shocked at

Father's lack of financial concern for the family. I was far more shocked at what Mother had done. I wondered if she was insane.

Propped up comfortably, Father took his tea in short nervous sips. His hands were trembling.

I sat down on the edge of the bed. It had been bought second hand and it creaked under our combined weights.

'Is your chin feeling better?' I inquired.

'Yes, thank you.'

'Mother told me what happened about your wages.'

'Yes?'

'I am sorry, Daddy. Sorry for you and sorry for Mother.'

He did not reply.

I plunged in. 'I don't know how you and Mother are going to make it up. But it's like a boil which has burst and has drained. Perhaps things might heal a bit now.'

'I'm sorry, Helen. Your mother fritters money so. There seems no point in giving her any more.' Despite the apology he sounded defensive.

Frittering money away was something both my parents were good at, I thought sadly. Aloud, I said, 'She's very tired, Daddy, because really in the final analysis everything falls on her shoulders. And she's had seven children – and a very severe illness after Edward was born.'

'I'm tired, too.'

'I know,' I soothed. 'You must be exhausted. You've been dreadfully ill. You have both had a very bad time.'

I took the empty cup from him and put it on the side chair. I picked up one of his limp, cold hands and began to rub the circulation back into it. 'You know, you and Mother really need each other. There's a tremendous shared experience between you – and you've somehow stuck it out all these years, despite the fights.' I laughed softly, and he managed a rather grim smile.

In the glare of the unshaded bulb hanging from the middle of the ceiling, I sat talking with him for about an hour, reminiscing about the nicer things that had happened in his life before he went bankrupt. I pointed out that our lives were slowly improving now, and that if Mother stayed at home, she would be less tired and consequently less testy. 'You could find some interests in common and could have a little social life together.'

'I doubt it,' he said, in response to my last remark.

'Well, after all the frightful things that have happened to you, you have probably not given it much thought,' I suggested.

On I went, driven by pity for my mother and my drifter of a father. It spurred me to cajole, to mend his shattered pride, to give him ideas of how to bridge the gap between him and his wife.

Finally, I said fairly briskly, 'Edward will be in soon, I expect. I think I should put the hot water bottle in your bed, to warm it up for you, and then tidy up this bed for Edward, so that he does not know anything is wrong. I'll help you move.'

Before he could protest, I picked up the cup and whipped out of the room. I was, after all, going to put him firmly back into the bed he shared with Mother, and he probably would not be very happy about it.

He did, however, move without comment. Since we had no extra bed linen, I took the pillowcase off my own pillow to replace the bloody one on Edward's, and by the time he and Tony and Avril came breezing in from the houses of their respective friends, all was in order. I made cups of cocoa for them and sent them to bed.

I then sat down to my sewing machine, to fill in the time until Mother should arrive.

She arrived, around midnight, with Fiona, whom she had met at the end of our road. Fiona was, for once, walking back from a village dance by herself, and Mother did not hesitate to pour out her troubles to her, being bent on enlisting her on her side. This was an unpleasant custom both parents had, of making the children take sides in their quarrels.

At their entrance, I stopped turning the machine handle and looked up. Fiona gave me the faintest wink, and I nodded back. It was enough to indicate trouble, to each other.

Mother was still talking to Fiona, as she took off her coat, expressing her bitterness. Yet it seemed to me that some of the steam had gone out of it.

I had earlier made up the fire, and both women went to warm themselves by it, while I made more cocoa.

We sat round the fire for hours, drinking the sugarless, almost milkless, concoction, while Fiona reiterated to Mother much that I had already said to Father. I chimed in occasionally.

Both Fiona and I had the same instinct, to try to hold the family together. Poor as we were, together we had certain strengths; separated, we were puny individuals who could be individually crushed, and, after her experiences in the aircraft factory, nobody knew this better than Fiona.

CHAPTER THIRTY-TWO

How the months of the war dragged! Like many other women I was waiting it out. Servicemen were shipped abroad to threatened India and to Singapore, in the latter case, to man guns which had been fixed facing the sea, the traditional source of danger to the little island, while the Japanese came through the jungles behind them. So many men went to North Africa that it seemed like a bottomless pit swallowing human lives.

Stories of horrifying Japanese atrocities were, at first, only half believed, and tales of military bungling came from all directions, to add to the restlessness of troops, like Eddie and his friends, still cooped up in England.

With our minds filled with nightmares of what would happen to us if Britain were invaded, it was difficult to sustain hopes of what we would all do when the war was finished. We felt that, on the other side of the English Channel, the German troops were drooling over what they would do to us, once they got a footing on our shores.

I was tied, by Government decree, to an organisation which would be dissolved when the war ended; the men recruited from the oil companies would want their positions back, and the droves of young women at present doing their jobs would be out of work.

I felt that I ought to be studying to prepare myself for a better future. Yet where was the time? To eat, to have travelling expenses, to clothe myself, to help with the high rent of our bungalow, I had to sew in my spare time. By the end of the evening, my eyes were red-rimmed, my body stiff from sitting all day in front of a desk, and, later, in front of the sewing machine. No wonder I walked or danced so late in the evenings. Both were very necessary exercises, and could be done after ten o'clock at night.

We missed Brian's lively presence very much. For a long time, he sailed with a crew made up largely of Newfoundland fishermen, few of whom could write, though they were superb sailors. He wrote their letters home for them, and became known throughout the ship as The Professor. He was trained as a Gunner AA2, to defend the ship from aerial attack, and it still makes my flesh creep to know that, during action, he was chained to his gun. He used to wear a crucifix and a tiny glass black cat, on a chain round his neck, perhaps to beguile the powers of both light and darkness into protecting him. Something did protect him. He was in almost every major theatre of the war, including the invasion of Normandy, and came out unhurt.

I do not know how Father and Mother made up after their dreadful quarrel, nor what explanation Father gave to the younger members of his family, to explain away his bruised and cut face. But, after a period of sullen silence, they began to treat each other more normally – for them. There were many small spats between them and occasional shouting matches. Mother, however, never went to work again, and there is no doubt that Father began to be more careful about how much he drank. He stayed at home more and found solace in a steady stream of library books about other wars. Mother continued to go to the cinema.

We began to have family jokes, incomprehensible to others, yet guaranteed to make us all laugh.

Tony and Father were masters of the absurd,

Tony verbally and Father of mimicry and wild improvisations.

With a towel wrapped round his head, Father could instantly transform himself into, say, an Indian prince being received by the King. The prince with the utmost gravity and with a drawling Oxford accent, invariably got the better of our stuttering King. The same towel tied round his waist and a kitchen knife in his hand, made him into two surgeons trying to remember which leg they were supposed to amputate. Hands clasped together, as if in prayer, eyes half-closed and with the indignant expression of a camel ordered to get up, he was an Egyptian queen ordering a breakfast of fried asps – hot. He was quite capable of mentally climbing inside an indignant camel and answering his camel driver back. It was as if he had, in some part, regained a boyish sense of fun. Even Mother managed to smile at his antics.

Eddie continued to write to me, sometimes from the heights of optimism, occasionally from the depths of despair, as he realised that he was well into his thirties, which could have been his best years, and was stuck in a castle feeding rice pudding to two cats.

When he had only a short leave, he would arrange to meet me under the clock in Lime

Street station, and we would go out to tea at some nearby restaurant, to eat baked beans on toast or sausage and mash, followed by sponge cake which tasted exactly like sawdust. The cafes were always stuffy and underheated, filled with men in damp uniforms and women in clumping utility shoes and too much lipstick.

He had undergone training as a Commando, part of a group specially trained in silent, hand-to-hand fighting, to carry out small but devastating raids on particularly sensitive enemy positions. He was pleased at being considered tough enough to belong to such an elite group. In a dark corner, on the way to Central Station to see me on to my train, a corner which a more enterprising man might have used to press for favours, he obligingly taught me how to kill a man, barehanded, from behind. 'Could be useful if we're invaded,' he told me gravely, as I ruefully rubbed my sore throat.

'I sometimes think I should do more for the war effort – join the ATS,' I told him once, over a cup of limpid liquid which was supposed to be coffee.

'You? You're mad! You stay right where you are. You're doing part of my job, aren't you?' He was quite angry and his face went even redder than usual.

'I'm much fitter than I was, Eddie.'

He replied indignantly, 'A little thing, like you? Those bloody, lesbian NCOs! They'd make your life a hell. You'd be lucky if all they did was walk all over you. What on earth am I holed up in a bloody castle, keeping cats for, if it isn't to save you from things like that?'

'Eddie!' I protested, suppressing a desire to laugh.

He scowled. 'You don't know what you'd be up against. You stay here like a good girl, and leave the war to me.'

A chuckle burst from me. 'Eddie, there are a few other people fighting the war,' I gurgled.

The grimness left his face and the pair of us began to laugh immoderately. Two elderly ladies sitting almost touching shoulders with us, frowned, and tried to redistribute the margarine on their toast, with loudly scraping knives.

At the back of my mind, I thought with some wonderment, he cares, he really does. And yet he's never even kissed me, even as a friend might kiss me.

At another meeting, he said savagely, 'I wish they'd start the Second Front and get it over with. It's sitting doing nothing that gets me. It's like waiting to be guillotined.'

Such a pang went through me, because I knew his

unit was not made up of men who had seen much fighting, despite its fearsome training. They could easily be killed by more seasoned German troops. Though Eddie was known at the Installation as a hard-fisted brawler, he had yet to kill a man.

'Perhaps the Russians will be able to put paid to the Germans, without there ever being a Second Front,' I suggested.

He replied gloomily, 'The Russians'll be lucky if they're not ploughed under themselves.'

He became obviously quite troubled about me when, at one point, I became a Test Case between the Petroleum Board and the Employment Exchange. The argument of the Government was that older women could do the jobs of the younger women employed by the Board, and that all the girls working on the Installation could then be redirected, either to factories or to the Forces. The Petroleum Board responded by saying that they had already lost most of their male staff to the Forces, and had had to train their current female staff to take over. It would disrupt their organisation to an intolerable extent, if they had to train a fresh female staff. The fact that I was the rabbit thrown to the governmental hounds to be chewed over, made me wonder if our almost invisible General Manager on the Installation had remembered the impertinent young woman who would not wear stockings and had caused him to have to back down.

While the Government's tribunal tried to make up its mind, I spent two uncomfortable days in the cold, smelly waiting room of the Employment Exchange with another fellow sufferer, from a sugar company. This girl had been directed to a sugar manufacturer and had found that the sugar penetrated her shoes, causing her feet to swell abnormally. Her doctor had recommended that she seek different employment. The Employment Exchange clerks had refused to permit this. So she sat beside me, clad in her father's carpet slippers, to be judged by as supercilious, self-righteous a group of people as I have ever met in a chequered life.

If they are so keen on factory work, why aren't they doing it themselves? I wondered crossly.

Acutely aware of my lack of education and, therefore, the certainty that wherever I was sent I would be at the bottom of the pile, I sat, wooden-faced, in front of the tribunal and let them talk at me. The more caustic the tribunal became, the more I silently raged within. It was obvious that if they could not make the oil companies yield up their young women, they were determined to make as many as possible volunteer for factory work. But I had seen what had happened to Fiona. It was not going to happen to me.

Eddie had heard the news of the impending call-up, and nestling in my handbag was a hastily scribbled note to me.

'Let the oil companies fight it. You are not to volunteer. They'll probably try to shame you into joining the ATS or some bloody factory. It will kill you. Be shameless, little lady, be shameless. You are doing as good a job as anybody, already.'

I clutched my handbag in my lap, and answered the patronising tribunal in monosyllables. After two wasted workdays, I was allowed to return to the office, while the oil companies consulted their legal representatives. The unfortunate girl with swollen feet was told that there was a war on, and was sent, weeping, back to the sugar company.

As we went out together, I said to her, 'Get your doctor to sign you off until they change their minds. That's what my sister did. You don't have to suffer so.'

She stopped crying, and a big grin dawned across her wet face. 'Thanks, pal,' she said. 'I'll do it.'

The oil companies talked to higher echelons of government, bypassing the local tribunal. They simply said that they could not guarantee their distribution system, if the girls were removed, and the whole war effort would, in consequence, come to a slow stop.

Ernest Bevin's administration knew when it was wise to give a little, so I went back to my desk, and hundreds of other girls in other parts of the country stayed in front of theirs, for the duration.

The experience had tired me immeasurably, and I realised that, despite canteen lunches and a more bearable situation at home, I did not have as much endurance as many girls did.

Civilians bore their own particular difficulties without a great deal of complaint. Perhaps the lack of fuel was the greatest hardship. We queued for coal at the railway stations, gas jets flickered down to a tiny, almost useless flame; and, despite dropping shillings into the electric meter, the lights often went off. Nothing lay between our bungalow and the sea, except windswept marshes and the dike, and the gale howled through the uninsulated structure, while every wave hitting the dike made the bungalow shudder on its cement raft.

The smallness of the soap ration also bothered us. There never seemed to be enough to wash clothes properly, and we would use the water from the wash to scour the floors.

The question on the billboards, 'Is your journey really necessary?' became rhetorical. If they did not have to do so, few would put up with the acute discomfort of cold, slow, packed trains and buses.

In the winter winds, our bare legs got increasingly chapped and sore, and we had to admit that one of the very few advantages of being in the Forces would be to have thick woollen bloomers and woollen stockings. Our Wizard-of-Oz type manager continued to forbid us to wear trousers in the office, and we, fools that we were, obeyed him.

I continued my habit of buying bits of old, hand-knitted garments from second-hand shops and unravelling them. Whether sitting or standing during my train journeys to Liverpool, if I had enough elbow room, I knitted gloves, cardigans and jumpers, either for myself or for various members of the family. Considering how the trains shook, it was surprising that I never impaled a fellow passenger on a knitting needle!

Since I had no clothing coupons, I watched the small advertisements pinned up in the window of the village tobacconist, in order to buy second-hand shoes. Because shoes were often trodden out of shape by their original owners, it meant that to find a reasonably comfortable pair, I had to follow up several advertisements. I was plagued by chilblains on my heels and toes, caused by exposure to the winter weather. To get a blister from an ill-fitting shoe, on top of a chilblain, and have it turn septic, which it usually did, was very painful.

All through the war, late at night, I danced. I danced with men from every nation in Europe, and they had one attitude in common; they never talked about what they would do after the war. Perhaps they accepted, what I feared, that they would be killed.

CHAPTER THIRTY-THREE

Civilians were not the only people who fell ill and had their sickness made worse by overcrowded conditions and poor food. Alan, travelling home on leave, was stuck in a train which became mired in an enormous snowdrift in Derbyshire. There were many children on the train who became fractious with cold and hunger. Alan volunteered, with some other servicemen, to walk through the waist-high snow covering the bare fields surrounding the train, in the hope of finding help. They came upon an isolated farm, which provided milk, bread and candles. Unfortunately, it did not have a telephone, though they promised to send out a messenger to the nearest phone, some miles off, to try to hasten help to the stricken train. Back in the freezing train, Alan and the other men were unable to dry their sodden uniforms, and when he arrived home, forty-eight hours later, he had pneumonia.

Because of the tremendous snowfall, we were unable to get him to the transit camp hospital. Their telephone lines were down and the lanes leading to the camp were choked. Our local doctor was out at a confinement, and by the time he saw poor Alan, the crisis was approaching and the family was nearly beside itself with worry. The doctor examined the tossing young man, who was extremely thin from overwork and poor food, and said flatly that he doubted if he would live. When Mother burst into tears, he said uneasily that he had a sample of some new tablets put out by May and Baker, which might help, though he was not sure. A powder with the same base had been used by the Russians, to pack wounds before removing their men from the battlefield, and they had had great success in lowering the rate of infection in the wounds.

Unanimously, we pressed him to give Alan the tablets.

Within two days, Alan was nearly free of fever, though weak; and we were the first family in our village to bless the names of Fleming and Florey, the discoverers of penicillin.

A long-distance telephone call at the office brought

me into touch with another group which was sometimes sick.

'Could you get over to Doncaster tonight?' asked Eddie, without preamble. 'I've got to bring another POW up for treatment, and I could spend all day there . . .'

'But Doncaster's in Yorkshire. I'd have to travel right across country overnight.'

'I know, but I won't get any leave for months.'

The ears of my colleagues had pricked up, and grins of amusement spread from face to face.

I blushed with annoyance. Then I asked, 'Where shall I meet you?'

'If we arrive first, we'll be in the General Waiting Room, provided some blasted MP doesn't get over-fussy. If you arrive first, wait in the Ladies' Waiting Room.'

I hesitated, and a very humble voice at the other end of the phone pleaded, 'Please, Helen.'

When the office manager had received the call, he had, of course, recognised the voice, and had actually said, 'Hold the line, Eddie.' So everybody knew that I felt strongly enough about the man to make one of the more difficult train journeys in the north, overnight, to see him. Gleefully, they spent the day telling me horror stories about him and his unknown brother.

I escaped at lunchtime and went to the Post Office to withdraw all I had saved, and to telephone Fiona to say that I would be away overnight.

'You haven't got any night-clothes, and Mother will think you are spending the night with him.'

'I won't be staying anywhere. I'll be travelling both nights. And I've got makeup with me.'

'Well, I'll tell Mother,' Fiona promised, 'But I think you're dotty.'

In the early hours of the morning, a disconsolate German prisoner of war, so young and so drawn of face that pity immediately welled up within me, and a sleepy Eddie with a chin frosted with golden beard, his uniform crumpled, sat on a bench outside the General Waiting Room, both of them slouched forward, arms resting on knees.

Even the prisoner seemed glad to see me, because both their faces lit up, as I was carried towards them by a surge of luggage-carrying passengers. They both sprang up, and Eddie clasped my hand and put an arm round my waist as he turned to introduce me to his companion, who clicked his heels politely and bowed. The prisoner was muffled up in pullovers and, with his greenish coloured trousers, could have passed as an Englishman in a reserved occupation.

'The porter says there's a little cafe across the road which serves breakfast,' announced Eddie, and hustled the pair of us through the station barrier.

Except for a cup of tea on a Manchester railway station, while I waited for a connection, I had had nothing to eat since the previous day's lunch, and I went happily with my odd companions into the steamy little cafe.

In good English, the prisoner said that, to give us a little privacy, he would sit at the next table, where Eddie could see him. He smiled at me, and added, 'I only wish my girl were here, too.'

I laughed, and said thank you, and thought that, judging by his emaciated frame, it would be a miracle if he ever saw his fräulein again.

'TB,' Eddie told me, as he seated me in a worn wooden chair. 'In the lungs. I've brought him for treatment.'

Sick or not, even the prisoner ate a hearty breakfast of porridge without milk or sugar, scrambled dried egg on card-boardlike toast, and two pots of weak tea. I doubt if the fat, languid woman who waited on us realised she was dealing with an enemy prisoner.

It was a memorable meal. Eddie cheered up immensely, once he had been fed, and, while he drank his last cup of tea, he held my hand under the table, and talked about a film he had seen.

I omitted to tell him of my struggle to get there, of being faced with having to change stations in Manchester in the blackout, and being unable to find a taxi.

A kindly Flight Sergeant in charge of some eighty men had realised my predicament and inquired which station I wanted. When I told him, he bundled me into the double-decker bus waiting for his contingent, and up the stairs. 'Hey, you,' he ordered an aircraftsman, 'you look after her.' The aircraftsman got me a seat and stood hanging from a strap by me, as if he were afraid the rest of the grinning, teasing gang with us would rape me.

At the other end of the bus trip, the Flight Sergeant came up the stairs and said that he would be handing over the men to another Flight Sergeant. 'So you wait while everybody gets off and he's real busy. Then you slip off quietly.'

This I did and passed unnoticed into the station.

I eased myself on to the train for Sheffield, where I expected to change again. This train was filled with troops being moved overnight, presumably because they were less visible at night. The less the enemy knew about troop movements the better it was. The only light on the blacked out train was given by miserable blue bulbs which made it impossible to read. The soldiers seemed tired, too.

Just outside Sheffield, the train stopped, because the city was being bombed. The passengers, at first, did not know where they were, and we sat uneasily listening to the roar of planes. The lights went out. Planes swept along the railway track and between the scream of the bombs coming down and their explosion, came the sharp rat-tat of machine gun fire. I sat, terrified, with my face pressed into my lap, between two soldiers cursing softly into their own laps, while machine gun bullets whipped along the side of the train, and somewhere further in front of us glass shattered as a windowpane was broken.

I thought the men might panic and try to get out of the train, since the railway line was an obvious target.

In no other raid had I ever felt so helpless. Confined in the non-corridor train, with blinds drawn over painted windows, the dim blue lights turned off, the heavy breathing and muttering of the men round me, and the smell of the sweat of fear, I felt trapped. Every minute seemed hours long, every bullet seemed destined for our crowded little compartment.

Very slowly, the train began to back, its wheels

squealing. After a little while, it stopped. The noise outside was more distant, and within, a collective sigh of relief went up, as we slowly straightened ourselves.

A pair of army boots was vaguely outlined in front of my face, as the man travelling in the luggage rack above me also sat up. ''Ave a dekko, Joe, and see where we are,' a disembodied voice urged.

The soldier next to me heaved himself up, brushing my face with coarse khaki. He wound down the window and looked out. Immediately, there was a rush of fresh air into the tiny compartment and a glimmer of light, probably from the moon.

Feet crunched along the track outside, and Joe shouted down, 'Where are we?'

'Near Sheffield.'

'Are we going in?'

'Na. They'll reroute us.'

Panic struck me. Where would I end up? The man outside had stopped by the door, to answer Joe, so I tugged at the overcoat in front of me, and whispered, 'Ask him how I'll get to Doncaster.'

'Lady here wants to know how to get to Doncaster.'

'Tell her to stay on train. That's where you're going.'

It seemed as if we spent hours backing and

shunting and then slowly making our way to Doncaster. The ten or so men in our compartment grumbled steadily about being hungry and thirsty; and I was thankful when a faint light through the painted windows told us it was morning, and I heard the women porters shouting, 'Doncaster, Doncaster, all change.'

I wondered what had happened to the train I was supposed to have changed on to in Sheffield. Perhaps it lay burning, amid twisted railway lines and shattered glass from the railway station roof.

I shivered. It was comforting to hold Eddie's warm hand, and see the light of mischief dancing in his greenish eyes. His attitude was different at this meeting, more easily friendly. I caught the prisoner viewing us with amusement, and felt shy and reticent. With a sudden pang, I remembered Harry's remark about my being as distrustful as the ship's cat. And yet, I reminded myself, I had come on a long and difficult journey, very much on trust, just to spend a few hours with the soldier holding my hand.

He was saying casually, 'I must have been nuts to ask you to come – but I'm glad you did.'

I waited at the gate of the hospital, while Eddie delivered his prisoner. The man had faltered, as we marched him between us through the streets crowded with people going to work. I said impulsively to Eddie, 'He's very sick. Let's go more slowly.'

Eddie had stopped immediately, and the prisoner had leaned thankfully against a soot-encrusted stone wall, to get his breath. After that, we proceeded at a gentle amble. I did not talk to the prisoner and neither did Eddie. At the gate, however, I had said, 'Auf Wiedersehen.'

He gave a small mocking salute, and trailed up the path, beside Eddie.

Eddie and I spent the morning in a windswept park, with last winter's leaves whirling round our feet, as we walked. He talked and I listened. After the usual groans about the High Command keeping the Army penned up in Britain for years, he began to talk about his childhood and his home. 'My Dad died when I was twelve,' he said. 'Lucky for Mum, we owned the house, and there was a little money and her Widows' Pension.' He grinned. 'She's had her hands full with my brother and me. But once we were both earning, she didn't have to worry so much about money.'

'Is your brother married?'

'No.' He was quiet for a moment, and then he said, 'Neither of us will get married while the war is on – wartime marriages never seem to work.'

I thought of my parents' unhappy wartime union, and replied, 'I think you're right.'

He looked at me in surprise, the heavy, fair eyebrows nearly shooting up to touch the cowlick of golden hair sticking out from under his forage cap.

'I thought all girls wanted to get married, regardless.'

'Not this one,' I replied, feeling a glint of amusement. I had told him long ago that I had lost a fiancé in the Atlantic, so after glancing at me, he said dryly, 'I suppose not.'

It began to rain, so we scuttled back to the little cafe where we had had breakfast, and ate a mysterious stew with mashed potatoes for lunch. Then we enquired about a return train for me. There was one at 4.30 p.m., which meant that, barring air raids, I would be home by bedtime. The train Eddie would catch went in the early evening.

As we wandered out into the light rain, I realised that Eddie's army greatcoat was getting very wet. I was better clad, in a macintosh, though my feet were wet. Nevertheless, we walked on for a little while, until I saw, peeping above a row of shops, a church spire. I caught Eddie's arm, and asked, 'Do you mind sitting in a church?'

'No.' He laughed.

'Well, it would be dry, and we could talk if we are very quiet.'

The small Anglican church was open. A fat woman in a big black apron was placidly polishing the pews at the front.

We slipped into the cold gloom of the back pew. While Eddie put his arm round me, the fat woman surveyed us unsmilingly, and then went back to her polishing.

Behind the thick stone walls, it was incredibly quiet, and as we sat cuddled together, the peace of it washed over us, two tired people stepping out of the hurly-burly of the war for a few minutes. We did not talk much, yet there was no sense of boredom. Occasionally, he would shift himself and hold me more tightly. I wondered if he felt the rising sense of passion that I did, and the unspoken question was answered when I looked up, because he bent over me and kissed me.

The polishing lady had reached the matching pew to ours on the other side of the aisle, and Eddie said heavily, 'I suppose we'd better get over to the station. We might get you a seat, if we're there early.'

I nodded, and he kissed me again, and this time

I kissed him back. The polishing lady clucked, presumably at the length of the silent kiss.

I slowly slipped from his encircling arm on to the faded embroidered hassock in front of me. I closed my eyes and prayed intensely for the safety of one Private Edward Parry.

A small thud beside me. To my utter astonishment, Eddie knelt beside me, put his arm round me again and closed his eyes. Perhaps this tough, hard-headed man realised that, once the Second Front was opened, the odds for him were not very favourable. And like many another unbeliever, he turned to the faith and hope his mother had taught him as a child. I put my arm round him.

He did not kiss me goodbye. But a new relationship had been established. I was bewildered by it, uncertain that anything would come of it. And was not even sure that I wanted it to flower.

CHAPTER THIRTY-FOUR

In a wooden hut, which stood apart from other buildings on the Installation, dwelt two laboratory assistants, fondly known to the Payroll Department as the lab assists. They checked the quality of the oil and petrols being imported. They also obligingly filled our cigarette lighters with some of their samples. The petrol was of such poor quality that we used to lay bets on how many strikes our lighters would need before they flared. At all times of day, these technicians made tea on their bunsen burners, and anybody was welcome to a cup.

They swore soulfully that they were both dying of loneliness, because the wife of one and the fiancée of the other were in the Forces.

In despair, they began to plot how to get their womenfolk home on leave, so that infants might be fathered and the mothers discharged into civilian life. They had long conversations on the efficacy of everything from garlic to ginseng to increase the chance of a pregnancy, and offers of help from the other male members of the staff were plentiful.

The female staff asked if anyone had inquired of the ladies concerned whether they wanted a family – or the concomitant discharge.

Our inquiries were met with deep scowls.

The ladies were shipped abroad for the duration, and, despite embarkation leave, their husband's efforts came to nought.

One fine spring day there was a sharp explosion. We all leapt to our feet wondering which way to run; an explosion in a petrol installation is not an event which one stops to watch.

A girl ran to the window. 'It's the lab,' she shrieked.

Flames engulfed the only entrance, and two tattered figures flew through them, to roll on the ground outside, to put out their burning clothes.

The men in our department tore out to help the technicians, and the fire alarm went.

The Installation had its own auxiliary fire brigade and the flames were soon put out. The poor scorched young men were rushed to hospital.

The burns were fortunately light, but they were

extensive, over their faces, heads, necks and hands. Though painful, their injuries were not serious, and they returned to work swathed in bandages, looking rather like a couple of Air Force pilots caught in the flames of their shot-down plane.

That was it. They had a wonderful time. The general public thought they were, indeed, injured air crew, and nothing was too good for them. No tram conductor would take a fare from them. They rode free. They had only to go into a pub and, with pitying glances, the barmaids would shove full pints of the best ale across the counter to them, and refuse payment. Cigarettes rolled out from under shop counters. Cinemas? Theatres? The best seats at no charge.

'We tried to explain to everybody,' they assured us, in chorus. 'But it was no good. Everybody thought we were being modest. So what could we do?'

Even when the bandages were off, it was some time before their hair, eyelashes and eyebrows grew again and their skin looked normal, so they enjoyed several weeks as heroes, while we teased them unmercifully.

When they looked quite well again, they returned to making cups of tea and trying to seduce us into visits to drink it.

When repairs to their hut were made, nobody considered the wisdom of supplying them with two exits; employee safety was not high on the list of wartime priorities. So short were we of timber and spare parts that it was always averred that, apart from the personal ingenuity of our invisible manager, the Installation was held together by bits of string and chewing gum.

Unlike the lab assists, office boys were called up at seventeen and a quarter. They were usually Grammar School boys, who came to us at sixteen. They were not quite so knowing or so worldlywise as the overalled products of the elementary schools, who formed the outside staff.

We had one amiable roly-poly of an office boy whose innocence was so great that he became a target for the workmen. One man said to him, pointing out of the window, 'You see that big crane on the dock? Well, it isn't a crane. It's the new fog lifter.'

The boy looked at his instructor open mouthed. 'You don't say?'

'Yes. Invented by a chap who works in the docks. When they get a bad fog, they attach the hook to it and simply roll it up. Works like a charm, I tell you. Super magnetic, that hook – that's the secret of it.'

'Well, I never!'

Another day, the foreman borrowed his services and sent him speeding from workshop to workshop on the Installation to borrow a left-handed spanner. Another time, they sent him to the garage where the big Scammell lorries were repaired, for a long stand.

'Mr Jones wants a long stand,' he told the foreman there.

'All right. You just wait here.'

A wearisome hour later, he was told he could go back to Mr Jones.

'Where's the stand?'

'You've had it.'

Very forlornly he returned to our yard, to be received with laughter by the hands, and to be consoled, with sweet biscuits with his tea, by the girls in the office.

One favourite youngster, who was called up, returned, six months later, to visit us. His khaki uniform was loose on him and he looked years older.

'The rumour is that we're going to Palestine,' he said unhappily.

'But you're so young,' I said.

'I'm not. I'm eighteen.'

To cheer him up, we opened up the office safe and carefully poulticed off its door, with the aid of the washroom towels, our favourite centrefold from a men's magazine, a voluptuous blonde in a transparent black nightgown, lying in a languorous pose on a fur-covered settee. We dried her out on the radiator, folded her carefully and put her in an envelope, for him to carry her.

Laughing, he went back to his unit.

We were left with a sad sinking feeling that we would never see him again.

The permanent staff welcomed back a colleague whose health had broken and who had been demobbed.

I shall never forget my dumb amazement when I saw him seated at his desk on the first morning of his return. He wore a beautifully cut beige suit, perfectly pressed, with a blue tie and blue socks, and from his jacket pocket peeped a pale blue silk handkerchief. His fair hair shone with brilliantine and his shaven face was as smooth as pink icing.

We had totally forgotten the high standards of dress required by employers before the war. This man had got ready for work with the same care that he must have exercised in 1939, before he was called up. He had taken out one of his suits from his pre-war wardrobe, unaware that few civilians had anything left that was remotely comparable.

We looked at the other men in their shabby

sports jackets, frayed collars, crumpled, mended trousers, and shrunken pullovers. We girls suddenly saw ourselves through his eyes – our shiny skirts, yellowed blouses, and our truly awful collection of cardigans, mostly a musty grey. We were neat, and one girl had a better collection of dresses than many, also from a large pre-war wardrobe, but this vision of sartorial perfection left us low and dispirited. We realised how far we had slipped.

He was a very pleasant person and never complained of his ill-health. We watched with glee his frequent changes of suits and ties.

'The only way he could get a shave like that,' remarked one irate man, 'is by having a girl friend in a chemist's shop, to get him razor blades.'

The crews of the American tankers which brought the oil and petrol to our installation were great smugglers and continued to provide us with such luxuries. But their prices were very high – some girls would give a week's pay to get a pair of nylon stockings.

Our contact was still the dipper. He was the man who climbed the narrow metal steps to the tops of the great storage tanks to dip the contents of the tank, so that the quantity of petrol or oil could be checked. He carried his dipstick in a box slung on his shoulder. Like the policeman guarding the gate, he was part of the landscape and nobody noticed him particularly.

But when a tanker was in, we would corral him in a quiet corner of the grounds and happily rifle his dipstick box, which looked to us like a pirate's treasure trove.

Another small treasure came our way, when a freighter in the river jettisoned its deck cargo of oranges. They had either been ruined by the ship being driven off-course by the Germans and consequently taking too long to get home, or by machine gun fire. It did not pay to sort through them, to retrieve the fruit which might be still good.

Leaving our shoes and stockings on the river bank, we spent a merry lunch hour, paddling in the shallows, gathering the oranges as they floated in. Many were, indeed, bad, but I was able to take several home.

'Eat fruit which has been in the river? You must be mad. Throw them out at once,' Mother ordered. But the rest of the staff washed theirs and ate them, and nobody was sick.

A cook on one of the tankers brought a whole frozen sheep, but was defeated in his smuggling efforts when the tanker was redirected to the Herculaneum Dock next door, where the Customs Officers were much more in evidence.

The story of the sheep flew round the office. Our mouths watered. Real mutton! Consultations were held between the tanker crew and our representatives who went aboard.

'I'll cook it!' announced the frustrated smuggler. 'And you can all come down and eat it for lunch.'

A price was settled, and the number of Installation officials who felt it necessary to inspect the cargo, talk to the ship's master, or take samples, was innumerable.

'When can we go down?' the girls demanded.

The men, sleek from lovely mutton stew, said in shocked tones, '*Girls* can't go! You'd have to eat in the crew's quarters – and they eat from communal dishes. It wouldn't do at all for a girl.'

'We don't care.'

'You forget. They're Americans. They're not like us!'

'They won't touch us.'

'You never know!'

So we sulked, and at teatime we made sure that the men's cups of tea were stone cold.

Wartime rations did not allow for much breakfast, and in the mornings, with canteen lunches still hours away, we were often hungry. One sunny summer day, the whole staff was complaining about empty tummies. In desperation, one of the male clerks went to the nearest corner grocery shop, and came back triumphantly with a newly baked white loaf and a tiny pat of tightly rationed margarine.

'Sweet talk,' he explained.

We did not ask him what he had had to pay for such a nice treat. We joyfully tore the loaf into fair shares and dipped our hunks into the fishy-tasting margarine.

In his spare time, this man was a well-known water colour artist, and I often saw his delicate landscapes in a city art store. I would dearly have loved to own one, but, like the water colour paints that I longed for for myself, they were too expensive. My artistic attempts were limited to drawing tiny pencilled cartoons to amuse the staff.

One spring, the same man went down to Shropshire to visit his evacuated wife and children. When he returned, he brought with him, for each girl, a large bouquet of primroses centred with a knot of violets and edged with the big, green primrose leaves. We were all so moved that we did not know what to say. Our world was such a depressingly grey place that we had forgotten that spring comes each year, no matter what men do.

As I carried the precious gift home in the train, I nearly cried with longing for the primrose woods, the sweeps of bluebells, the masses of wild anemones, amid which I had walked as a small child – another world which had gone forever.

Civilians and servicemen in the train exclaimed at the flowers, and leaned over me to smell them. Mother was entranced by them, and nursed the little yellow and mauve flowers carefully in a soup bowl until they faded, and the last one or two violets were put in an egg cup until they, too, died.

CHAPTER THIRTY-FIVE

One wet and windy day, the Installation fire brigade decided that, since it would be on duty overnight, anyway, it would give a New Year's Party in the basement of one of the offices. All firewatchers and all the girls in our Department were invited.

After eating our evening meal in the canteen, the girls streamed back to the office, to monopolise the little sink and badly distorted mirror, while they washed and made up their faces, and redid their elaborate hairstyles.

In a time of great shabbiness, beautiful hair was of prime importance. I now wore mine in sweeps combed upwards from my face, with an arrangement of soft waves and curls on top, all secured with hair grips from the dipstick man. The back hair was shoulder length, curled and gathered into the nape of my neck by a fine tortoiseshell hairslide. A friend had found the slide in a tiny shop in a Cornish village, where she had been for a holiday, and had brought it home to me as a gift. It was my most prized possession.

We crowded down the narrow stairs into the small basement room encumbered by old desks, a table and odd chairs. The ceiling was a web of pipes, heavy with dust, and, to one side, the furnace loomed darkly.

The firemen had lit the room with a few candles. Dressed in their navy blue uniforms, peaked caps pushed to the back of their heads, they handed us each a drink. Mine tasted of lemonade powder, and I did not ask what else was in it, but sipped it slowly. The cigarette smokers lit up and soon the room was a sea of smoke. I sat gravely on the corner of a desk, sticking shyly close to the firewatchers from our Department. From darker corners came an occasional protesting squeak, from girls less nervous than me.

Unexpectedly, the chief fireman produced a violin and began to play. He went through popular songs, bits of *Carmen* and some light, classical pieces which I did not know.

The bow flicked up and down in the soft light of the candles, and I sat spellbound, so happy to hear live music instead of the tinniness of the radio. Occasionally the guests would hum the chorus of a song, but for the most part they sat quietly in a rare moment of relaxation. The music seemed a special New Year's gift.

At five minutes to twelve, the fireman put down his magic bow, and we broke into applause, which sounded thunderous in the confined space. Then, we all stumbled up the dark staircase and out of the office, towards the postern gate, normally kept locked, which led into Grafton Street above the Herculaneum Dock.

The weather had cleared up, though the sky was still overcast, and it was extremely dark. The river was invisible, except for an occasional glint of a wave. Below us, in the dock, there was the sound of voices; a ship was in.

Men peered at their wrist watches, trying to see the time.

'Don't worry, every hooter and siren on the river'll go off when it's time,' a fireman assured them. Then he nudged me. 'Keep your eyes on the river. You're in for a surprise.'

Not quite in unison, the hooters and ships' sirens did go off. We all laughed and shouted Happy New Year to each other and to the invisible ships.

And then the miracle occurred. From end to

end of our line of sight, all the ships switched on their lights, giving a glimpse of a peacetime river lasting about five seconds. Then they all went out, and we were left shivering in the dark.

Bemused, we clasped each other's hands and formed a circle.

'Should auld acquaintance be forgot and never brought to mind . . .'

We swung our hands up and down as we sang and I was happy, with friends whom I loved dearly, and yet, in the back of my mind there was a silence as if part of me could not join in. There lay a memory of someone who was not there and never would be.

I missed the last train from Liverpool, and had to cross the river on the ferry boat to the Birkenhead terminal. From there, I walked home through the sleeping town, past fields and villages where nothing stirred. There was no traffic and it was absolutely dark. Only the grey macadamed road showed as a faint line ahead of me. It was a curious beginning to a new year.

'How did they manage it – the lights, I mean?' I asked one of my colleagues at the office the next morning.

'It wouldn't be too difficult. Messages go up and down the river all the time between ships and shore. The sparks talk to each other.'

'It was so quick. I don't suppose the wardens would have had more than time to blink before it was over.'

'Nor the ships' masters, either.'

I could almost hear the protests, if the authorities inquired amongst the ships' crews. The rumpled, bleary faces of the morning after New Year, would protest, 'Me, Sir? Never touch a light switch. Not my job.' Or, 'No, Sir. Nobody come in and switch 'em on. I were here meself. I'd know.' Or, 'I never saw nothin' unusual. Anyway, I were too busy.' The flow of Liverpudlian denials would be so uniform that any self-respecting officer would retire in honourable defeat.

The switching-on of the lights was a lovely joke, a school-boy cocking of a snoot at authority, and for weeks afterwards we would occasionally refer to it.

Soon after the New Year, I frightened my colleagues by fainting at my desk, as a result of a particularly painful menstrual stomach ache. I was put to bed on one of the firewatcher's beds, and, when I came round, one of the girls offered me two tablets, which I gratefully swallowed.

They were Codeine, and she told me where to buy them. They released me from a great deal of regular suffering.

None of the girls realised that the tablets were

a derivative of morphine and sometimes addictive. They could be bought at any chemist's, though one sometimes had to sign the Poison Book when purchasing them.

I gave some of the tablets to my father, when he had salmonella poisoning, from eating improperly processed American dried egg. Our doctor was out on another case, and Father was rolling on the bed, clutching his stomach. He was covered with perspiration, and a further pain in his chest threatened another heart attack. He had been vomiting, but he managed to keep three tablets down, and the pain vanished.

Stomach upsets were very common during the war and for some years afterwards. Standards of hygiene were very low in cafes, restaurants and canteens, and more people were eating away from home, partly because of the long hours of work and partly to augment inadequate rations.

As men were called up and fourteen-year-olds found they could earn more in factories, the innumerable small shops and cafes had difficulty in getting help. Complicated by a sea of Government regulations, it was difficult to find time to keep such places properly clean and food adequately stored. Anyone selling sweets, for instance, had to count, and thread together with a needle and cotton, coupons about a quarter of the size of a postage stamp, before sending them to the Ministry of Food. It must have driven shopkeepers, mostly women, nearly mad. Concentrated bombing, with its subsequent heavy dust fall and its disorganisation, did not help.

In the spring of 1943, the first marriage in our family took place. Alan was to be posted to North Africa and decided to marry his sweetheart, an ATS girl serving on a gun post, before he left. Like many wartime marriages, the arrangements were made so quickly that our family could not get to the ceremony, held in the south of the country. He did, however, bring her to stay with us for a few days' honeymoon.

There was a hasty doubling up in an already overcrowded house, so that we could give them a bedroom where the roses were growing right across the window, the only pretty thing we could offer in our shabby home.

Though we three sisters were delighted by the new bride, it took very little time for her to become the victim of Mother's vicious temper; and Father was by no means nice to her. He seemed to think she was just a housemaid.

This sickening situation was the beginning of a clear separation between my family and myself.

I had always kept my own counsel, but now I intensified my independence. When the war was over and life in Britain had settled down, I would try to build a home of my own – it was as well that I did not realise that it would be many years before life in Britain returned to normal! All I knew was that I could not stomach such unkindness towards a stranger, and it brought home to me what my future life would be, if I stayed with my parents. Occasionally, I would tell myself that I might marry, anyway, and that would take me away – but I was not going to count on it.

CHAPTER THIRTY-SIX

After Christmas, 1943, London became the target of a new German weapon, an extremely fast and destructive pilotless plane, which the British named the Doodlebug. A number of Londoners fled to the north, amongst them the sister of Alan's wife, and her little daughter. It was decided that they should stay with us.

It took only a week or two for this terrified woman to decide that the Doodlebugs were preferable to Mother, and she returned to London.

Eddie came on leave, and I waited for him under the clock in Lime Street station. I wondered how he would behave, after our last meeting.

It was as if nothing had changed. He took me to our usual cafe, and we gossiped about everything under the sun, except what lay between us.

'The invasion won't be long now,' he told me jubilantly.

'How can you be so cheerful about it?'

'Well, if you know you're going to be hanged, it's a relief to have some idea when!' He then went on to tell me that he had been returned to his own unit, half way through some advanced Commando training. 'I'm too heavy. Every time I climb a tree, for sniping, the bally tree bends and tells the world that I'm there!'

From later conversation, however, I gathered that probably the main reason the Commandos did not want him was that he was older and, consequently, not as quick and agile as a youngster would be. He said flatly, 'If I'm killed, it will be because I can't move fast enough.'

With the aid of the greasy menu, a teaspoon and a piece of string, he instructed me in how to climb a quarry wall or the side of a cliff, or even a building. At first I laughed at him. But then I sobered, as I saw, mentally, men struggling through surf, to reach a sandy shore overshadowed by well-defended cliffs. The invasion, I thought, could be another Dardanelles, another botched effort, like Dieppe, where under-trained men had been simply butchered by the Germans. He must have seen it, too, because he put the spoon down quietly and shoved the menu to one side.

Seeing his expression suddenly harden, I asked quickly, 'How are the kittens?'

He grinned. 'They've got great-great-grand-children. The ruddy castle's rotten with them – they all hunt for themselves. Our sergeant found one on his bed last week, and he was properly put out. Told us we could get some practice wringing the little tykes' necks. Says the Old Man himself is saying there are too many pets, and that they've got to be cleaned out.'

'Never mind,' I comforted. 'There's probably not a mouse in the place. If you're right about the invasion, it'll soon be over, and you can come home. What are you going to do then?'

'Go back to Shell, I suppose, if I've any sense. The way they pay, it would be beer money at least.' He grinned wickedly at me, and I was again reminded how alike we were – he could have been my brother, with his greenish eyes, his big nose and thin, reddish skin. We shared an underlying endurance, too, a particular inner strength. His young life had not been easy either. We shared, also, an inner reserve; his covered by a humorous defiance of life, mine by a highpitched chattiness or a nervous silence. I liked immensely the man behind the facade, his interest in everything going on around him, his care for his mother, his general exuberance.

Two evenings later, he came over to our bungalow, and spent the evening talking with Father and me. The old soldier and the new one got on surprisingly well. He stayed so late that he missed the last train to Liverpool, and had to walk to the ferry.

He continued to write to me in an ordinary, friendly way. And it seemed as if the invasion of Europe was as far away as ever.

While Eddie's unit continued to climb up and down quarries, and I worked and sewed and danced, Alan toiled up the leg of Italy and spent the bitter winter of 1943–44 in the Apennine mountains.

Brian was at sea, and went to the United States to be part of the crew of a minesweeper being built in Seattle. They had a rough passage bringing the little tub back to British waters, where, for a while, he swept mines.

On 5th June, 1944, he was minesweeping along the coast of France, a ready target for German guns. He saw the British invasion at Arromanches, and helped to pull the dead and dying out of the water. A day or two after the landing was assured, he went ashore, found a post office still in business, and sent Mother a picture postcard.

Mother nearly collapsed, when she saw that the card was from France, but she kept it for years.

After seeing the hideous results of the attack on France, to send a post card, as if on holiday, seemed to me to be the epitome of the British stiff upper lip. The sallow-skinned little boy who suffered from nightmares grew up to live them through his youth. He fought in the Atlantic and the Pacific, walked through Tokyo, after it was burned to the ground by one of the biggest fire storms ever created by man and afterwards walked through the cold ashes of Hiroshima. Later, he served in a ship cleaning out pirates from Chinese waterways. There, the starvation was so intense that the women porters, loading the ship's coal in baskets on their heads, fell in their tracks from hunger, and the sorely distressed British crew had to be forbidden to hand over their rations to them. He saw slain or burned servicemen and civilians under almost every possible situation, and found that, all over a desperate, ruined world, a few cigarettes from his ration would buy anything.

Eddie was not under any illusion about *his* near future. He said, while on one leave, 'The poor bloody infantry are going to get it, as usual.'

I felt sick. Despite his tough reputation, I could

not imagine Eddie killing anybody; yet he would have to, if he was not to die himself.

On his final leave before the invasion of France, he again missed the last train to Liverpool, so I walked down to the bus stop with him. We were just in time to see the bus vanish into the gloom.

'Never mind,' he said comfortably, 'I'll walk to the ferry.'

'Then I'm going to walk some of the way with you.'

I had not anticipated going more than a mile or two, but we were so quietly companionable and the starry night was so pleasant that we swung along together, regardless of the distance.

At the foot of Bidston Hill, Eddie paused and looked around the quiet fields and the empty road. Satisfied, he looked down at me. 'Helen,' he said, 'I want to ask you something.'

'Yes?'

'Helen, after the war – when I've got started again, Helen would you marry me then?' he blurted out.

I was astonished. After all the tales I had heard, I had expected that some time or other he would proposition me. I never thought he would ask me to marry him. I stared doubtfully up at him.

'I know I'm no catch, Helen.' He sounded anxious

when I still did not reply, and went on, 'I can earn a living for you, though. And I want to settle down.'

No word of love?

I took a big breath and smiled at his confusion. 'I didn't think you had holy matrimony in mind,' I finally responded lightly.

'Holy or unholy, I've got it in mind.' He put his arms round my shoulders and eased himself close to me. 'I want to come back to you, Helen. Nobody else.'

He bent and kissed me tentatively, and such desire shot through me that the rigidly maintained self-control I had learned in my sorrow threatened to crumple. With a great effort, I drew myself back, though he still held me loosely. In the faint light, I could see the wicked grin on his face, and the knowledge that he would probably win. I blushed scarlet.

It was my turn to be confused. Here was a man who would never remember birthdays, take for granted much that a wife would do for him, sire children without a thought.

Yet, and yet, perhaps I was being too hard. When times got rough, I thought, he was not the kind to desert me, and he was a great deal more civilised than he liked to make out.

'Yes,' I said, and put my arms round his neck.

He kissed me again, and, though I knew it would be different from all my young girl's hopes, I felt it would be all right.

I expected him to whoop his satisfaction to the shivering trees in the churchyard nearby. But he kissed me long and soberly and then let me go. 'I'll take you home to see my mother next time I'm on leave. And we can buy a ring, if you'd like one.'

Slowly we turned and walked on until the wind rose and it became cold. He insisted that I turn back, so we kissed again, and I watched him jog steadily down the long straight road until he was out of sight. He did not look back.

With a heavy heart, I began the long walk home. I feared to lose what I had just gained.

I never saw him again. His next leave was cancelled, as everyone was confined to barracks or to training grounds, preparatory to the invasion of France. Letters there were, oddly loving and funny. 'We'll get married next leave. Be ready.'

He survived the invasion itself. I got letters scribbled in haste, so funny it was hard to believe that they were written on the battlefield. Then a very sad one telling me how one of his old friends had been hit by a sniper's bullet and had died in his arms. Fortunately for his mother, Eddie's brother was still in England.

Life at home went on as usual, but we all waited for the BBC's Nine o'clock News every night, with nervous intensity. The news reader reported the give-and-take of the invasion battles as if it had nothing to do with killing or dying. Not a hint was there of the further horrifying suffering inflicted on both German and Allied troops, all men of my generation, who died slowly, went mad under misdirected shelling or bombing, or to this day lie in hospital beds or are confined to wheelchairs. Not a word of those unseasoned conscripts who faced battle for the first time, civilians who had never killed before.

In July, British and Canadian troops bled the Germans, by drawing their reserves into the battles of Falaise and Caen. This enabled the Americans to sweep through the Germans' weakened defences, into the heart of France.

The British then got bogged down.

There were only four bridges across the River Orne on which Caen stood, and there is a limit, even under the best of circumstances, to the amount of traffic which can pass over a bridge in a given time, a point which was apparently mislaid in the group military mind. When the bridges became choked, the Germans saw their chance amid the all-enveloping dust and mix-up of vehicles. Many,

many British and Canadians died in the resultant chaos before the city of Caen fell to the Allies.

After the war, I saw the city before it had been rebuilt. It must have been a dreadful battle. Looking out over the rubble, from the top of a hill, stood, almost undamaged, the twin churches built by William the Conqueror and Matilda, his wife, in gratitude for his winning the Battle of Hastings and for the subsequent conquest of Britain. The British, I thought forlornly, had paid a terrible price to liberate the Conqueror's city.

I had caught, at the time of the invasion, a bad dose of flu and was subsequently confined to bed. An infection in my throat and ears followed and, without the help of sulfa drugs, took a long time to get better. It left me with more rheumatism in my legs. The doctor ordered a slow convalescence, while I gained strength.

I had got to the point where I was taking little walks up and down the road and then getting into bed immediately after tea, when, one evening, Father kindly brought the *Liverpool Echo* in to me, to read. He then retired to the sitting-room, which he regarded as his own particular room.

It was quite late and I first lit my bedside candle, then leisurely turned the pages of the paper.

Finally, I came to the section referred to by Liverpudlians as the Hatches, Matches and Dispatches. The Dispatches section was frighteningly long. Almost without thinking, I ran my finger down the names.

And there it was.

'No,' I whispered. 'No! Not him!'

Mother must have heard my cry, because she came running from the kitchen, her hands dripping.

'What is it?'

I lifted the paper towards her. 'It's Eddie.'

Then I turned my head into the pillow, so full of anguish that I could not speak, could not cry. I just wanted to die myself.

Mother was incredibly kind. She had never held me in her life and she did not now, but she stroked my head and whispered, rather helplessly, that everything would be all right after a little while.

In such a situation, words have no meaning, but one sometimes remembers them later on and is grateful for them. I was vaguely aware of other members of the family milling around the bedroom. But it was Mother who was left with the task of helping me.

With frantic, unleashed energy, I began to thrash around in the bed, like a butterfly skewered on a pin. Finally, I sat up, and said, 'I have to get up.'

I stumbled into my clothes, vests, pullovers, cardigan, the layers with which people in those days sustained themselves in icy homes.

While Mother watched me anxiously, I looked wildly round the confining room. 'I think I must go out, Mum – into the fresh air.'

'I'll come, too.'

'No, Mummy,' I told her gently, between gasps for air. 'I need to be by myself – very badly. I'll be all right.'

Mother did not try to deter me, though the rain was lashing the bedroom window panes, bubbling from the downspouts, flooding our waterlogged district.

More clothes were pressed upon me, a second cardigan, a mackintosh, rubber boots, gloves, an umbrella.

'Don't worry, Mum. I'll just walk for a little while. I'll be home soon.'

Putting up the umbrella, I dived out of the house, with no idea where I was going, only the desperate need to run away from my pain.

Despite the torrent of rain, it was better outside. Like an Indian about to die, I wanted to lie on the ground, to gain comfort from the feel of earth and grass. But deep puddles already glistened on our little lawn, and I sloshed down to the gate, pulled it open and went out.

Though weak from illness, the same weird energy carried me mile upon frantic mile. Through dear, familiar Meols, Hoylake and West Kirby, I strode without meeting a single other pedestrian – only a couple of shadowy vehicles with shaded lights.

'Eddie,' I cried, to the slashing, unheeding rain, 'Eddie, darling.'

At Caldy Hill, I faltered, and then slowly began to climb. At the top, there is a sandstone pillar, a marker for sailors using the Dee Estuary. Panting, I leaned on a wall nearby, to look out at an invisible sea. Any tiny glowing of the coming summer dawn was masked by the weeping clouds.

What was I going to do? How was I to assuage the tearing grief inside me? With one arm clutched across my stomach, the other holding the dripping umbrella, it was as if I had stumbled into a torturing, wet hell.

What instinct turned me homeward, I do not know, but back I went, some mechanical ability keeping me from tripping over the usual pedestrian hazards, as I stumbled through the dark.

As I entered the unlocked back door into the kitchen, Mother in her dressing-gown rose from her chair by the kitchen fire, which she had kept unusually high for my return. She looked old and haggard.

'You poor girl,' she said, and took the sheathed umbrella from me and put it to drip in the sink. I took off my mackintosh, shook it in the lean-to shed which lay against the back door and then hung it, mechanically, over the door to dry. I was wet to the skin, like a bedraggled dog.

'Take your shoes off,' Mother ordered.

I did as I was told.

She helped me undress in front of the blazing fire and put on my nightgown. 'Now,' she said, 'I'm going to make you a really strong cup of tea and give you three aspirins, and you'll feel a little better in the morning.'

I could not speak. I felt that if I once opened my mouth, I would have hysterics. But it was as if she truly understood what was happening to me. This strange, bitter, violent woman was, for the first time in my memory, mothering me. Of course, I did not consider this at the time – I was immersed in shock. But I remembered it afterwards and forgave her much, in consequence of it.

Three cups of tea and three aspirins later, warmed by the fire, I said to Mother, 'I'll go to work tomorrow. Perhaps they'll have more news of him.'

She accepted this decision with a quiet nod, and drained the contents of the teapot into her cup.

Except for my dry sobs, we sat silently together, looking into the hot coals in the fire-grate.

Mother cleared her throat, and began to speak, at first hesitatingly, and then, when she saw she had caught my interest, with more confidence.

'You know, before the war, long before I met your father, I was engaged. He was the youngest of seven sons of a widowed lady, who had been left a cotton mill by her husband. In the first two years of the war, she lost all her sons in battle, except him. He was allowed to stay at home and run the business. His mother was an Indian lady, whom his father had met in India and brought home with him, so you can imagine he was very handsome. I loved him very much.

'One day, he was walking through the mill, when the floor above him collapsed under the weight of the machinery – and he was crushed to death.'

For a moment I was shaken out of my own suffering. 'Oh, Mum,' I cried in horror. 'How dreadful! How awful for you. And his poor mother?'

'She lived out the rest of her life in complete seclusion – cut herself off completely, except for a couple of old servants.'

'Oh, God!'

On Mother's face I glimpsed a dreadful look of abject despair, and then it was gone.

'I'm so sorry, Mum. I had no idea.'

She smiled slightly, and got up and collected the teacups and put them in the washing up bowl, for attention in the morning.

After a couple of hours of deep sleep and an inadequate toilet, I was running along the cinder track beside the railway. Though it had stopped raining, my leg makeup and shoes were mired as I ran through the puddles, past the abandoned quarry and the market gardens. On the station, I piled into a crowded carriage with my girl friend, who had arrived earlier.

'Are you feeling quite well again?' she asked.

I jumped. Had she read the *Echo*, too? Then I realised that she was referring to my influenza bout, and that I would have to tell her about Eddie.

But not today, I thought, not today. I replied simply, 'Yes, thanks.'

'You look awful.'

'I feel weak.'

I hung on to a strap and swayed with other standing passengers, and let her talk, while I looked in my mind at the shattered pieces of my hopes. And, ever burning in the fore-front of my mind, was the prayer that Eddie had died instantly.

CHAPTER THIRTY-SEVEN

That morning, I wept openly in the office, when Eddie's name was sadly mentioned. And, later, when I was seated in the steamy canteen with two of my colleagues, and faced a lunch I was sure would choke me, I asked my companions bitterly, 'Why did it have to be him? He was so bright and intelligent. Why didn't God take a fool like me, instead?'

In the ensuing silence, I played around with my meal. Then one of the men, a Methodist, said cautiously, 'Perhaps God has something special for you to do yet.'

It pulled me up short. I never forgot it. If I believed in Almighty God, then I must accept that He knew when my use in this world was ended, and would take me then, not before.

I held the speaker in great affection, and through sleepless, tossing nights and long, dreary days, his remark stayed with me.

He also mentioned that he had been to see Eddie's mother.

Eddie's mother? She probably did not even know I existed.

What should I do? What could I do?

For some days the matter was settled for me. My throat flared up with a new infection, and I took once more to my bed. A week later, however, though still weak, I returned to work and to the problem of Eddie's mother.

My mother had, seeing my grief, drawn up a truce regarding Eddie's character, but it was her opinion, she said, that Eddie's mother was probably not a very refined woman. I should stay away from her.

Refined or not, she was probably going through hell. So, armed with a bouquet of summer flowers begged from a neighbour's garden, I set out for the north end of Liverpool.

Eddie's home was much bigger than I had expected, a fine Victorian house set back from a quiet road. I walked up and down the pavement several times, before working up enough courage to open the handsome cast-iron gate, go slowly up the path, and ring the old-fashioned bell.

A tall, slender, elderly lady answered the door. Her face was pink-flushed as Eddie's had been, and Eddie's eyes stared down at me. She wore a black dress and a fine necklace of grey, natural pearls.

'I'm Eddie's girl friend,' I said, in a trembling voice. Suppose he had had other girl friends beside the one he had asked to marry him.

She put out a welcoming hand. 'Oh, my dear,' she exclaimed. 'I'm so glad you've come. Come in.' She opened the door wide, and I stepped into a house not unlike the home I had left so precipitately when Father had gone bankrupt.

Wordlessly, I handed her the bouquet, and she buried her nose in it. When she looked up, there were tears running down her face.

I was led into a large drawing-room, furnished in good Edwardian taste, with Japanese flower-patterned wallpaper, unchanged, I guessed since Mrs Parry had first moved into the house. Everything was extraordinarily well kept.

I must not cry, I warned myself. I have come to help.

Mrs Parry bent down to plug in an electric fire, though the day was far from cold. 'I'm so glad you've come,' she repeated. 'We didn't know how to find you, you know. Fred – that's Eddie's elder brother – told me about you, and we were nearly frantic with worry. You see, Eddie's things haven't been sent home yet, so we had no address.' Her voice broke, and for a moment she remained bent over the glowing electric fire. Then she laughed softly, 'Officially, I didn't know anything, of course, but I guessed from odd things Eddie let slip before he went back last time, that something was in the wind. All Fred knew was that he had a girl he was very keen on, living in the Wirral.' She smiled up at me, and then straightened herself, and took a hanky from the sleeve of her dress and wiped away her tears.

'Well, now. Do sit down. I'll put the kettle on and we'll have a cup of tea.'

I sat down and smiled up at her, confidence returning. 'That would be lovely,' I assured her.

A dragon? A Tartar? Really, Eddie! She was a fine, well-bred, northern lady, and she was being heart-warmingly kind. I loved her on sight, and continued to love her until her death. She provided for me a warmth and affection that Mother, even at her best, had been unable to give me.

'You're so like Eddie,' she would sometimes say. 'I can't get over it. I wish I had had a daughter like you.'

I think that in a vague way, she hoped that her burly elder son would take a fancy to me. Though we did become quite friendly, there was none of the natural attraction that there had been between Eddie and me. He did, however, eventually bring her a very sweet daughter-in-law.

She showed me Eddie's room and his books. She had the same ready sense of the ridiculous that Eddie had had, and she told me lots of funny stories about his various escapades.

When Eddie proposed to me, I accepted him on chance. But he knew what he was doing. I would have fitted into his life very well. Though he might swear like a docker and play tough, I knew now who had taught him the attitudes which had endeared him to me.

'Losing their father so young had a profound effect on both the boys,' Mrs Parry told me. 'I knew it but I could not do much about it. Without a father, it is harder to learn how a man should behave, and they were quite wild, and I was very worried about both of them. I used to lay down the law like a High Court judge! But it's surprising. In the last few years, they both settled down quite well. And then, of course, the war came . . .' She fell silent after such confidences, and I would hold her hand until she felt better. I did not know what else to do.

CHAPTER THIRTY-EIGHT

As the Allies advanced in Europe and Asia, we became impatient, and asked each other, 'Will it never end?' And when faced with a task we did not want to undertake, we would say, 'I'll do it after the war,' as if, by saying that, we would never actually have to do it.

Our family worried that, during this last lap of the conflict, we might lose either Alan or Brian. And we simply prayed that neither of them were sent to the East, because of the tales of Japanese atrocities.

The son of a friend of mine died of beating and starvation while doing forced labour for the Japanese, on the Burma Road. She was so stricken, when a scarred survivor came to tell her what had actually happened to her boy, that she was unable to speak or eat for several weeks, and lay in hospital being artificially fed like some poor suffragette.

Pictures of the death camps in Germany and Poland, taken as the Allies released the survivors, raised the hatred of the Germans, in Britain, to new heights.

Despite the feeling of the general public that the war would never end, Government and business were planning for that happy day. A civil servant called William Beveridge had designed a plan to overhaul the entire health and welfare system of the country, and when, after the war, it was implemented, it changed the lives of almost every man, woman and child in the country. The Petroleum Board was preparing to dismember itself, and I was told, at the end of the Japanese war, that there would be a post for me with one of the companies.

I remember laughing, when I was told that the post was a pensionable one. After the atomic destruction of Hiroshima and Nagasaki, nobody expected to survive long enough to draw a pension. Long before that, another war would obliterate us.

Our tight little group in the Wages Department was restless. Some of the camaraderie began to wane, as faces new to many of us began to appear.

Unfit men were being demobbed and returned to civilian life.

On 8th May, Churchill announced that the war in Europe was over, and someone took a picture of the girls in our Department. We still looked young; yet in many ways we were old, just as our parents had been after World War I.

While the war still raged in the East against the Japanese, many people began to get married, to househunt without much hope – to look for peacetime employment.

I was twenty-five years old and, once again, my life was going to change. Like everybody else, I was tired to my very bones, and almost any effort seemed too much. I sat in the train, amid a very merrily drunk group of Air Force men who had been celebrating the victory, and wondered what to do with my life.

Though Mother had been very kind in helping me when Eddie was killed, like the leopard she still had her spots, and when I arrived home she was very cross at being left alone on a day of rejoicing. As I sat down to two shrivelled sausages and a small mound of potatoes, she asked fretfully, 'And what are you going to do?'

'Do you mean this evening?'

'Yes.'

'I thought I'd finish the dress for Mary.'

'Well, I hope she pays you for it. She'll be out of work soon – they won't want any munitions.'

I looked up quickly. She was right. My dressmaking business could shrink, even vanish, once properly trained dressmakers returned to their peacetime occupation. The girls for whom I had made so many dresses would never again earn such high wages as they had enjoyed in the war.

My salary had increased slowly during my time with the Petroleum Board, but I had not realised until recently how really low it was. I had tried to save a little by contributing to war savings bonds through payroll deductions, and had long ago given Mother the money for a set of artificial teeth. I do not know what she spent it on, but she never had any false teeth, and, once she had discovered that I could save, she had been merciless – and often successful – in squeezing extra money out of me.

Mother poured herself another cup of tea out of the pot I had made. She was nearly fifty, yet she looked like a very old woman. Her dyed, black hair contrasted strangely with a heavily lined face and toothless mouth. Her hands, like mine, were ruined by too much scrubbing of floors and rubbing of washing. She was running to fat, and her shoulders stooped. She did not seem to care much what happened to her, as long as she had cigarettes and cinema money.

As I listened to her monotonous, nagging voice, I thought, 'My God, I *must* pull myself together. I must try for a real career. Otherwise, in a few years' time, I'll be just like her.'

It was a salutary idea. And at that moment, in quiet despair, afraid of being hurt again, I gave up all hope of marriage as an escape route. I would work and save for a home of my own.

In Liverpool, 8th May – VE Day – had been celebrated with street parties and dances, and it became a custom to give a street party for returning servicemen.

Kitchen tables were put end to end along the centre of the road, followed by almost every chair in the neighbourhood. Children had a great time making fancy dresses, while their mothers used precious rations to bake rock buns and scones. Hoarded tins of Spam and sardines were sacrificed to make sandwiches, and anything green was tossed into a salad. If anybody owned a piano, it was dragged on to the pavement, so that there could be music for singing and dancing. Otherwise, they made do with accordions or mouth organs. The local publicans were under great pressure to produce a barrel of beer. For years afterwards, one would come across brick walls with *Welcome home Joey* or *George* or *Henry*, splashed across it, in drippy, faded whitewash.

I never saw such a message painted for the Marys, Margarets, Dorothys and Ellens, who also served. It was still a popular idea that women did not need things. They could make do. They could manage without, even without welcomes. But these were the women who would give impetus to the feminist movement. At the time of demobilisation they did not realise it, but they were going to do a lot more marching.

The 15th August, 1945, was declared VJ Day, the end of the war with Japan. The same six girls in our office had their photograph taken, this time with a returned soldier in the centre of the picture. How quaint we look, in our heavy utility shoes and our ill-fitting dresses. One of the six had been widowed and, like me, must begin again, one had a merchant seaman for a fiancé, mercifully spared, one was engaged to a civilian, and two were still fancy free. I smiled for the photographer, but I remember that I wanted to scream at the unfairness of life.

That night, I sat down at the kitchen table and wrote replies to every advertisement in the *Liverpool Echo*, for secretaries.

Firms that had closed for the duration or who had gone over to war work, now re-opened, like crocuses in the sun. I had several replies, and accepted a post as personal secretary to an electrical engineer, at double my previous salary. It was the first step in a long climb which led me, eventually, into the packaging industry, a fascinating world for a woman to be in.

When I left the warm companionship of my friends in the Petroleum Board, I was stepping out blindly into a rapidly changing world.

I felt dreadfully alone.